Labor, Class, and
the International System

STUDIES IN SOCIAL DISCONTINUITY

Under the Consulting Editorship of:

CHARLES TILLY
University of Michigan

EDWARD SHORTER
University of Toronto

The list of titles in this series continues on the last page of this volume

Labor, Class, and the International System

Alejandro Portes

Department of Social Relations
Johns Hopkins University
Baltimore, Maryland

John Walton

Department of Sociology
University of California
Davis, California

ACADEMIC PRESS
A Subsidiary of Harcourt Brace Jovanovich, Publishers
New York   London   Toronto   Sydney   San Francisco

ACADEMIC PRESS, INC.
111 Fifth Avenue, New York, New York 10003

United Kingdom Edition published by
ACADEMIC PRESS, INC. (LONDON) LTD.
24/28 Oval Road, London NW1 7DX

Library of Congress Cataloging in Publication Data

Portes, Alejandro, Date.
   Labor, class, and the international system.

   (Studies in social discontinuity)
   Bibliography: p.
   Includes index.
   1. Economic development. 2. Underdeveloped areas.
3. International economic relations. 4. Social history
--1945- . 5. Economic history--1945- .
I. Walton, John, Date. II. Title. III. Series.
HD82.P58   337'.09'048   80-2772
ISBN 0-12-562020-9   AACR2

PRINTED IN THE UNITED STATES OF AMERICA

81 82 83 84   9 8 7 6 5 4 3 2 1

To
Adreain
and
Casey,
old friend,
young daughter

Contents

4

Ideologies of Inequality and Their Transformation in the Periphery: The Case of Latin America — 107

5

The Internationalization of Capital and Class Structures in the Advanced Countries: The United States Case — 137

6

Conclusion — 187

Preface

This book is a product of our individual research and collaborative efforts over the past 10 years to lend some coherence to the study of international development. Although it is impossible to date such events, the book was actually begun sometime before the completion of our earlier volume, *Urban Latin America*. As we neared completion of that work, we became increasingly uneasy with those geopolitical categories of convenience that easily confound and sometimes distort an understanding of the general conditions of development and underdevelopment. Although we have no reason or desire to recant earlier views, nor certainly to discourage geographically limited studies, we learned in these early efforts that our own theoretical instincts would only find satisfaction in an interpretation of development as a world-historical process.

Naturally, we did not arrive at this position single-handedly. The period spanned by our collaborative work coincides with remarkable progress in this field, which went from imperious conceptions of backward and underachieving nations and jaundiced assessments of dependency to a novel but sweeping overview of the world-system. In some ways, our own changing notions recapitulated these developments. At the same time, we have continued to turn our own interpretive prism in the light of theoretical advances and, particularly, the sobering discoveries of an accumulating research literature. The holistic elegance of recent theory is, by any standard, an impressive achievement, but the grudging realities of crafted research never fail to force revision and novelty upon current theoretical fashion.

Accordingly, this book should be understood as an ongoing confrontation of empirical synthesis and theoretical stretch. We provide less new evidence here than codification of extensive and often disparate material drawn from our own and others' previous research. Nor do we propose any original grand theory of the historical process of uneven international development. Indeed, our view is that the remarkable work of the last decade has yielded a relative surplus of general theory and intriguing—if somewhat disparate—research, and that the most compelling task now is the integration of these streams in concrete areas. In the individual chapters, we endeavor to provide exemplars of the interplay between the best available current theory and research, demonstrating in each instance that the theory can be refined to provide cogent and fertile explanation. In the ensemble of chapters, and from selected points of triangulation, we hope to provide a modest contemporary reformulation of certain classical concerns about imperialism and uneven development (discussed in the Introduction), where we stand now, and where this vein is leading (as suggested in the Conclusion).

To reach these objectives, we have gambled on the strategy of pursuing selected lines of inquiry that correspond to our areas of interest and research, rather than attempt a survey of a variety of conceivable major topics in development. We analyze in detail the issues of international migration, the urban informal economy of peripheral societies, ideologies of inequality, and social class in core societies under influences of the internationalization of capital; they are *some* of the major issues on which we feel adequately informed to reach critical, factual, and theoretical interpretations. Doubtless, there are other major issues that could be added, perhaps even substituted. We are convinced, however, that all of these topics are intertwined in historical process, and that the discoveries that emerge and cohere across a representative selection of issues are likely to uncover even more general truths. In this sense, we pursue what Polanyi called "a pattern of plausible reasoning."

Although this book is in every sense an equal and collaborative effort, we have taken individual responsibility for the principal preparation of separate chapters: Portes for Chapters 1–4, and Walton for Chapters 5 and 6. An essay by Walton on revolutions in the Third World, originally planned as a chapter, ran to excessive length and somewhat oblique purpose for inclusion here, although its results informed portions of the concluding chapter. Through a number of revisions we have continuously made critical comment on one another's work, and many key points in our separate texts owe their inspiration to the other. Accordingly, the plural pronoun that recurs in these pages is more than an editorial convention.

Our indebtedness, of course, extends far beyond this amicable partnership. As consulting editor of the Studies in Social Discontinuity series, Charles Tilly provided us with many valuable suggestions ranging from abrupt lessons in grammar and style to erudite observations on the broader directions of the path we had come upon—all of this offered in an easy and thoroughly professional manner. Our intellectual debt to theorists and researchers responsible for the great advances in the study of development and underdevelopment over the last decade are clear in the pattern of citations. Finally, we wish to thank a number of friends and colleagues for comments on portions of the manuscript, including Robert L. Bach, Howard S. Becker, Charles Bergquist, William L. Canak,

Nancy DiTomaso, Walter Goldfrank, Gary Hamilton, James Hawley, Ronald Herring, Charles Hirschman, Larissa Lomnitz, Bryan Roberts, Allan Schnaiberg, Paul Singer, Carol A. Smith, Atul Wad, Craig Walton, and Erik O. Wright. Their varied and valuable contributions to our thinking on the different topics are gratefully acknowledged. By the same token, they are individually and collectively absolved of any of this book's shortcoming.

To Maria Patricia Fernandez, the first author owes a special debt; she combined critical support and commentary with a willingness to help in proofreading when time was short. Last but not least, Charlene Anderson, Fifi Gonzalez, and Wava Fleming bore the brunt of successive revisions at the typewriter with unfailing patience and grace. Over many months, they earned our respect and our gratitude.

Labor, Class, and
the International System

1

Introduction

If there is a significant convergence between the journalistic and academic literature in recent years, it is in the growing recognition that events in the international arena play a decisive role in the internal course of events in both poor and advanced nations. The dizzying pace of change in the world situation during the last decade has progressively discredited a number of comfortable generalizations. The apparently firm lines of battle between East and West gradually dissolved with the defection of countries such as China—previously the most radical and most feared member of the Eastern camp—and of Iran—supposedly a Western rock of stability and military might in the Middle East. The alternative North–South debate over the partition of the world's wealth became blurred with the rise of OPEC, the emergence of "semi-imperialist" powers in the Third World, and the simultaneous "underdevelopment" of some previously advanced, industrial nations.

The course of détente between the two superpowers has been anything but predictable in recent years, sometimes suggesting a growing communality of interests behind the public rhetoric while at other times pointing ominously to nuclear confrontation. In one Third World region—Latin America—the expectation of popular mobilization and a rapid turn toward the left in the aftermath of the Cuban Revolution was almost immediately negated by the rise of a new brand of military-bureaucratic regime in close alliance with international capital.

For those whose perceptions of the world are shaped by the morning papers and the array of journalistic instant analyses, the 1970s must surely have come to an end in a state of confusion. Regardless of one's ideological leanings, it was increasingly difficult to identify either international friends or enemies, or to predict even short-term trends. A serious analysis of the state of the world could not begin without questioning the solemn official truths that change, in tone or content, on convenience.

Equally important, however, is the need to identify—behind the accelerating

1

pace of events—those basic regularities characterizing the present structure of world exchanges and governing their long-term development. During the same decade, the scholarly literature—in particular that dealing with relationships between advanced and backward nations—has undergone important transformations. It is this particular literature and the problems that it deals with which will concern us. The advancement of scholarly inquiry, often bearing little relation on the surface to the latest set of international events, offers the only reliable promise of clarifying some of its long-term determinants. As part of this process, the definition of national "development" has itself undergone change—less as a response to latter-day news than as the outcome of growing understanding of basic forces in the world economy.

Since its emergence, the field of comparative international development has been marked by a duality between parallel but seldom interacting, currents. At one level, there has been an interest in broad processes of structural change involving comparisons between historical periods or between large geopolitical units. At the other, interest has centered on concrete local issues, generally involving a spatially identified community—nation, region, village, tribe, or urban neighborhood—and the way it copes with the problems of a backward economy.

These two parallel lines of investigation have endured shifts in basic theoretical perspectives. At the time when modernization was the dominant perspective on international development, macrostructural theories focused on the question of the European transition from feudalism to capitalism and urban-industrial society. The gap between "modernity" and "tradition" in these theories represented the latest version of a series of similar antinomies developed since the nineteenth century to grasp the European passage into industrialism.

Historical concern with postfeudal European society was followed by studies of the modernization of former colonies, such as the United States, and the major non-Western societies such as China, Japan, and the Ottoman Empire.[1] The counterpart of these studies in U. S. sociology was a series of cross-national surveys seeking to identify psychosocial "modernism" or "achievement" syndromes said to be both consequence of prior modernization and major forces for accelerated national development.[2]

1. Marion J. Levy, "Contrasting Factors in the Modernization of China and Japan," in *Economic Growth: Brazil, India, and Japan*, ed. S. Kuznets (Durham, N.C.: Duke University Press, 1955), pp. 496–536; Seymour M. Lipset, *The First New Nation* (New York: Basic Books, 1963); S. N. Eisenstadt, *Essays on Sociological Aspects of Political and Economic Development* (The Hague: Mouton, 1961), pp. 9–53; Robert N. Bellah, "Religious Aspects of Modernization in Turkey and Japan," *American Journal of Sociology* 64(1958): 1–5; Robert N. Bellah, *Religion and Progress in Modern Asia* (New York: Free Press, 1965).

2. David McClelland, "The Impulse of Modernization," in *Modernization: The Dynamics of Growth*, ed. Myron Weiner (New York: Basic Books, 1966), pp. 28–39; Alex Inkeles, "Making Men Modern: On the Causes and Consequences of Individual Change in Six Countries," *American Journal of Sociology* 75(September 1969): 208–225; Everett E. Hagen, *On the Theory of Social Change* (Homewood, Ill.: Dorsey Press, 1962).

At the level of specific research concerns, the modernization perspective generated an abundant empirical literature dealing with such topics as the diffusion of innovations in rural areas, the adaptation and socialization of marginal rural migrants in the cities, and the sources of higher or lower achievement orientation among local entrepreneurs. This literature tended to regard underdevelopment as a social "problem," on a par, say, with crime or urban sprawl, but localized in other nations.[3]

As a consequence of this view, development research guided by the modernization perspective tended to concentrate exclusively on problems internal to Third World countries, rather than on the mechanisms tying them to the advanced nations. The latter were not the subjects of research for they were not affected by the "problem" of underdevelopment. Advanced Western countries were regarded by this school as models that the Third World should imitate and toward which it would move, once its maladaptive features were corrected.

The more recent theoretical literature has justly criticized this and other features of modernization theory. This literature has redefined the concept of development as a process embedded in the structure of the world economy and having consequences for both advanced and backward societies. Hence, the study of development should not be limited to underdeveloped countries; but it should include, as a primary concern, structure and processes in the centers of the international system.[4]

Although they successfully criticize the static features of modernization theory, the more recent perspectives have not overcome the original dualism. As in earlier times, broad theories of societal change and a derivative empirical literature—with nation-states as units of analysis—proceed with little or no regard for concrete processes of change within specific countries or regions. Studies at the level of the community, region, or nation have begun to make use of concepts stemming from the new structural perspectives; but they have had, in turn, little bearing on the development of theory.[5]

Specific studies of development thus remain as isolated pieces of empirical

3. See Bert F. Hoselitz, *Sociological Aspects of Economic Growth* (Glencoe, Ill.: The Free Press, 1960); Szymon Chodak, *Societal Development* (New York: Oxford University Press, 1973); Daniel Lerner, *The Passing of Traditional Society: Modernizing the Middle East* (New York: Free Press, 1965).

4. Theotonio Dos Santos, "La Crisis de la Teoria del Dessarrollo y las Relaciones de Dependencia en America Latina," in *La Dependencia Politico-Economica de America Latina*, ed. H. Jaguaribe (Mexico D.F.: Siglo Ventiuno, 1970), pp. 147–148; Immanuel Wallerstein, "A World-System Perspective on the Social Sciences," *British Journal of Sociology* 27(1976): 343–352; Terence K. Hopkins and Immanuel Wallerstein, "Patterns of Development of the Modern World-System," *Review* 1(Fall 1977): 111–145.

5. See, for example, the collection of research articles in the special issue of the *American Ethnologist* 5(August 1978) dedicated to political economy. Other examples are Robert L. Bach, "Mexican Immigration and the American State," *International Migration Review* 12(Winter 1978): 536–558, and Bryan R. Roberts, "The Provincial Urban System and the Process of Dependency," in *Current Perspectives in Latin American Urban Research*, ed. A. Portes and H. Browning (Austin: Institute of Latin American Studies and University of Texas Press, 1976), pp. 99–132.

information. Regardless of their significance, they are seldom organized in a manner that directly addresses the more general problems confronted by the new theories. The result is that the literature on world-level processes of change has tended to develop in relative isolation, accumulating hypotheses at a highly abstract level, but deprived of contact with, and potential insights from, close-range empirical investigation.

The World-System Perspective

Criticisms of modernization theory during the late 1960s and during the 1970s have run their course by now. They accomplished a shift in emphasis from cultural values and the presence or absence of ideological *leit-motifs* as determinants of economic growth to a view of development and underdevelopment as parts of an integral totality. This overarching unit—the world capitalist economy—simultaneously depends on and recreates conditions of economic inequality worldwide.

In U. S. sociology, this shift of perspectives is commonly associated with analyses of the "development of underdevelopment" by Andre Gunder Frank and, more recently, with the study of the origins of the world capitalist economy by Immanuel Wallerstein.[6] Although these are important contributions, the world-system perspective was not born with them nor is it limited to these studies.

The emergence of a structural perspective on development in American sociology amounts to a rediscovery and elaboration of theories and debates dating back to the nineteenth century. Whereas others might undoubtedly find even more remote origins, we identify the advent of a world-system perspective with the theories of imperialism, first advanced by Hobson and Lenin, and later developed by the writers of the Second International. It was at this point when studies of economic development in the advanced capitalist countries ceased to be self-contained. From this point onward, they had to take into account events and interrelationships with colonies and semicolonies around the world.

Hobson's work dealt with England and the British Empire. His was the first exhaustive account of a qualitative shift in the economic relationships between the industrial and nonindustrial worlds. Whereas before such relationships had

6. Andre G. Frank, *Capitalism and Underdevelopment in Latin America* (New York: Monthly Review Press, 1967); Immanuel Wallerstein, *The Modern World-System I: Capitalist Agriculture and the Origins of the European World-Economy in the Sixteenth Century* (New York: Academic Press, 1974). See also Phillip O'Brien, "A Critique of Latin American Theories of Dependency," in *Beyond the Sociology of Development: Economy and Society in Latin America and Africa*, eds. Ivar Oxaal, Tony Barnett, and David Booth (London: Routledge and Kegan Paul, 1975), pp. 7–29.

been those of trade and commodity exports, by the late nineteenth century they were increasingly dominated by the massive export of capital from the advanced countries. Prefiguring Keynesian theory, Hobson identified the central problem of the advanced economies as the growth of a mass of surplus capital lacking outlets in the domestic economy for profitable investment.[7]

The rise of financial capitalism over industrial and commercial capitalism in Britain thus coincided with a transformation in the role of the nonindustrialized world: from a source of cheap foodstuffs, raw materials, and a market for manufactures to a receptacle for surplus capital in search of profits. Whereas France specialized in the export of capital at usurious rates to Russia and other Eastern European countries, England chose the path of colonialism. Hobson documented how little indeed the country as a whole benefited from colonial conquest and trade, but how profitable these activities were for financial capital and "the single and peculiar race" that controlled it.[8]

Lenin's analysis of imperialism was based in part on the empirical materials provided by Hobson. Lenin sought to demonstrate, however, that imperialism and the expansion of capitalism on a world scale emerged as the logical consequence of the laws of motion of capital discovered by Marx. Imperialism could not be understood without the rise of monopoly capital, and the latter could not be comprehended without reference to the continuing processes of capital accumulation and concentration:

> The capitalists divide the world, not out of any particular malice, but because the degree of concentration which has been reached forces them to adopt this method in order to get profits. And they divide it in proportion to "capital," in proportion to "strength," because there cannot be any other system of division under commodity production and capitalism.[9]

Monopoly not only made possible the "division of the world," the financing of vast foreign ventures, it also had consequences for class struggle in the advanced countries. Under conditions of competitive capitalism, analyzed by Marx, rises in productivity were followed by price reductions in the respective commodity, this being the essence of capitalist competition. The rise of conglomerates made possible the control and division of markets, the working of "agreements" to avoid the mutually deleterious consequences of competition. From 1880 onward, the rise of financial imperialism coincided with the decline of price cutting as the key element of competition. In the future, productivity

7. J. A. Hobson, *Imperialism* (Ann Arbor: University of Michigan Press, 1971), chaps. 6 and 7.
8. *Ibid.*, chaps. 7 and 8.
9. V. I. Lenin, *Imperialism, the Highest Stage of Capitalism* (New York: International Publishers, 1939), p. 75.

increases in monopoly industries would be translated into both higher profits to capital and higher wages to labor.[10]

Higher remuneration to the working class in the advanced countries was in part made possible by the higher returns to investments in the colonies and semicolonies. The profitability of foreign investments in plantations, mining, railroads, and so forth was, in turn, traceable to the higher rates of surplus extraction from workers in these areas who were kept at the level of subsistence. Thus, the rise of monopoly, financial imperialism, and the "aristocracy of labor" coincided and required the initiation of what was later to be labeled "unequal exchange" between the centers and periphery of the world-system.[11]

Lenin's analysis of imperialism was not limited, however, to the asymmetrical relationships between advanced countries and their colonies, but took into account the situation of intermediate nation-states. Anticipating by decades contemporary notions of the "semiperiphery," Lenin noted the case of Portugal, which though formally independent was "in actual fact, for more than two hundred years, a British protectorate."[12] Similarly, Argentina had become at the time so dependent on London that it was described as almost a British commercial colony.[13]

Leninist theory identified the central feature of imperialism as the effective completion of the territorial division of the world among the great powers. With capitalism consolidated as truly a world-system, no new areas for colonial expansion existed; henceforth, only redivisions of existing territory and spheres of influence became possible.

Later Marxist theorists of imperialism did not always pay attention to the cleavages in modes of production among the different constituent areas of the world economy and the uses of these cleavages by capital. Bukharin, for example, applied to the world-system notions of equilibrium similar to those which led to his defense of "balanced" development policy within the Soviet Union and the acceptance of a capitalist class in agriculture.

Bukharin equated the world-system of capitalism with the elimination of alternative modes of production and, hence, the applicability of classical equilibrium theories on a global scale.[14] He failed to note that the world economy contained, and indeed required, exchanges between different modes of production.

10. *Ibid.*, chap. 5.

11. Samir Amin, *Unequal Development: An Essay on the Social Formations of Peripheral Capitalism* (New York: Monthly Review, 1976), p. 170.

12. Lenin, *Imperialism*, pp. 85–86.

13. *Ibid.*

14. Nikolai Bukharin, *Imperialism and World Economy* (New York: International Publishers, 1929); Nikolai Bukharin, *Economics of the Transformation Period* (London: Pluto Press, 1975); Nikolai Bukharin, "Notes of an Economist," trans. K. Smith, *Economy and Society* 8(November 1979): 473–500.

In the Bukharin–Preobrazhensky debates over Soviet industrialization, it was the latter who correctly noted the fallacy of balance theories and identified the character of international exchange as involving "the exchange of a smaller quantity of labor by one system of economy . . . for a larger quantity of labor by another system."[15]

This notion was to be fully developed by Rosa Luxemburg. The merit of her work lies precisely in abandoning an exclusive focus on the capitalist mode of production (then the topic of most Marxist economics). She showed how the process of accumulation and expansion of markets in the industrial countries took place simultaneously with the continuation of primitive accumulation in the colonies and semicolonies. Capitalism as the hegemonic mode of production relied on its articulation with economic structures different from it. Through this articulation, surplus value could be simultaneously extracted from the urban working class in the industrial countries and from peasant labor in the backward ones. For Luxemburg, maintenance of the rate for profit through imperialist expansion could not be explained by reference to the classic "laws" of capitalist accumulation, as Bukharin believed.[16]

There is a direct linkage between the work of Preobrazhensky and Luxemburg and contemporary analyses of unequal exchange and accumulation on a world scale. It is important, however, to consider an intermediate stage stemming from the work of the United Nations Economic Commission for Latin America (ECLA) and the reactions to it. It was in the reports of ECLA during the 1940s and 1950s, and especially in the writings of its leader, Raul Prebisch, where the concepts of "center" and "periphery" found their first systematic application to modern development theory.[17] What ECLA did in essence was to rediscover and document within orthodox economics the inadequacy of classical principles of international trade, a task undertaken by the Marxists two decades earlier.

The law of comparative advantage and the anticipated increases in industrial productivity had led orthodox economists to predict improving terms of trade for the periphery. Peripheral primary goods could be exchanged for an expanding amount of manufactures, as the latter were cheapened by technological innovation. ECLA economists empirically disproved these classical notions as applied to Latin America. Employing time-series data, they showed the continuously deteriorating terms of trade for the region. The benefits of improved productivity were being kept in the centers in the form of profits and higher wages. Increased

15. Evgeny Preobrazhensky, *The New Economics* (Oxford: Clarendon Press, 1965) as cited in Amin, *Unequal Development*, p. 147.

16. Rosa Luxemburg, *The Accumulation of Capital* (London: Routledge and Kegan Paul, 1951).

17. Raul Prebisch, *The Economic Development of Latin America in the Post-War Period* (New York: United Nations, 1964). See also ECLA, *Development Problems in Latin America* (Austin: University of Texas Press, 1969) and Celso Furtado, *Development and Underdevelopment: A Structural View* (Berkeley: University of California Press, 1971).

productivity in the periphery was, on the other hand, exported in the form of cheaper primary goods.[18]

Prebisch's main contribution is generally associated with his critique of conventional assumptions concerning income elasticity of demand. It was assumed in classical theory that the centers' demand for primary goods would grow at least as fast as income, if not faster. In fact, the demand for many primary imports in the industrial countries proved more inelastic than the demand for imported manufactures in the periphery. Although some of Prebisch's dire predictions appear exaggerated from the vantage point of the 1970s, the core of his thesis remains valid: There is no law that requires that income elasticities of demand for a given country stay constant over time.[19]

The ECLA analysis of terms of trade in the world economy contained, however, a contradiction: Technical innovation, which led to a rise in workers' income in the industrial countries, simultaneously produced its decline in peripheral ones. The latter was attributed to increases in the surplus population caused by advanced technology. As Amin pointed out, there is no reason why the same process could not occur in the centers.[20] In other words, there is no reason, within the ECLA framework of analysis, why employers in the advanced countries could not also use increases in productivity to displace labor and, hence, force an increase in competition for available jobs among workers.

What ECLA economists failed to take into account was precisely the central thesis advanced by Marxist theorists of imperialism: the rise of monopoly capital that shifted competition away from price reductions and permitted the partial transfer of productivity rises into wages in the centers. Similarly, the process of reproduction of the labor force in the periphery was not adequately explained by ECLA's use of the notion of surplus labor. Such incomplete analyses would lead to major errors in ECLA's predictions about the consequences of industrialization for Latin America and to subsequent extensive critiques of its eclectic position.

The brand of "dependency" theory associated in the United States with Andre Gunder Frank is in part a reaction to the shortcomings of ECLA development policies. Based on the experience of countries such as Brazil and Argentina during the Depression and World War II, ECLA had advocated import-substitution industrialization as a means to escape deteriorating terms of trade. This kind of industrialization, oriented as it was to a small high-income market, did not lead to national autonomy but to increasing foreign dependence.

Luxury imports, which could be previously dispensed with, were now pro-

18. Raul Prebisch, *The Economic Development of Latin America and Its Principal Problems* (New York: United Nations, 1950); ECLA, *Development Problems in Latin America.*

19. David Booth, "Andre Gunder Frank: An introduction and appreciation," in Oxaal *et al.,* eds., *Beyond the Sociology of Development,* pp. 50–85.

20. Amin, *Unequal Development,* p. 170.

duced locally and required heavy inputs of foreign machinery, technology, and even raw materials. Foreign exchange reserves accumulated during World War II and favorable prices for the region's products in the postwar years were able to finance the new imports for a while. By the mid-1950s, however, the situation had shifted, leading to repeated balance-of-payment crises and plunging one country after another into growing foreign indebtness.[21]

Frank analyzed the world-system as a structure determined by the sustained expansion of capitalism and the destruction of precapitalist economies. Underdevelopment was not an original sin of countries "left on the shelf"[22] by industrialization, but an active process determined and modified in its form by the requirements of capitalist expansion. Frank's "development of underdevelopment" thesis had an important corollary: If countries became underdeveloped because of capitalist penetration from the centers, it followed that those periods when they were less integrated into world-economy networks would afford the best chances for autonomous development.

This was exactly what had happened in Latin America during the Depression and World War II. What ECLA mistook for a unique departure toward industrialization was in fact part of a cycle that had occurred several times before. Once the central countries recuperated from war and depression and reasserted their world hegemony, Latin American economies were plunged again into stagnation.[23]

Most of Frank's historical research was directed at documenting the "development of underdevelopment" thesis and at identifying those moments of core retrenchment where peripheral development became possible. His analysis suffered, however, from serious limitations. Because he took his analytic point of departure not from Luxemburg, but from the brand of U. S. Marxist economics associated with Paul Baran, he viewed capitalism as a uniformly destructive system, which wiped out in its advance everything that had preceded it. Thus, for him, it was impossible to speak of "feudal" or precapitalist structures in Latin America since such institutions as the *hacienda, encomienda,* and plantation slavery were the direct creation of core capital.[24]

As his critic Ernesto Laclau pointed out, Frank focused exclusively on capitalist exchange structures neglecting the existence of alternative modes of production and their patterned interaction with the hegemonic one. He thus gave up a basic conceptual tool for understanding the actual processes of repro-

21. Furtado, *Development and Underdevelopment;* F. H. Cardoso, "Las Contradicciones del Desarrollo Asociado," *Revista Paraguaya de Sociologia* 11(Jan.–Apr., 1974): 227–252. Theotonio Dos Santos, "El Nuevo Caracter de la Dependencia," *Cuadernos del CESO,* Santiago, #10, 1968.

22. Charles Bettelheim, "Lettre a Rossana Rossanda," cited in Amin, *Unequal Development,* p. 197.

23. Frank, *Capitalism and Underdevelopment in Latin America;* Andre G. Frank, *Latin America: Underdevelopment or Revolution* (New York: Monthly Review Press, 1969).

24. On this point, see Booth, "Andre Gunder Frank," pp. 66–67.

duction of the peripheral labor force and, hence, the maintenance of low-wage economies. The result was a sweeping denunciation of world capitalism in terms charged with emotion, but containing little that significantly advanced the analysis beyond ECLA. [25]

Frank's vision of the world-system encompassed a single chain of exploitation, which "extends the capitalist link between the capitalist world and national metropolises to the regional centers, and from these to local centers, and so on to large landowners who expropriate surplus from small peasants or tenants, and sometimes even from these latter to landless laborers exploited by them in turn."[26] As Booth noted, the actual mechanisms through which this vertical chain of expropriation occurs and the underlying structures sustaining it are never satisfactorily explained.

Against this giant metaphor, critics could rally a multitude of examples showing the survival and growth of exploited regions and the preservation of precapitalist formations in some of the areas most heavily penetrated by capitalism. Further, Frank's model was a static one lacking any conceptual tools to explain historical changes in relative positions of hegemony and subordination between countries and regions within the world economy. [27]

Contemporary analyses of the world-system have returned to the lines of argument pioneered by Lenin and Luxemburg and have generally succeeded in overcoming the limitations of both the ECLA and the Frank models. In particular, the work of economists such as Arghiri Emmanuel has identified a central mechanism for the exploitation of peripheral regions in the process of "unequal exchange."[28] Emmanuel's analysis begins, in a sense, where Frank's had ended. He succeeds in documenting the routine processes through which—independent of political exactions or financial indebtness—surplus value finds its way from peripheral production into the core.

Unequal exchange according to Emmanuel does not occur because of different capital investment or differential productivity in advanced and peripheral countries, but because of different levels of remuneration to labor. Assume two countries producing the same commodity for the world market with equal production techniques (fixed capital), but with returns to labor that in country A are

25. Ernesto Laclau, "Feudalism and Capitalism in Latin America," New Left Review 67(May–June 1971): 20 pp. Andre G. Frank, Lumpenbourgeoisie: Lumpendevelopment: Dependence, Class, and Politics in Latin America (New York: Monthly Review Press, 1972).

26. Frank, Capitalism and Underdevelopment in Latin America, pp. 7–8. Cited in Booth, "Andre Gunder Frank," pp. 67–68.

27. O'Brien, "A Critique of Latin American Theories of Dependency"; Laclau, "Feudalism and Capitalism in Latin America"; Roberts, "The Provincial Urban System and the Process of Dependency."

28. Arghiri Emmanuel, Unequal Exchange: A Study of the Imperialism of Trade (London: New Left Books, 1972); Arghiri Emmanuel, "Myths of Development versus Myths of Underdevelopment," New Left Review 85(May–June 1974): 61–82.

one-fourth of those in B. The commodity must have one price—that which prevails in the world market. The rate of surplus value extraction is thus higher in country A with the effect that the worldwide rate of profit is increased.[29]

The lower prices in the world market for peripheral commodities are directly traceable to remunerations to labor that are a fraction of those prevailing in the core. The exchange of commodities embodying different amounts of surplus labor in the world market amounts to a "hidden" transfer from peripheral to central countries of the order of many billions of dollars annually.[30]

For Samir Amin, exports produced under low-technology conditions also enter into the unequal exchange process since, though productivity is low, rewards to workers in this sector (mostly peasants) are still lower. Relative surplus value extracted in this sector is actually higher, given the low content of capital goods in the final product:

> Altogether, then, if exports from the periphery amount to about $35 billion [in 1966], their value, if the rewards of labor were equivalent to what they are in the center, with the same productivity, would be about $57 billion. The hidden transfer of value from the periphery to the center, due to the mechanism of unequal exchange, are of the order of $22 billion, that is to say, twice the amount of "aid" and the private capital that the periphery receives.[31]

Unequal exchange thus takes place whenever labor of equal productivity receives proportionally lower wages in the periphery. The benefit is particularly significant for multinational firms and major banks involved in international production and trade. The logical question posed by the unequal exchange argument, however, concerns the nature of the arrangements permitting the remuneration of labor in the periphery at a fraction of its "cost" and at rates lower than those presumably required for subsistence.

A number of theorists, including Meillassoux, Wolpe, Wallerstein, Amin, and de Janvry have provided explanations of this situation. All of these are based, ultimately, on the thesis of articulation of different modes of production within a single world economy. Though particular formulations vary, the essence of the argument is that maintenance of a surplus labor force in the periphery requires the preservation of precapitalist structures that absorb a substantial share of the costs of reproduction of the labor force. This involves both absorption of "redun-

29. Emmanuel, Unequal Exchange: A Study of the Imperialism of Trade; Amin, Unequal Development, chap. 3.

30. Alain de Janvry, "Material Determinants of the World Food Crisis," Berkeley Journal of Sociology 21(1976–77): 3–26.

31. Amin, Unequal Development, p. 144.

dant" workers and raising the new generation at no cost to the capitalist sector. [32]

Without exception, these existing interpretations of the process identify precapitalist modes of production with enclaves of subsistence agriculture in peripheral rural areas. It is there, according to the theory, where the bulk of the labor force for industry is reared and where workers displaced from the urban capitalist sector return. Through this system, capital saves the "indirect wages" involved in reproduction of the labor force in its unproductive years. As we will see later on, the role assigned to subsistence enclaves by the theory is seriously divergent with actual experiences in many peripheral countries.

The continuing analysis and debate over unequal exchange and the structural arrangements in the center and periphery that sustain it represent the present state of world-system theory. Seen from this vantage point, the contribution of Immanuel Wallerstein constitutes a valuable recapitulation of the origins of this system in the sixteenth century, but cannot be identified by any means with this perspective as a whole. Wallerstein's account of the origins of the capitalist world economy has itself been challenged at several important points. The emphasis he places on the Atlantic trade as a determining factor in the origins of capitalism can be questioned, for instance, on the basis of other interpretations which stress the internal disintegration of the feudal mode of production. [33]

Similarly, Wallerstein's analysis of the "strong core states" emphasizes their capitalist character and their role in world capitalist expansion. On the contrary, Perry Anderson's careful study of these absolutist states show them to be late-feudal formations and instruments for continuing domination by the nobility under the new socioeconomic conditions. [34] In general, the view of world capitalism associated with Wallerstein is one of a single and expanding system, born in the sixteenth century and developing through cycles to the present. The analytic utility of this sweeping approach is limited for it tends to disregard major "breaks" in the process and important political and economic distinctions.

Following the lead of Anderson, Amin, and others, it would seem more appropriate to envision the absolutist states and mercantilist trade as protocapitalist formations leading to the gradual demise of a feudal mode of production. Capitalism proper emerged with the series of events associated with the Industrial Revolution and the rise to hegemony of the bourgeois class. A

32. Claude Meillassoux, "From Reproduction to Production," *Economy and Society* 1(February 1972): 93–105; Harold Wolpe, "The Theory of Internal Colonialism: The South African Case," in Oxaal *et al.*, eds., *Beyond the Sociology of Development*, pp. 229–252; Immanuel Wallerstein, "Semi-peripheral Countries and the Contemporary World Crisis," *Theory and Society* 3(1976): 461–483; Amin, *Unequal Development*, chaps. 3 and 5; de Janvry, "Material Determinants of the World Food Crisis."

33. Amin, *Unequal Development*, chap. 1; R. Brenner, "The Origins of Capitalist Development: A Critique of Neo-Smithian Marxism," *New Left Review* 104(1977): 25–92.

34. Perry Anderson, *Lineages of the Absolutist State*, (London: Verso Editions, 1979).

capitalist world economy found its base in mercantilist trade and colonization, but reached full development only with the shift to financial imperialism in the monopoly era. It was then that the internal organization of production and structures of class domination in the periphery became directly molded by core capital. Investments abroad were to permit, from that point onward, the routine extraction of surplus via the mechanisms of international trade, unequal exchange, and fiscal indebtedness.

Subprocesses in the World-System

The preceding cursory review should make clear that the "new" perspective on world development emerging in U. S. social science has roots that date back for at least three-quarters of a century. With increasing recognition, there has been an acceleration at present of theoretical debates concerning the origins of this system, its present features, and its likely future course. Such critiques and reinterpretations tend to occur at a high level of abstraction where the world economy as a whole appears as the only viable unit of analysis. Research directed at buttressing one or another position also focuses at this broad level and tends to produce sweeping conclusions applicable in appearance to the entire system.

An example is the search for "secular trends" in the world-system pioneered by Wallerstein and his associates and the concomitant study of the number and duration of waves or cycles in the system. The debate focuses at present primarily on the "long-waves" identified by the Russian economist Kondratieff and includes conflicting diagnoses of whether the present state of the world economy is "up" or "down." The debate has been joined by orthodox Marxist economists like Ernest Mandel, conservative ones like Walt Rostow, and a research collective associated with Wallerstein.[35]

The result of analyses and debates dealing exclusively with the world level is the perpetuation of the gap between research and theory inherited from modernization times. Such gap creates two major problems. First, the lack of concern with concrete subprocesses has slowed down the application of the new general perspective to specific research topics. There is at present a manifest disjuncture between general theory, where the world-system perspective has become dominant, and the myriad lower-level focused studies—national, local, and thematic—based, on the earlier modernization model.

35. Immanuel Wallerstein, "Kondratieff Up or Kondratieff Down?" *Review* 4(Spring 1979): 663–673; See also in the same issue the statement by a Research Working Group, "Cyclical Rhythms and Secular Trends of the Capitalist World Economy: Some Premises, Hypotheses, and Questions," pp. 483–500; Ernest Mandel, *Late Capitalism* (London: Verso Editions, 1978), chap. 4; Walt Rostow, *The World Economy: History and Prospects* (Austin: University of Texas Press, 1978).

More important, this self-contained speculation on secular trends and long waves forgets that it was insights developed in the study of concrete historical processes that informed and gave rise to the original theories. It was the critique of classic political economy and, later on, of culturalist sociology as they failed to predict concrete outcomes at the national or regional levels that paved the way for the emergence of the new ideas.

The progressive formalization of models of the world-system today contrasts markedly with the practice of historical materialist analysis by Lenin or Luxemburg. The attention and study of delimited subprocesses in the world-system is not simply a matter of working out the fine points of an essentially "final" theory. It is rather a matter of correcting the theory in response to concrete economic and political conditions worldwide. The theory of imperialism, as developed by Lenin, represents precisely this kind of readaptation to changed conditions of analytic principles discovered by Marx in earlier inquiries on the capitalist mode of production.

Formal theories of the world system, as the one outlined recently by Hopkins and Wallerstein,[36] appear closer to classic political economy than to the practice of historical materialist analysis. The lack of attention to intermediate subprocesses within the global system leads to interpretive failures and to frequent "surprises" as concrete events overtake the theoretical axioms. Four examples of these limitations may be cited. First, the critique of the Ricardian theory of trade departed from the untenability of the assumption of perfect mobility of the factors—labor and capital—in the world market. This assumption had led to the predicted equalization of both profits and wages worldwide, a prediction held by Marxist economists such as Bukharin. ECLA and dependency economists pointed out the absurdity of this assumption since workers in the center and periphery are separated by legal and geographic barriers and are restricted by powerful structures of political control.[37]

Based in part on this contribution, the theory of unequal exchange assumed perfect mobility of capital and relative immobility of labor as the key to the process of surplus extraction. The consistent subremuneration of workers in the periphery depends on the stability of legal–political and economic arrangements confining them to specific locations. As usually described, unequal exchange is a process involving unequal rewards not only to capital and labor, but also to labor restricted to different national patches within the world economy.

Though accurate for the years following World War II, the assumption of differential mobility of the factors has become less tenable in recent years with the massive displacements of peripheral labor toward the centers. These

36. Hopkins and Wallerstein, "Patterns of Development of the Modern World System."
37. Booth, "Andre Gunder Frank," p. 55; Prebisch, *The Economic Development of Latin America in the Post War Period*.

movements, legal and illegal, have had the twin consequences of lowering production costs in the center while simultaneously reducing the size of the "surplus labor" in peripheral countries of emigration. The character of these large-scale movements and the mode in which they affect exchanges between core and periphery have not been systematically incorporated into world-system theories. In recent formulations, labor migration continues to be regarded, if by default, as a secondary process rather than the theoretically central one that it is.

Second, the uniform assignment of responsibility for the reproduction of the peripheral labor force to rural subsistence enclaves is subject to clear empirical challenge. Precapitalist agricultural production is associated with a segment of the world population, which is itself rapidly diminishing and which, in some peripheral countries, is already insignificant. In most world-system writings, the capitalist sector of peripheral economies is associated with the cities and a segment of technologically advanced agriculture, whereas the precapitalist sector is identified with the remainder of the rural population.[38] The latter, however, is rapidly decreasing. In particular, that segment of the peasantry producing exclusively under subsistence arrangements is disintegrating in many countries.[39]

The question for theory then is this: How can an economic sector, which is itself stagnant or declining, absorb the costs of production and reproduction of an ever-expanding urban labor force? Wallerstein has taken the problem to its logical conclusion by making the full proletarianization of the peripheral working class the main "secular trend" in the capitalist world-system leading to its eventual demise.[40] Such analyses and predictions fly in the face of the growing, not diminishing, gap in real wages between core and peripheral countries (including even the most "advanced" of the latter group) and between workers in the modern capitalist and traditional sectors in the periphery.[41] These expanding gaps attest to the vitality of the structures keeping unequal exchange in place and show the inadequacy of present interpretations of peripheral labor processes.

Third, the circulation of ideas in the world-system has received much less attention than the circulation of either commodities or capital. References to ideologies that justify class inequality or unequal exchange abound, but they are mostly casual and restricted to a national context. The significance of legitimacy and the legitimizing potential of ideologies has been recognized by all exponents of structural theories of development. Still, the emphasis on material interests

38. de Janvry, "Material Determinants of the World Food Crisis"; Amin, *Unequal Development*, chap. 3; Wolpe, "The Theory of Internal Colonialism: The South African Case"; Wallerstein, "Semi-peripheral Countries and the Contemporary World Crisis."

39. Evidence of this trend is presented in chap. 3.

40. Immanuel Wallerstein, "The Rise and Future Demise of the World Capitalist System: Concepts for Comparative Analysis," *Comparative Studies in Society and History* 16(September 1974): 387–415.

41. These trends and the empirical evidence supporting them are discussed in chap. 3.

and processes of political domination has relegated the circulation of ideas to a secondary and fairly obscure place.[42]

The question of ideology is less a problem than a gap in the world-system perspective. It is indeed within national contexts that ideologies of inequality and development become major instruments of legitimation. The extent to which hegemonic ideas are believed in by subordinate classes has much to do with the stability of the political order and, hence, the ability of a country to fulfill its "role" in the world economy. In the contemporary world-system, however, the production of ideology has ceased to be a national affair to depend, increasingly, on exchange and circulation across the globe. The flow of ideas from core to periphery and its articulation with the changing structures of economic domination is a central topic so far unexplored from this perspective.

Fourth, contemporary interpretations of unequal exchange and accumulation on a world scale tend to present an overly schematic account of class structure in different regions of the system. In particular, the class structure of the centers is portrayed as basically stable since many of its contradictions are "exported" to the periphery. Economists working from the unequal exchange perspective have focused on the partial transfer of productivity gains into wages by monopoly firms in the centers, thereby co-opting their domestic working class. They thus speak of "articulated" economies in the centers—meaning an organic convergence between the interests of core capital and labor—in opposition to the "disarticulated" economies of the periphery.[43]

Such arguments are contradicted, however, by an extensive empirical literature on effects in the structure of employment of the advanced countries of the internationalization of capital. It is difficult, for example, to reconcile benign descriptions of "articulation" between capital and labor with the deteriorating situation of large segments of traditional and competitive sectors of the American working class. This situation can be traced directly to contemporary worldwide strategies of capital. Central among the latter are the export of production and employment abroad and the importation of peripheral labor to combat the organizational efforts of the domestic working class.

Because they are couched at a high level of abstraction, world-system analyses of class structure often fail to take into account internal divisions within the working class in both center and periphery. In particular, they fail to note that the segment of the core working class employed by monopoly firms and, hence,

42. Indeed Wallerstein explicitly discounts the significance of ideology as a vehicle of legitimation and stability. In his view, legitimacy is primarily a matter of co-optation of the cadres rather than persuasion of the masses. See *The Modern World-System: Capitalist Agriculture and the Origins of the European World-Economy in the Sixteenth Century*, pp. 143–144.

43. Alain de Janvry and Carlos Garramon, "Laws of Motion of Capital in the Center-Periphery Structure," *Review of Radical Political Economics* 9(Summer 1977): 29–38.

benefiting from productivity increases represents a small and diminishing proportion of the labor force. The character of relationships between the rest of the core working class and the international economy is not satisfactorily captured by the concept of articulation.

We should note, finally, that the dualism between global theorizing and intermediate subprocesses is not being overcome by efforts to "test" these theories on the basis of quantitative cross-national data. Such efforts stem from the transformation of historically grounded analyses of the expansion of capitalism into "schools" of research. This transformation has been undertaken by scholars who endeavored to adapt what they viewed as intriguing but untested ideas into the molds of positivist science. The result is a burgeoning empirical literature where world capitalism or "dependency" become independent variables predicting such effects as GNP *per capita* and domestic inequality. [44]

These studies are typically based on aggregate data from nation-states, defined as sample units. The analysis ignores historical differences across these units, assuming that the operationalization of variables is not only valid for the whole, but valid equally for the different countries. The need to find comparable data for a sufficiently large number of countries tends to restrict the analysis to fairly short time periods bearing no relation to the character of historical processes explored in the original theoretical analyses.

The fundamental flaw of this derivative empirical literature is the transformation of a *perspective* on international processes into a "variable." As Gereffi has observed, the condition of peripheral countries was never conceived in the original writings as a continuum from "more" to "less"; instead, it referred to a distinct historical situation. Given a *context* of dependency, relationships between specific economic and political factors may have certain predictable outcomes. [45]

The consequence of the forced transformation of complex national situations into a "variable" has resulted in statistics often at variance with painstakingly acquired knowledge of individual countries. Fernando Henrique Cardoso has noted that the long-term effects of this empirical literature has not been to prove

44. See, for example, the peculiar conclusions arrived at by Jacques Delacroix in his "The Export of Raw Materials and Economic Growth: A Cross-National Study," *American Sociological Review* 42(October 1977): 795–808. On the basis of cross-national data with independent variables lagged only 15 years (1955–1970), Delacroix concludes that it is not the position of countries in the world economy, but internal factors, such as secondary school enrollment (an indicator of "information processing capacity") that play a significant role in national development. For a review of this literature, see Robert L. Bach, "The Reproduction of Triviality: Critical Notes on Recent Attempts to Test the Dynamics of World Capitalism," mimeo, Department of Sociology, State University of New York at Binghamton, 1978.

45. Gary Gereffi, "A Critical Evaluation of Quantitative Cross-National Studies of Dependency," paper presented at the panel on "Dependency Theory," at the meetings of the International Studies Association, Toronto, March 1979.

or disprove the original theoretical insights, but rather to "consume" them.[46] Significant advances in the theory of imperialism and the world economy become hidden from view under a mass of contradictory and misdirected empirical "evidence." Results of all this empirical travail have seldom answered original theoretical problems nor challenged the conclusions reached by serious historical research.

The main objection to this expanding brand of world-system research is not to quantitative analysis per se, but to what might be called "contextless" quantification. The internal complexity of the units of analysis—nations or regions—makes ad hoc interpretation of statistical findings unacceptable. Appropriate interpretation in this area demands, at a minimum, prior knowledge of the historical context where measurements were taken.

A Research Agenda

The next question is one of substance. If intermediate level analyses are necessary to bridge the gap between grand theory and concrete situations, what are the specific topics that they must address? It would be pretentious to attempt a comprehensive answer here. Yet, some general lines of inquiry can be suggested, based on the preceding discussion.

Much recent theory on the state of the world-system has derived from the work of economists. They have contributed fundamental notions such as unequal exchange and articulation between hegemonic and subordinate modes of production. Historians and sociologists have made their contribution primarily in the study of institutions such as the state, trading companies, and, more recently, the multinational corporation.

The perspective common to most of these studies is one that views the world-system "from above" and that focuses on global strategies of industrial and finance capital and on the actions of core states in defense of the dominant order. In particular, the economic literature deals with the actions of capital, such as financial imperialism, surplus extraction, and terms of trade between core and periphery, in a manner frequently oblivious of the social and political structures that sustain such processes and the internal contradictions to which they are subject. Capital, in these analyses, appears as the *only* active factor of production.

No doubt we need more studies of capitalist accumulation and its interna-

46. Fernando H. Cardoso, "The Consumption of Dependency Theory in the United States," *Latin American Research Review* 12(1977): 7–24.

tional requirements; but, together with these, we need to focus attention on the labor process. By this we mean the modes in which workers are controlled and utilized in different areas of the world-system *and* their reactions to the changing organization of surplus extraction and political domination. In other words, we need additional analysis of class structures within specific nation-states as they are molded and in turn react to world-capitalist penetration. Included under this rubric are the shifting character of the working class in response to labor migration and the locational decisions of firms; contradictions within core and peripheral class structures provoked by the global strategies of capital; and the forms adopted by the class struggle in response to them.

A major paradox in contemporary social science is that important studies of class and class struggle tend to have a purely domestic focus, whereas studies of the world-system are pitched at such high levels of abstraction that they neglect concrete class formations. A focus on modes of labor utilization and control provides substance for the analysis of intermediate subprocesses. It is here where many hidden structures sustaining unequal exchange and global accumulation are found; it is also in the interaction between classes, not between nation-states, where the fundamental contradictions of the system are located.

The purpose of the following chapters is twofold: first, to explore the interface between the labor process, class structure, and the global requirements of accumulation as a necessary complement to the analysis of capital and dominant institutions; second, by focusing on this interaction to clarify some of the apparent contradictions and bring the general models in line with empirical reality. Each chapter addresses one of the four substantive problem areas previously identified: namely, international migration, precapitalist modes of production and the reproduction of the urban labor force, dominant ideologies of inequality, and class structure in the core. These topics are certainly not exhaustive of all those that an intermediate analysis could explore. They are, however, representative of those most urgently in need of attention for theoretical development and possess, in addition, substantive importance on their own.

Our analysis requires the intermixing of concepts and hypotheses derived from general theory with the available empirical knowledge on each particular topic. This approach should not be confused with a "test" of the general perspective, a task we do not believe appropriate or possible at this level. Our effort is aimed at two different goals: first, to explore how a world-system framework can help recast the state of knowledge in each particular area showing trends and relationships not identified previously; second, to examine how the assembling of empirical evidence can clarify problems in the general perspective and rechannel theoretical inquiry in new directions.

To do justice to each particular topic, we must immerse ourselves and the reader into the empirical literature. Though the empirical materials presented are themselves a digest from much wider sources, they may tax the patience of the theoretically oriented. We can only reply that this use of the relevant literature lies at the core of the type of intermediate analysis we have proposed.

We reserve the common lines of argument and new directions that emerge from the individual studies for the Conclusion. At this point, as a guide to the next chapters, it is possible to specify two theoretical axes along which the four selected topics fall. First, we consider the circulation of labor as it affects the social relationships of production and promotes internal divisions within the working class (Chapters 2 and 3). Second, we consider the circulation of capital and its consequences for the condition of workers in the countries where it originates and as it promotes the diffusion and adoption of particular ideologies of inequality (Chapters 4 and 5).

The task proposed here is an ambitious one and the path is still uncharted. It is for the reader to judge the extent to which we have succeeded. In presenting the following four studies, we are less concerned with their being complete or final statements on each individual topic than with their opening the way for a new and necessary type of analysis. It is by simultaneously considering global theory and concrete reality that our present understanding of the world-system can be advanced and the promise of this general perspective actualized.

2

International Migration: Conditions for the Mobilization and Use of Migrant Labor under World Capitalism[1]

Introduction

The movement of human populations has been an intrinsic component of major processes of structural change throughout history. Whether in response to political or economic imperatives, whether spontaneous or coerced, whether involving entire nations or selected groups within them, the displacement of people through space has accompanied every major transformation of the social order. Thus defined, migration is almost coterminous with history.

Since the advent of capitalism and especially during the last 150 years, attention has been concentrated, however, on a particular form of migration. This migration possesses several distinct characteristics. First, it does not encompass entire nations, but particular sectors of them. Second, it does not generally occur through coercion but through inducement and spontaneous decision. Third, it is not directed toward unknown or hostile nations but occurs fundamentally between units articulated into the same international system. Fourth, the forces underlying it are fundamentally economic and produce a patterned movement, sustained over extensive periods of time and predictable as to direction and size. Fifth, and most important, it is migration of *labor*, that is, of individuals whose purpose in moving is to sell their work capacity in the receiving areas.

It is this last characteristic that has come to define modern population movements. Although many other types of migration have existed, today the word has become synonymous with the displacement of labor. This distinction is important since a purely demographic definition of migration invariably obscures the very different economic roles that such "migrants" play.

1. An earlier version of this chapter appeared under the title, "Migration and Underdevelopment," *Politics and Society* 8(1978): 1–48. Adapted by permission.

The articulation of a global economic order during the last centuries is the factor underlying the increasing dominance of labor migration. Tilly estimates that from 1800 to World War I the net size of European labor migration abroad was of the order of 50 million or 65 million, if return migration is taken into account.[2] In this chapter, we examine selected characteristics of long-distance labor migration as a process routinely accompanying the development of the international economic order. The features we will highlight do not comprise a "theory" of international migration but rather challenge standard interpretations of the phenomenon by orthodox and even critical theories. In this sense, this chapter corresponds to the common attempt of this book to show the utility of an internationalized global perspective on processes previously studied exclusively from a domestic standpoint.

The advent of labor migration as the dominant form is a relatively recent phenomenon. The earlier development of mercantilism on a world scale had also promoted other forms of economically motivated movements. Unlike labor migration—where the specific intent is to sell human work in an established market—these other forms have, as a common feature, geographic displacement to areas where appropriate natural resources and labor were more readily available. They can be generically termed "colonizing migrations." Several specific forms exist.

Omvedt, for example, distinguishes between the earlier commercial colonizations—where the primary purpose was the appropriation of gold, spices, and other objects of trade—and the industrial type—where the goal was the stable supply of raw materials and the creation of markets for manufactures.[3] Along similar lines, Stein and Stein differentiate between direct colonizations by the Spanish and Portuguese in Latin America and the indirect forms preferred by the British in the nineteenth century.[4] In addition, there are colonizing migrations where the primary intent is the exploitation of natural resources using the colonists' own labor, and there are those where the goal is the appropriation of value produced by the work of subjected populations.

Colonizing migrations were the dominant form of economically motivated population movements for two centuries. They were the concrete manifestation of the expansion of an European-based mercantilist economy into outlying territories. The gradual decline of colonizing movements, especially in the last century, coincided with the exhaustion of such isolated areas and with the

2. Charles Tilly, "Migration in Modern European History," in *Human Migration, Patterns and Policies*, eds. William H. McNeill and Ruth Adams (Bloomington: Indiana University Press, 1978), pp. 48–72.
3. Gail Omvedt, "Towards a Theory of Colonialism," *The Insurgent Sociologist* (Spring 1973): 1–24.
4. Stanley Stein and Barbara Stein, *The Colonial Heritage of Latin America* (New York: Oxford University Press, 1970).

incorporation of the world into a single capitalist economic system.[5] It can be argued, however, that the present period of labor migration, far from being independent from earlier colonizing movements, was ushered in by the latter. This occurred as colonists procured replenishment for an exhausted domestic labor supply or as they so disrupted a preexisting native economy as to force migration of a newly created "surplus" population.

Early Labor Migrations

Early scholarly attention to the migration of labor centered on the question of consequences of the movement for exporting countries. The mercantilist school opposed emigration from the home country on the grounds that it would weaken the national economy. By the second half of the seventeenth century, this school had articulated a position that identified strength with numbers and saw, in Sir Joshua Child's words, "the riches of city or nation as lying in the multitude of its inhabitants."[6]

The movement that mercantilists opposed was, by and large, one of members of the domestic working class going as colonists abroad. Undermined first by the Malthusian analysis of population, mercantilism came under full attack by nineteenth-century political economists. They argued that emigration, far from weakening the home economy, would strengthen it since it would open new markets for its products, and bring relief from overpopulation. For English economists, such as Torrens, colonization was essentially the application of redundant capital and population of England to redundant lands of her empire.[7]

The most cogent defense of this position was presented in John Stuart Mill's *Principles of Political Economy*, which viewed the export of population, as well as capital, as ways of counteracting the tendency of profits to fall to a minimum. The release of part of the circulating capital and labor to the colonies would alleviate the pressure on the fertility of the land and, hence, retard the trend toward decreasing profits.

Mill argued that emigrant labor could be profitably employed by capital in the colonies provided emigrants were prevented by the state from becoming land proprietors and working for themselves. Use of political means to guarantee this economic function of emigrant labor was deemed by Mill important enough to warrant infringement of the dominant postulates of *laissez faire*.[8] As will be seen,

5. Immanuel Wallerstein, "Rural Economy in World-Society," *Studies in Comparative International Development* 12(Spring 1977): 29–40.

6. Brinley Thomas, *Migration and Economic Growth* (second edition), (London: Cambridge University Press, 1973), p. 1.

7. *Ibid.*, chap. 1.

8. John Stuart Mill, *Principles of Political Economy* (London: Longmans, 1909), Book III.

his position was in no way foreign to the actual usage made of immigrants in the United States, Brazil, and elsewhere.

Classical economic theories of immigration in the nineteenth century occurred in a context in which core industrialized nations, such as England, were also sources of emigration. Thus, control of investment capital and of the immigrant labor required by that capital abroad rested in the same hands at the centers of the system. Throughout the nineteenth century, the United States, Canada, and Australia received both investment capital and labor from England; a positive correlation existed between the two flows. In Tilly's words, the British Isles were "the champion exporters of humankind and the chief Purveyors to America."[9] Their poor inhabited large tracts of all the newly opened continents. Theories of immigration, no matter what their divergences, dealt invariably with this situation in which labor flowed from the economic center to the periphery.[10]

Changes in this situation emerged in the United States during the second half of the nineteenth century as a result of two processes. First, there was a progressive autonomy relative to the earlier dependence on foreign (British) capital. Second, new sources of labor began to be tapped in eastern and southern Europe. Contrary to the pattern of earlier European immigrations, new migrants did not originate in the laboring classes of the advanced economies, but came instead from backward agricultural regions in process of transformation.[11] The end of the slave trade—brought about by colonization of West Africa and the denial by the British of this source of labor to their competitors—meant the closure of a then viable alternative. In a most poignant instance of this relation, peasant labor from northern Italy directly replaced slaves in Brazil's coffee plantations.[12]

In the northern region of the United States, peasant labor could be employed because technological innovations made it profitable to substitute skilled workers with poorly paid unskilled laborers. The low wages paid to the new immigrants discouraged, in turn, the continuation of emigration by the better trained, or at least, more urbanized, workers from the industrial countries of Europe.

At this point, the sources of investment capital and of free immigrant labor ceased to coincide. In rough terms, immigration finally ceased to be a "colonizing" movement from the centers of expanding commercial imperialism and became, instead, a movement from peripheral countries and regions in response

---

9. Tilly, "Migration in Modern European History," p. 58.

10. Thomas, *Migration and Economic Growth*; Mill, *Principles of Political Economy*.

11. Gerald Rosenblum, *Immigrant Workers: Their Impact on American Labor Radicalism* (New York: Basic Books, 1973).

12. Jorge Balán, "Regional Urbanization under Primary-Sector Expansion in Neo-Colonial Countries," in *Current Perspectives in Latin American Urban Research*, eds. Alejandro Portes and Harley L. Browning (Austin: Special Publications Series of the Institute of Latin American Studies, University of Texas, 1975), pp. 151–179.

to the needs of new industrial centers. This shift in the nature and origins of immigration was to consolidate itself during the twentieth century.

The progressive disappearance of unincorporated areas and economic frontiers after the consolidation of world capitalism thus transformed immigration from a movement of "advanced" populations settling backward lands, to one in which "backward" populations were induced to fit the needs of more advanced economies. The shift also marked the obsolescence of classical political economy as an approach to immigration and, though seldom noted in contemporary writings, signaled the emergence of new conceptual frameworks underlying all contemporary theories.

Theoretical Perspectives: A Critique

The advent of contemporary demographic and sociological studies of migration have not necessarily improved our understanding of the process since, as a whole, they fall far behind the breadth of scope of nineteenth-century political economy. The most common empirical trend is that of studies that search for causes of migration in individualistic factors. Quite clearly, individuals migrate for a number of different causes—desire to escape oppression or famine, financial ambition, family reunification, or education of children. Nothing is easier than to compile lists of such "push" and "pull" factors and present them as a theory of migration. The customary survey reporting percentages endorsing each such "cause" might be useful as a sort of first approximation to the question of "who migrates?" In no way, however, does it explain the structural factors leading to a patterned movement, of known size and direction, over an extensive period of time.

The same literature has tended to accept geographic and juridical distinctions at face value. Coupled with the trend toward specialization, this has led to compartmentalization of the study of migration along lines that obscure the basic similarities of apparently diverse movements. Thus, separate bodies of research exist on legal and illegal immigration, on internal and international migration, on working-class emigration and the so-called brain drain with little or no articulation between them and little or no understanding of their related structural determinants.

Static methodologies of research have led to a rigid conceptualization of migration. The image portrayed by conventional demographic accounts is that of an uni-directional flow that "empties" certain regions while filling others. This image does not generally take into account phenomena such as return migration, division of time between urban and rural employment, and displacement to third cities or regions. More generally, it fails to cope with the full complexity of migration as the convergence between economic constraints and the strategies of human groups to deal with them.

At a higher level of generality, other scholars have defined migration as the outcome of broad economic and political forces. There is agreement at this level that labor migration is a response to structural inequalities between nations and regions. Several perspectives compete, however, for explanation of the dynamics and consequences of migration. Earlier ones invariably described the process as involving the interaction between two distinct sociospatial units: that which expels labor and that which absorbs it.

The first and better-known perspective views labor migration as a way of restoring equilibrium between spatial units. Migration decreases the pressure of population in low-growth areas and provides for the labor needs of the growing regions, thus helping restore balance between human and capital resources. Mill's analysis of population movements represents an earlier instance of equilibrium theory. Conventional economics defines migration as, in principle, a self-regulating process through which spatial differences in labor demand and supply adjust themselves. Higher wages in urban areas stimulate out-migration from the subsistence rural sector. The new abundance of workers results in a shift of urban industries toward labor-intensive methods, therefore providing employment for the first waves of migrants.

A continuation of the process yields, however, an overabundance of labor. If unfettered by other constraints, the market will react by a rapid reduction of wages, which in turn decreases the attractiveness of migration for those still in the subsistence economy.

For W. Arthur Lewis, the "rigidity" of wages in urban areas—brought about by prolabor legislation and the organization of the workers—is the factor responsible for continuing migration and urban unemployment.[13] In the absence of self-regulation by the market, industrial wages are maintained at an artificially high level. There is no way then that the traditional subsistence sector can continue to retain excess labor and not dump it into the urban market. At the same time, high wages discourage industrial investment in labor-intensive methods, thus leading to the rise of unemployment.

A variant of equilibrium theory exists in sociology under the general rubric *modernization*. The penetration of Western-style values and forms of consumption in backward regions leads to the emergence of new aspirations among their most dynamic sectors. Mobilization for attainment of these goals takes place, inevitably, in the larger cities where the glittering prospects of modern life can be

13. W. Arthur Lewis, "Unemployment in Developing Countries," Lectures to the Mid-West Research Conference, 1964, cited in Paul Singer, *Economia Politica da Urbanizacão* (third edition) (São Paulo: Editora Brasiliense, 1976), p. 42.

fulfilled. Exposure to Westernism thus produces a split in the population of backward areas: those clinging to the ways of the past are labeled "traditional"; those willing to adapt themselves to the new trends are recognized as "modern." For Daniel Lerner, "empathy," or the ability to put oneself in the role of Western man, is the mark of modernity.[14] Migration is the logical outcome of this value split: It restores equilibrium by moving those more attuned to the advanced world to advanced centers and leaving the traditional population behind.

In both its economic and social versions, equilibrium theory has been the object of severe criticism. Economists have noted that this orthodox perspective does not satisfactorily explain why migrant labor flows are not much larger than they are: "Given the existing income differential and the ease with which employers seem to be able to tap new sources of labor to sustain a given demand, it is impossible to understand in conventional terms why that demand is not much more extensive."[15] Other critics have not questioned the existence of regional inequalities, nor of motivations that lead to migration in search of higher wages or modern advantages. They focus, however, on the consequences for outmigration areas, which, in the modern world, are invariably those of the periphery.[16]

The counterperspective on migration was popularized by Gunnar Myrdal under the label *cumulative causation*.[17] "Backwash effects" by which surplus is drained from underdeveloped areas are not self-regulating but cumulative, leading to an ever-greater impoverishment and depopulation of these regions. In a manner similar to Mill, Myrdal portrayed population and capital resources as flowing in the same direction and from identical sources. In mid-twentieth century, however, these flows did not originate in the core, but in the periphery and did not function to develop peripheral areas, but to deepen their underdevelopment.

This general idea was further elaborated and documented by Paul Baran and other Marxist scholars in the United States and by dependency writers in Latin America. Their argument was again that trade relationships and the flow of investment capital from advanced to peripheral countries did not lead to eventual

14. Daniel Lerner, *The Passing of Traditional Society, Modernizing the Middle-East* (New York: Free Press, 1965).

15. Michael J. Piore, *Birds of Passage, Migrant Labor and Industrial Societies* (New York: Cambridge University Press, 1979), p. 30.

16. Singer, *Economia Politica;* Gunnar Myrdal, *Rich Lands and Poor* (New York: Harper & Row, 1957), Andre G. Frank, "The Development of Underdevelopment," in *Latin America: Underdevelopment or Revolution* (New York: Monthly Review Press, 1970), pp. 3–94; Alejandro Portes, "Modernity and Development: A Critique," *Studies in Comparative International Development* 9(Spring 1974): 247–79.

17. Myrdal, *Rich Lands and Poor.*

parity or equilibrium between them but rather to the progressive subordination of the weaker regions.[18] The surplus of peripheral economies was continuously drained off, with the result that they stagnated or grew at rates slower than did central ones and in terms dictated by the latter.

The importance of these writings for the study of migration is that they provided a unifying framework on the causes of superficially diverse processes. In agreement with the metaphor of a worldwide hierarchy of exploitation, domestic rural–urban migration followed the one-way flow of economic surplus and reflected the domination of rural areas and smaller cities by the national metropolis. International labor migration, in turn, reflected the struggles of impoverished populations of the subordinate countries to gain access to advanced industrial consumption. Finally, the brain drain of professionals from the Third World was just one more manifestation of the exploitation of these societies and their continuous loss of resources to the central ones.[19]

Students of dependency went on to disaggregate the factors grouped under Myrdal's "backwash effects." For Paul Singer, two sets of factors account for labor migration: factors of change and factors of stagnation.[20] The first have to do with the penetration of capitalist techniques of production into areas of traditional agriculture. The new techniques displace labor, which is forced to move toward regional or national centers or even to foreign countries. Factors of stagnation operate when the growth of population exceeds the productivity of the land thus forcing the displacement of the surplus labor.

The merit of the cumulative causation-dependency perspective was to present a coherent interpretation tying together apparently disparate phenomena. The approach is both simple and appealing in making of labor migration an integral aspect of the operations of an international system to exploitation. However, several limitations have become apparent in recent years that reduce the applicability of this perspective.

First, it shares with equilibrium theory the basic view of migration as a process occurring between two distinct spatially defined units: that which is exploited and

18. Paul A. Baran, *The Political Economy of Growth* (New York: Monthly Review, 1957); Andre G. Frank, *Latin America: Underdevelopment or Revolution* (New York: Monthly Review, 1970); Harry Magdoff, *The Age of Imperialism* (New York: Monthly Review, 1969); Celso Furtado, *Development and Underdevelopment* (Berkeley: University of California Press, 1971); Osvaldo Sunkel, *Capitalismo transnacional y desintegración nacional en América Latina* (Buenos Aires: Nueva Visión, 1962); Theotonio dos Santos, "La crisis de la teoría del desarrollo y las relaciones de dependencia en América Latina," in *La dependencia político-económica de América Latina* (México, D. F.: Siglo Veintiuno Editores, 1970), pp. 147–187; Fernando Henrique Cardoso and Enzo Faletto, *Dependencia y desarrollo en América Latina* (México, D. F.: Siglo Veintiuno Editores, 1970).

19. John Walton, "Urban Hierarchies and Patterns of Dependence in Latin America: Theoretical Bases for a New Research Agenda," in *Current Perspectives in Latin American Urban Research*, eds. Alejandro Portes and Harley L. Browning (Austin: Special Publications Series of the Institute of Latin American Studies, University of Texas, 1976), pp. 43–69; Singer, *Economia Politica*; Andre G. Frank, *Latin America*, chap. 2.

20. Singer, *Economia Politica*, chap. 2.

exports labor and that which exploits and receives labor. This polarity between places of origin and places of destination leads to a static conceptualization of concrete processes of migration: Power and capital flow in one direction; economic surplus and labor in the other. After a while, it is not clear what is left in the periphery or how such places can survive. Empirical evidence, on the contrary, indicates that dependent regions can maintain themselves and even grow under these conditions. Such areas may not necessarily lose population, but may gain it through vegetative growth, migration from less developed places, and return migration from core regions.

More important, the dependency conceptualization of relationships between center and periphery, including labor migration, does not make clear how existing conditions can change. This approach is partially static in that it ends with the image of an entrenched and essentially unalterable system of exploitation.[21] Historical evidence shows, on the contrary, that the conditions of labor migration have changed significantly and continue to do so under capitalism.

More recent writings offer promise of overcoming the difficulties of the cumulative causation–dependency perspective without returning to those of conventional equilibrium theories. Recent statements of the world-system perspective, for example, convey with full force the fact that labor migration, such as related exchanges, does not occur as an external process between two separate entities, but as part of the internal dynamics of the same overarching unit. This unit, the world-capitalist system, is constantly changing according to forces that allow its components to modify their relative positions without significantly altering the basic dynamics of the accumulation process.

Further, these recent writings have specified with greater clarity the nature of the change forces at play. Here, they essentially restate the classic Marxist analysis of the laws of motion of capital with emphasis on territorial expansion. In brief, existing peripheral areas are bound ever closer to the centers via a series of financial and trade mechanisms controlled by the latter. Although the purpose is always maximization of the surplus, the net result is an ever-growing articulation and interdependence between the different economic units of the system.[22]

21. Philip O'Brien, "A Critique of Latin American Theories of Dependency," in *Beyond the Sociology of Development: Economy and Society in Latin America and Africa*, eds. Ivar Oxaal, Tony Barnett, and David Booth (London: Routledge and Kegan Paul, 1975), pp. 7–27. See also Fernando Henrique Cardoso, "The Consumption of Dependency Theory in the United States," *Latin American Research Review* 12(1977): 7–24.

22. Samir Amin, *Accumulation on a World Scale*, 2 Vols. (New York: Monthly Review Press, 1974); Immanuel Wallerstein, *The Modern World-System I: Capitalist Agriculture and the Origins of the European World-Economy in the Sixteenth Century* (New York: Academic Press, 1974); Terence K. Hopkins and Immanuel Wallerstein "Patterns of Development of the Modern World-System," *Review* 1(Fall 1977): 111–145. Fernando Henrique Cardoso, "Associated Dependent Development: Theoretical and Practical Implications," in *Authoritarian Brazil* ed. Alfred Stepan (New Haven: Yale University Press, 1973), pp. 142–178; Jonathan Friedman, "Crises in Theory and Transformations of the World Economy," *Review* 11(Fall 1978): 131–146.

The penetration of capitalism in evermore recondite corners of the planet, the monetization and reorganization of the most peripheral economies, and the growing information among peripheral populations of events and conditions in the centers, all have significant consequences for the character of labor migration.

Within this general perspective, the study of contemporary international migration involves the issues of mobilization, transportation, and utilization of a disposable labor force within territorial units that have been brought under the same economic system. The general process can be analyzed under four headings:

1. Conditions under which labor migration can be induced
2. Conditions under which labor can be released and transported
3. Conditions under which migrant labor can be profitably utilized
4. Conditions under which workers themselves can put migration to economic advantage

Each problem is examined in the following sections of this chapter through specific studies used for illustrating general points. Disparity in time, place, and content of the examples discussed represents an intentional attempt to show how common forces underlie superficially different movements. Each of the headings just listed encompasses a wide-range of topics, which cannot be appropriately covered here. The purpose in each case is to advance theoretical propositions that, though tentative and open to modification, serve to integrate disparate strands of the empirical literature and to summarize its essential characteristics.

A world-system perspective on international migration leads to a series of propositions not otherwise encountered in the literature. Corresponding to each of the above headings, the following four propositions will be advanced:

1. International labor migration does not occur through "invidious" comparisons of economic advantage between separate, autonomous countries, but requires the penetration of economic and political institutions of peripheral areas by those of the core.
2. The articulation of capitalism on a world scale has led to two convergent subprocesses: (*a*) dominant classes in sending regions have found it increasingly advantageous to allow, rather than resist, the release of labor; (*b*) costs of transportation and the risks of the journey have been increasingly assumed by the migrants themselves.
3. The effective utilization of migrants as a source of cheap labor depends in most concrete instances, on deliberate political manipulation designed to ensure a condition of vulnerability *vis-à-vis* capital.
4. Migration as a means of survival and of gaining access to economic advantage is most appropriately defined, at the individual level, as a process of

network building. Such networks allow workers to search for opportunities distributed unequally in space and facilitate exploration of avenues of gain outside the formal economy.

The significance of these propositions will be clarified by discussion and selected examples.

Inducement to Migration

External Disequilibrium and Internal Imbalancing

Perhaps the most interested simplification of the process of labor migration advanced by classical equilibrium theory is that it occurs between two societies that are autonomous and internally integrated, but at different levels of economic development. The search for economic advantage then motivates workers in the poorer society to move to the richer one. This market explanation runs consistently against the fact that many "backward" economies throughout history have not spontaneously exported labor and that, when labor has been needed, it has had to be coerced out of them.[23]

Sustained labor migration requires the penetration of the political and economic institutions of the dominant unit—nation-state or region—into the subordinate one. This penetration creates imbalances between sectors and institutions of the subordinate unit, which lead eventually to labor displacement. Imbalances are induced from the outside, but become *internal* to the structure of the weaker societies. These internal imbalances, not invidious comparisons with the wealth of more developed regions, are what underlie sustained processes of labor migration.

To clarify the point, one can examine characteristics of migration accompanying each of three "ideal" stages in the incorporation of outlying areas into the capitalist world economy. During the first stage, the society has not yet entered into contact with capitalist expansion. There is, of course, no migration since whatever differences in wealth exist are unknown to the outlying population. Such areas constituted the norm during early stages of formation of the capitalist economy and represented the object of "colonizing" migrations.

During the second stage, trade relationships are established between a colonial power and the outlying society. The latter still conserves its social organization intact and remains governed by its original rulers. Although there is now

23. Francis Wilson, "International Migration in Southern Africa," *International Migration Review* 10(Winter 1976): 451–488. Robert Blauner, *Racial Oppression in America* (New York: Harper & Row, 1972); Balan, "Regional Urbanization."

awareness of the existence of other advanced economies, spontaneous migration does not occur. Labor may enter as a commodity into commercial relationships with the external powers, but its transfer is mediated by local chiefs who organize it and benefit from it. A classic example of this situation is the trade enclaves established by Portugal in the Indian Ocean beginning in the sixteenth century. Contrary to Spain, Portugal deliberately avoided a colonization policy in many instances, preferring the highly profitable external trade with native states.[24]

The establishment of *factorias* on the African coast during the years of the slave trade documents a different situation in which labor is the principal commodity of the exchange, but its displacement is not voluntary. Though the *factorias* frequently promoted tribal wars in order to increase the number of prisoners turned into slaves, their dealings were still directly with the local chieftains.[25]

In a third stage, the outlying area is incorporated, as periphery, into the orbit of a capitalist power. Its internal structure is altered, new local classes emerge, and the economy is remolded to fit external demands. There are concomitant changes in cultural values and normative expectations. Structural imbalances between newer and older elements eventually produce migratory pressures.

If labor displacement occurs, its key feature is that it is neither coerced nor mediated by local authorities, but a product of voluntary decisions. Migration becomes an *economic* movement for migrants themselves as well as for users of their labor. Economic inducements frequently lead workers to self-transport to areas where their labor is needed and to assume the risks of the passage. This "spontaneous" migration naturally cheapens costs relative to earlier forms of labor procurement.

Imbalancing of peripheral societies can take many forms—from deliberate measures to produce labor migration to displacements which are the unintended consequence of other forms of penetration. U. S. Marxists have tended to describe capitalist penetration as a uniform process of destruction of traditional modes of production and their substitution by strictly capitalist relations. Thus, Paul Baran advanced the theory of the decomposition of precapitalist structures and the dependency writings of Andre Gunder Frank incorporated the idea in the thesis of a single chain of exploitation from the international centers of capital to the most isolated rural regions.[26]

More recent economic anthropology and economic history have shown how flexible the process can in fact be: Dominant capitalist structures may not only coexist with precapitalist modes of production but, under certain circumstances,

24. A. H. de Oliveira Marques, *History of Portugal* (New York: Columbia University Press, 1972).

25. *Ibid.*; Lino Novas Calvo, *El Negrero, vida novelada de Pedro Blanco Fernández Trava* (Buenos Aires: Espasa-Calpe, 1944).

26. Paul Baran, *Political Economy of Growth*; Frank, *Latin America.*

will actively promote them. A typology can thus be constructed of the relations of capitalism with newly subjected regions of which only one, settler colonization and the destruction of the preexisting traditional economy, corresponds to the dependency analogy. Other situations are: (a) the extraction of surplus, via tributation, from a still intact precapitalist economy; and (b) its use as a source and reserve of labor.[27]

In Volume 2 of *Capital*, Marx states:

> No matter whether commodities are the output of production based on slavery, of peasants . . . or of half-savage hunting tribes, etc. . . . as commodities and money they come face to face with the money and commodities in which the industrial capital presents itself. . . . The character of the process of production from which it originates is immaterial. They function as commodities in the market, and as commodities they enter into the circuit of industrial capital as well as into the circulation of surplus value incorporated into it. . . . To replace them . . . they must be reproduced and to this extent the capitalist mode of production is conditional on modes of production lying outside of its own stage of development.[28]

Labor-power, like commodities, can be produced and reproduced outside the capitalist sphere. Under certain circumstances, the preservation of traditional subsistence enclaves is a most convenient form of rearing workers at no direct expense to capital and of avoiding high-cost formal systems of old age, illness, and unemployment compensation. Workers, drawn at a salary from the subsistence sector, can be returned there when no longer needed. As shown by Meillassoux, enterprises in the modern capitalist sector are thus able to pay only for the direct support of workers, avoiding the indirect wages necessary for their reproduction and maintenance in periods of enforced idleness.[29]

Use of precapitalist enclaves as sources of wage-labor involves a constant tension between the need to monetize them and partially imbalance their internal structure to promote migration, and the need to preserve their autonomous capacity for food production to enable them to absorb unneeded workers.[30] The best-studied case in point, that of South Africa, will be reviewed. It must be stressed that this is not the only form of penetration of peripheral areas, nor is the

27. John Clammer, "Economic Anthropology and the Sociology of Development: 'Liberal' Anthropology and its French Critics," in Oxaal et al., eds., *Beyond the Sociology of Development*, pp. 208–228.

28. Karl Marx, *Capital, Vol. II* (Moscow: Foreign Language Publishing House, 1962), pp. 109–110.

29. C. Meillassoux, "From Reproduction to Production," *Economy and Society* 1(1972): 95–105; C. Meillassoux, "Imperialism as a Mode of Reproduction of Labour Power," unpublished paper cited in Harold Wolpe, "The Theory of Internal Colonialism: The South African Case," in Oxaal et al., eds., *Beyond the Sociology of Development*, pp. 229–252.

30. Meillassoux, "Imperialism as a Mode of Reproduction of Labour Power"; Clammer, "Economic Anthropology and the Sociology of Development."

resulting migration limited to manual wage-workers. To illustrate this point, the case of highly skilled professional workers is examined next.

Imbalancing and Manual Labor Migration: The South African Case

Native migration in South Africa is a classic case of deliberate imbalancing of the subordinate society for the purpose of forcing a release of labor. To accomplish this, constraints were imposed on a previously self-sufficient economy to prevent it from fully providing for the maintenance of the worker and his family. The nature of these constraints was political, and the task of imposing them fell squarely on the state. Constraints were of two kinds: (a) the reduction of the ability of the traditional economy to provide for the costs of maintenance and reproduction of its members; and (b) imposition of new costs that a subsistence economy could not bear.

The origins of the present system go back to the opening of mines in the late nineteenth century. According to Wilson, patterns set then by the diamond mines of Kimberley and the compounds erected to house industrial Chinese workers on the Witwatersrand governed the course of events for the next six decades.[31] Early self-sufficiency is exemplified by the case of the Bantu households of Bechuanaland. Each household produced its own food by tilling the land and breeding livestock; it built its own huts and made most of its clothing and utensils. A simple division of labor among men, women, and children ensured fulfillment of these tasks. Although some specialized goods were made and bartered by craftsmen, no regular production for exchange in the market took place.[32] From about 1830, Europeans began to visit Bechuanaland. They introduced new material goods that were traded for native products, such as ivory and ostrich feathers. These early commercial contacts, however, did not imbalance the native economy and break down its self-sufficiency.

In 1885, a Protectorate was proclaimed for Bechuanaland and in 1899, the Administration established a hut tax for the first time. The measure coincided with labor shortages in the newly opened gold mines of the Witwatersrand. It imposed on the population the necessity of finding a regular sum of money each year. To obtain the necessary sums of money some natives took to selling produce to traders. This source of income, however, was not sufficient and had to be supplemented by some paid occupation. Given the very few opportunities offered by the local economy, migration to the mines emerged as the only alternative.[33]

The same deliberate "imbalancing" of subsistence economies occurred elsewhere. Malawians, like the Bantus, trekked down to the gold mines of the

31. Wilson, "International Migration in Southern Africa."
32. Issac Schapera, *Migrant Labour and Tribal Life* (London: Oxford University Press, 1947).
33. *Ibid.*

Witwatersrand and to the Zambian copper mines. The opening of the alluvial diamond mines in the Transvaal in 1928 attracted large numbers of not only men, but women and children from different tribes.[34] Recruiting was never confined to South Africa. By the turn of the century, about 60% of the workers in the Witwatersrand were from Mozambique. Lesotho had at the time 30,000 workers in the South African mines and railways.[35]

The artificial creation of new costs via taxation was reinforced in South Africa by the official program of expropriation of tribal lands. Land expropriations reduced the ability of subsistence economies to support their own populations. They increased, by the same token, the attractiveness of migration: By working in the mines, the individual could not only support himself, but also his family through periodic remittances.[36]

The state also intervened to ensure that the monetization of the tribal economies would not deviate from the desired path—that of increasing the labor supply. Arrighi documents the case of Africans who attempted to adapt to the new conditions through commercial farming and who were promptly priced out of the market by discriminatory subsidies for the white farmers.[37] Thus, "the rewards of remaining in the rural areas and accumulating surplus produce were arranged to be less than those of entering wage employment."[38]

Still tribal economies were not completely eliminated. To have done so would have meant the need by the capitalist sector to absorb the costs of welfare and reproduction of the labor force. In Bechuanaland, tribal authority over the native population was upheld by the high commissioner and requests and complaints by tribal chiefs in minor matters attended. The creation of protectorates and then vassal states turned indigenous South African workers into foreigners in their own land, forcing them to return after their contract period "abroad" had expired. The system of temporary contract labor and a complex set of internal passes and passports also ensured the periodic repatriation of foreign workers and the return of native ones to their tribes.[39]

The procedure employed by the two major recruiting organizations—the Native Recruiting Corporation (NRC) and the Witwatersrand Native Labour Association (WNLA)—was to induce migration by creating monetary indebtedness. Part of the cash advance went immediately to pay due taxes. Transportation

---

34. Michael Burawoy, "The Functions and Reproduction of Migrant Labor: Comparative Material from Southern Africa and the United States," *American Journal of Sociology* 81(March 1976): 1050–1087.

35. Wilson, "International Migration in Southern Africa."

36. Schapera, *Migrant Labour and Tribal Life*, chap. 2.

37. G. Arrighi, "Labor Supplies in Historical Perspective: A Study of the Proletarianization of the African Economy in Rhodesia," in *Essays on the Political Economy of Africa* eds. G. Arrighi and J. Saul (New York: Monthly Review Press, 1973), pp. 180–234.

38. Burawoy, "The Functions and Reproduction of Migrant Labor," p. 1058.

39. Wilson, "International Migration in Southern Africa."

to places of work, meals, and lodging were provided, but later deducted from the worker's wages. In 1943, the WNLA mine contract lasted 12 full months for which the native worker was paid £28. Up to 33% of this annual salary was consumed in repaying all initial advancements, including transportation, taxes, meals, and a residue in cash.[40]

The precarious balance between the deliberate penetration of traditional economies and the effort to preserve them as viable supporters and rearers of labor was not without costs. In South Africa, these were largely borne by the public sector, leaving the mines and a few other industries to enjoy the fruits: From 1911 to 1969 the real value of black cash earnings in the mines did not rise at all. In 1961, cash earnings for a full year of labor in the gold mines were R.146 or $168.[41]

Effects of induced labor migration coupled with attempts to preserve the viability of subsistence economies have not been positive to places of emigration. Despite assertions to the contrary, labor migration has resulted in growing dependence, impoverishment, and decomplexification of the source economies. This applies to both the internal colonies of South Africa and the countries of its periphery:

> Lesotho where on the one hand there are 86,000 migrant miners while on the other there is a country that cannot even begin to feed itself although it was once, at the turn of the century, an exporter of food. Nor is it able to provide employment for all of its citizens half of whose total male labor force is estimated to work on the mines and farms of South Africa. . . . Less than one-tenth (of new males in the labor force) will find employment in the country.[42]

The case of South Africa is a particularly poignant instance of structural imbalancing preceding labor migration. It is not, however, an isolated example, nor is the process limited to the migration of unskilled labor, as the following case documents.

Imbalancing and Nonmanual Labor: The Argentine Medical Emigration

The conventional literature has neatly separated study of wage-labor migration from that of professional workers, the so-called brain drain. This convenient distinction hides more fundamental similarities, for professional emigration is also the result of externally induced structural imbalances in the exporting countries. The brain drain illustrates a more subtle and more complex form of internal imbalancing. Unlike the case just reviewed, it does not depend on explicit

40. Schapera, *Migrant Labour and Tribal Life*, chap. 3.
41. Wilson, "International Migration in Southern Africa."
42. *Ibid.*, p. 479.

legal measures; also, it does not require the deliberate preservation of subsistence enclaves, but rather the thorough articulation of peripheral institutions with those of the center. Professional emigration is basically a consequence of the reproduction of the technical apparatus of advanced nations in underdeveloped ones. Implanted institutions come to function more in accordance with needs and requirements of the advanced nations than those of the country that receives them.[43]

Analysis of the brain drain illustrates limitations of both the equilibrium and cumulative-causation perspectives. Both have predicted a flow of professionals that increases with the wealth gap between sending and receiving countries. This is so because both depart from a comparison that is external to the units being compared. Thus, migration of professionals is either a way of restoring "balance" between countries or an integral part of the process by which advanced countries exploit and impoverish their periphery.[44]

The available evidence runs contrary to this prediction. Argentina, with a per capita annual income of more than $1100 and an economy considered the most advanced in Latin America, exported up to 7% of its annual output of physicians to the United States during the last decade; Chile and Brazil, with per capita incomes of less than $800 per year and less developed societies, exported a maximum of 3% and 2% of their yearly production, respectively.[45] In Central America, Panama, with the most developed economy of the region, lost the equivalent of 40% of its output of physicians in 1965. Honduras, the most underdeveloped Central American country, lost an estimated maximum of only 14% in the same year.[46]

The data in Table 2.1 offer additional evidence of the weak relationship between national development and professional emigration. Results come from an extensive, United Nations-sponsored survey of foreign students in advanced

43. This section is based on two previous articles by the first author. See A. Portes, "Determinants of the Brain Drain," *International Migration Review* 10(Winter 1976): 489–504; and A. Portes, "Modernization for Emigration," *Journal of Inter-American Studies and World Affairs* 18(November 1976): 395–422.

44. Myrdal, *Rich Lands and Poor;* Enrique Oteiza, "Emigración de profesionales, técnicos y obreros calificados argentinos a los Estados Unidos," *Desarrollo Económico* 10(January–March, 1971): 429–454.

45. Morris A. Horowitz, *La emigración de técnicos y profesionales argentinos* (Buenos Aires: Editorial del Instituto, 1962); Charles V. Kidd, *Migration of Health Personnel, Scientists, and Engineers from Latin America* (Washington, D. C.: Pan American Health Organization, Scientific Publication No. 142, 1967).

46. *Ibid.* Comparisons between developed and underdeveloped countries illustrate the same general point. Some countries considered developed lose more professionals—in absolute and relative terms—than less developed ones. The annual loss of British Ph.Ds in the sciences was estimated by the Royal Society to be 16% per year during the 1960s; a similar figure for the same period in Latin America did not exceed 6%. At the time when the loss of graduates in engineering did not exceed 8% of the annual output in Argentina, the figures for countries such as Switzerland and the Netherlands reached up to 17%. Horowitz, "La emigración de argentinos"; Portes, "Modernization for Emigration."

TABLE 2.1
Foreign Students' Plans and Level of Economic Development

Country	GNP (per capita 1973)[a]	Percentage of students who would "definitely return"[b]	Number of students interviewed[b]
North America			
Haiti	116	29	63
Jamaica	840	37	67
Mexico	774	52	25
Trinidad	1086	23	152
South America			
Argentina	1138	16	30
Brazil	539	69	220
Colombia	364	60	49
Venezuela	1290	63	29
Africa			
Cameroon	210	68	56
Ghana	223	89	76
Ivory Coast	400	71	48
Senegal	284	74	51
Asia			
India	101	34	300
Pakistan	113	52	116
Philippines	272	32	62
South Korea	338	33	116
Thailand	211	84	66
Middle East and North Africa			
Egypt	227	15	192
Iran	566	42	125
Lebanon	726	39	135
Tunisia	392	61	124
Turkey	444	27	35
Greece	1477	33	199

[a] *Source:* U.S. Department of State, *World Military Expenditures and Arms Trade, 1963–73* (Washington, D.C.: U.S. Arms Control and Disarmament Agency, 1974).

[b] *Source:* William A. Glaser and G. Christopher Habers, "The Migration and Return of Professionals," *International Migration Review* 8 (Summer, 1974): 227–244.

industrial countries in 1973. Table 2.1 presents percentages of students who indicated that they would "definitely return" to their countries on completion of their studies. GNP per capita in 1973 is employed as summary indicator of economic development.[47] Figures in the table indicate a most erratic relation-

47. Although criticisms have been leveled against GNP per capita as a measure of economic development, recent economic writings tend to recognize it as the single most efficient indicator. Given the pattern of associations detected, the following results are not likely to be affected by use of alternative measures. On the measurement of economic development, see A. Emmanuel, "Myths of Development versus Myths of Underdevelopment," *New Left Review* 85(May–June 1974): 61–82.

ship between commitment to return to the home country and level of development. Among countries enjoying a per capita GNP of U.S. $1000 or above, those definitely committed to return vary from 63% for Venezuela to only 16% for Argentina. At the other extreme, among countries with less than $250 of per capita GNP, commitment to return varies from 89% for Ghana to only 15% for Egypt. The African countries—the poorest group as a whole—show the highest level of commitment to return, a pattern directly contrary to the prediction.

International migration of highly trained workers does not occur because some countries are rich and others poor. The technological hegemony exercised by the United States and other advanced countries has meant the continuous reproduction of new procedures and professional practices in the periphery. Advanced training programs implanted in the latter are congruent with professional requirements of the exporting nations, but often at odds with those in receiving ones. Structural imbalances leading to emigration occur when labor market demand proves weak, or nonexistent, for the cohorts of workers trained in externally induced modes of practice.

The reproduction of new technologies in countries of the periphery presupposes the existence of a minimal technical infrastructure. It is for this reason that relatively "advanced" peripheral and semiperipheral countries—those most closely integrated into structural arrangements of the centers—are often the most susceptible to loss of professional workers. Countries such as Argentina, Egypt, and the Philippines have already acquired an infrastructure capable of absorbing technological innovations and training high-level manpower. They all lack, however, the economic and political conditions to absorb it. Outcomes of this "structural tension"[48] are migratory pressures, inevitably benefiting the countries where technology originated in the first place.

The case of Argentine physicians, a group noted for its tendency to emigrate to the United States, illustrates a particular form of structural imbalancing. Major Argentine schools of medicine, such as the University of Buenos Aires, have received from the United States both the format and orientations toward the teaching of medicine, with emphasis on science rather than healing art. Research, the use of modern and costly techniques, and familiarity with the scientific literature are emphasized over the mere everyday practice of the profession. The cognitive dichotomy that evolves among those so trained is between "good" medicine—with access to laboratories and modern logistical support—and "empirical" medicine—the more traditional practice based on observation and clinical interviews. Career orientations are tailored accordingly.[49]

The point is illustrated by career preferences of a small sample of Argentine physicians interviewed in Buenos Aires in 1973. Approximately half of this sample was composed of young doctors planning to emigrate to the United

48. Nilda Sito and Luis Stuhlman, *La emigración de científicos de la Argentina*, Bariloche, Argentina: Fundación Bariloche, 1968.
49. Portes, "Modernization for Emigration."

TABLE 2.2
Career Aspirations and Expectations of Argentine Physicians (percentage)

Variable	Emigrants (N = 24)	Nonemigrants (N = 33)	Total (N = 57)
Primary form of aspired professional activity			
1. Hospital practice	70.8	81.8	75.4
2. Research	16.7	0.0	17.6
3. Private practice	12.5	18.2	7.0
Total	100.0	100.0	100.0
Secondary form of aspired professional activity			
1. Hospital practice	13.6	20.7	17.6
2. Research and teaching	68.2	3.5	31.3
3. Private practice	18.2	75.8	51.1
Total	100.0	100.0	100.0
Difficulty of acquiring means for adequate medical practice in Argentina[a]			
1. Easy		15.6	
2. Difficult		53.1	
3. Very difficult		31.3	
Total		100.0	

Source: Portes' research in Buenos Aires, 1973.
[a] Question not asked to emigrants.

States; the other half was a roughly matched group of doctors planning to stay and work in Argentina.[50] Data in Table 2.2 present the preferred choices for career practice of both groups. "Hospital" medicine—meaning well-equipped institutions with adequate research facilities—is the overwhelming first choice of both groups of physicians. This type of practice is regarded as the way of maintaining close contact with scientific developments and is usually opposed to "private practice," which implies migration to the interior of the country.

As seen in Table 2.2, only a minority of both groups of physicians endorsed private practice as their first choice. Preference for private practice as the second choice among nonemigrants reflects their realistic appraisal of economic need; among those planning to leave, it was "teaching and research" that comes next to hospital practice as the preferred form of professional activity.

Argentine governments have so far maintained an open-admission policy in the public universities. In the Argentine political context, this has been a tra-

50. *Ibid.*

40

ditional way of symbolically compensating the working class for the actual absence of opportunities for mobility; de facto, the vast majority of university students come from the higher income groups. In a 4-year period, 1963–1966, Argentine universities graduated a total of 8144 physicians. The University of Buenos Aires alone graduated 4566 and the University of Córdoba, 1541.[51] The abundance of graduates ensures that many will not have access to the type of practice for which they were trained. The objective difficulty is subjectively perceived: In Table 2.2, 84% of nonemigrant doctors believed it would be difficult for them to reach their career aspirations.

Argentina has evolved into the paradoxical situation of having both a severe deficit *and* an oversupply of physicians. An urgent demand for medical attention in the interior goes hand in hand with emigration abroad of physicians from the capital. Scarce resources are spent in training students whose alienation increases in proportion with their professional expertise. Induced imbalances leading to emigration is, in this case, a direct consequence of the technological hegemony exercised by the United States.

Thus, the more advanced and scientifically oriented the curriculum of medical schools in Argentina, the more obsolete it has become for the nature and location of actual health needs. This is so because of the high costs of equipment required by such training and the orientations implanted in its graduates. Like other "advanced" peripheral nations, Argentina can afford to train physicians in expensive modern medicine, but cannot afford the infrastructure necessary to employ them. Thus, a significant contribution in manpower has been gratuitously made in recent years to the country from which such training was imported in the first place. In the United States, Argentine and other foreign doctors are often used as cheap skilled labor, staffing low-paid hospital positions and thus freeing native physicians for lucrative private practice.[52]

The Release and Transportation of Migrant Labor

Peripheral Ruling Classes and Labor Out-Migration

In addition to the inducements to labor migration examined above, two other aspects must be considered. They have to do, respectively, with the attitude of locally dominant classes in areas of labor out-migration and with the handling of

---

51. Pan American Health Organization, *Estudios sobre salud y educación medica: la enseñanza de la medicina* (Buenos Aires: Secretaría de Estado de Salud Pública, Serie 4, No. 3, 1971).

52. H. Margulies and L. S. Bloch, *Foreign Medical Graduates in the United States* (Cambridge, Mass.: Harvard University Press, 1969); Rosemary A. Stevens, Louis W. Goodman, and Stephen S. Mick, "What Happens to Foreign-Trained Doctors Who Come to the United States?" *Inquiry* 11(June 1974): 112–124.

the costs of transportation. The present and following sections will furnish some examples.

Contrary to equilibrium theory, dependency writings have asserted that labor out-migration results in the progressive impoverishment of underdeveloped sending regions. Cases such as the countries of the South African periphery, have already served to document this point. Examination of the consequences of migration for sending areas must make a distinction, however, between the interests of the local owning class and those of the mass of the population, since the two seldom coincide.

Statements on the interests of peripheral capitalists concerning out-migration are frequently contradictory, even within the same general perspective. Broad outlines of the dependency perspective have portrayed the local bourgeoisie as inextricably linked and subordinated to the interests of the centers. Hence, if labor migration is convenient for the latter, it will be endorsed by the former.[53] On the other hand, more recent writings on internal colonialism and historical case studies of dependency sustain that labor out-migration often occurs against the active opposition of locally dominant classes. It is noted that loss of workers frequently threatens the very basis of economic activity on which the power of these groups is based.[54]

Resistance to the loss of labor has been in fact registered in a number of historical cases. They range from the frequent, but seldom heeded complaints of tribal chieftains in South Africa's protectorates to the organized political campaign of Italian landowners at the turn of the century. Threatened by the mass emigration of peasants to North and South America, they petitioned the government to deny requests of passports from the area. Noting the miserable condition in which the peasantry was kept, De Pretis denied their request with the comment that "the rope much too strained, breaks."[55]

Contradictory positions on the interests of local ruling classes within the dependency perspective reflects the fact that, contingent on historical conditions, these groups have opposed, passively acquiesced, or even actively encouraged out-migration. Increasingly, however, local dominant classes have confronted the dilemma between the convenience of a cheap supply of labor and the political and social threat that it represents.

The general trend that appears to accompany the ever greater "boundedness"

53. Frank, *Latin America*; Edelberto Torres Rivas, "Poder nacional y sociedad dependiente: notas sobre las clases y el estado en Centroamérica," *Revista Paraguaya de Sociología* 29(January–April 1974): 179–210.

54. Nigel Harris, "The New Untouchables: The International Migration of Labour," *International Socialism* 2(1980): 37–63; Schapera, *Migrant Labour and Tribal Life*, chap. 3; Leslie Ann Brownrigg, "The Role of Secondary Cities in Andean Urbanism," mimeo, Evanston, Ill.: Center for Urban Affairs, Northwestern University, 1974.

55. José de Souza Martins, *A Imigração e a Crise do Brasil Agrario* (São Paulo: Livraria Pioneira, 1973), p. 76.

of peripheral regions to the centers of the system is a reduction in the resistance of local dominant classes to the loss of labor. This is not due, however, to their complete servility to the dictates of the centers, but to reasons of clear self-interest. Migration not only alleviates a threatening political situation as the labor force becomes increasingly mobilized, but its economic effects have become less negative.

There are four reasons for this: (a) the growing facilities to replace labor with machinery; (b) the increasing interpenetration between places at different levels of development, which permits recall of part of the migrant labor force in times of need or the tapping of labor reserves from even less developed regions; (c) the general adaptation of economic enterprise in the periphery to conditions set by an internationalized economy, of which migration is a central component; and (d), the role of remittances, both as a palliative to the condition of the work force left behind and, in the case of international migration, as a major source of foreign exchange. Thus, as the articulation of capitalism on a world scale has progressed, labor migration has come to serve simultaneously the interests of the ruling class in *both* peripheral and core regions.

This development underlies, for example, the political bargain between southern Italian landowners and northern Italian industrialists under which the latter accepted maintenance of the status quo in the south in exchange for the guaranteed southern labor reservoir, which has always been at the heart of Italian industrial expansion.[56] The same situation occurs at present with the flow of illegal workers from Mexico to the United States. Despite much publicized official concern in Mexico City about illegal migration, the fact remains that it has been amply permitted, when not encouraged by the Mexican state and bourgeoisie.[57]

Other examples document how periodic release of part of the labor force has become a precondition for the survival of some ruling groups. Landowners, for example, frequently come to depend on migration to the cities for alleviating population pressure on the land. Their situation is thus contingent upon the willingness and ability of the centrally located urban bourgeoisie to permit continuation of the movement. The question then becomes the obverse of the one with which we started: It is not whether ruling classes in the backward regions will oppose migration but rather whether those in the advanced centers will permit it. The well-documented history of the Peruvian highlands oligarchy furnishes a case in point.

56. Manuel Castells, "Immigrant Workers and Class Struggles in Advanced Capitalism: The Western European Experience," *Politics and Society* 5(1975): 33–66.

57. Ellwyn R. Stoddard, "A Conceptual Analysis of the 'Alien Invasion': Institutionalized Support of Illegal Mexican Aliens in the U. S.," *International Migration Review* 10(Summer 1976): 157–89; Francisco Alba, "Mexico's International Migration as a Manifestation of Its Development Pattern," *International Migration Review* 12(Winter 1978): 485–501.

Labor Out-Migration and Political Stability:
Rural Migration to Lima

A permanent situation of high population pressure in the Peruvian Sierra led governments sympathetic to the landowning oligarchy to concentrate on a policy of urbanization designed to improve the condition of Lima's squatters. Marginal improvements in the situation of the urban lower classes stimulated the continuous flow of peasant migration, thus easing the strain on threatened rural areas.

The first significant shift in this policy came during the government of Manuel Prado during the late 1950s. Prado, a member and close ally of the coastal export bourgeoisie, chose Pedro Beltrán as prime minister, a sophisticated conservative who was to shape Peruvian agrarian and urban policy during this period. The imminent political collapse of the situation in the highlands prompted the government to abandon the landowning oligarchy. Ironically, it was the conservative Beltrán regime that first gave impetus to agrarian reform in Peru through the creation of the Commission of Agrarian Reform and Housing in 1956.[58]

The commission's proposal spared the productive coastal *haciendas* and concentrated on the distribution of highland agricultural land to small landowners. The political goals of the government at this time were well reflected in the proposed agrarian reform: By granting small parcels of land, it stimulated the political conservatism of the Sierra peasantry, the most explosive sector in the country. The agrarian reform was also explicitly antimigratory: A solution to the rural problem would decrease migratory pressures and, hence, reduce the threatening growth of Lima's *barriadas*.

The next Peruvian government under Fernando Belaunde Terry committed itself during the early 1960s to a policy of broad national reform. Belaunde's antipathy to the traditional landowning classes found its reflection in an urban policy of deliberate neglect towards the squatter settlements. Despite protests by *barriada* organizations and opposition parties, the policy was maintained during the entire period. Its purpose, once again, was antimigratory: It attempted to reduce the attractiveness of the city to the rural poor and it concentrated resources, previously spent in urban improvement, in the development of the interior. Maintaining the pressure of the peasantry on the land was part of the overall governmental strategy to alter the structure of Peruvian agriculture against the landowners.[59]

Growing opposition to Belaunde by a broad coalition of forces culminated in the military revolt and ensuing reformist government during the late 1960s. The

---

58. David Collier, *Squatters and Oligarchs, Authoritarian Rule and Policy Change in Peru* (Baltimore: Johns Hopkins University Press, 1976); this section is based on Collier's excellent account of political power and exchange in urban Peru.
59. *Ibid.*, chap. 6.

military government, under General Juan Velasco Alvarado, attempted to avoid confrontation with the urban poor and tried to incorporate them instead into the overall government strategy. At the same time, the government never abandoned its efforts to discourage migration to Lima. It did so by concentrating resources on agrarian reform and other programs in the provinces and by opposing, as firmly as possible for a populist regime, new land invasions in the capital.[60] By this time, the power of the traditional oligarchy had been effectively broken.

Instances such as this document the importance of migration for maintaining the position of dominant classes in the periphery. The decline of landowning groups and the emergence of new centers of power in Peru were associated with an explicit antimigratory policy that eliminated this crucial safety valve and, hence, forced rapid transformation of the rural economy and political structure.

From Deliberate Recruitment to Self-Transportation: Recruitment Practices in the United States and South American Countries

Classical political economic theory spoke of a situation in which immigrant labor was in heavy demand in the expanding colonies. Contemporary writings on rural–urban migration in underdeveloped countries speak, on the other hand, of a situation in which the supply of migrant labor has far outstripped demand, even relative to the size requirements of the "reserve army."[61]

A range of situations exist in between these two theories. In a manner similar to the situation of ruling classes in out-migration areas, those in receiving regions may either actively encourage, passively permit or, at times, attempt to reduce migration. Just as the progressive articulation of the world economy has tended to increase relative benefits of out-migration to dominant classes in the periphery, it has had important consequences for employers of this labor.

Allowing for specific exceptions, the general trend has been toward increasing availability and ease of recruitment of labor in peripheral regions. This trend follows directly from their growing "boundedness" to core capitalist economies, with the twin consequences of high and increasing unemployment and exposure of peripheral populations to economic opportunities in the centers. Though the conventional literature has repeatedly deplored the effects of "excess" rural–urban migration and of illegal immigration into developed countries, there is little doubt that the trend has greatly benefited employers in core areas. Masses of self-transported migrants have cheapened labor costs relative to both domestic workers and earlier forms of labor procurement.

60. *Ibid.*, chap. 7. See also Anibal Quijano, *Nationalism and Capitalism in Peru, A Study in Neo-Imperialism* (New York: Monthly Review, 1971).
61. José Nun, "Superpoblación relativa, ejército industrial de reserva y masa marginal," *Revista Latinoamericana de Sociología* 5(July 1969): 178–235.

Means of tapping labor reserves available in outlying and peripheral regions include outright force, active persuasion, and mere regulation of a self-guided flow. Though it may seem surprising today, the rule from the sixteenth century onward was the need to recruit labor actively in the backward regions. Absolute gaps of economic advantage meant nothing to the population of outlying areas, for it neither could grasp their significance nor find the means of transportation to take advantage of them.

Labor migration through coercion or persuasion is usually more costly than that which is self-transported, since it involves establishment of a recruitment machinery and advances for the costs of transportation. The recruitment of African slave labor for sale in the American colonies offers, of course, the extreme case of organized and costly labor procurement. Yet, during the nineteenth and early twentieth centuries, migration was still, as a rule, an actively induced process involving labor agents and economic incentives. Bonuses, salary advances, and free transportation were standard techniques for recruitment. Although their costs were eventually borne by the workers, they still represented an initial capital investment.

In areas of expanding economy, agricultural and industrial interests usually attempted to shift these costs to the state. The general situation by the beginning of the twentieth century is exemplified by the cases of the southwestern area of the United States, the rapidly growing economies of Argentina and Chile, and the special case of Paraguay.

The banning of Chinese labor in the United States after the Chinese Exclusion Act and the later restriction of Japanese workers by the Gentlemen's Agreement of 1907 meant that growers and urban employers in the Southwest had to turn to Mexico as the only viable source of cheap labor. Paid-recruiters were sent to the border and to the interior of Mexico. By 1916, the *Los Angeles Times* reported that five or six weekly trains full of Mexican workers hired by the agents were being run from Laredo.[62] According to another author, the competition in El Paso became so aggressive that recruiting agencies "stationed their Mexican employees at the Santa Fe bridge where they literally pounced on the immigrants as they crossed the border."[63]

The Depression years brought an end to recruiting efforts and saw a reversal of the trend as government-organized deportations sent thousands of Mexican- and U.S.-born Mexican Americans back to Mexico. World War II, however, created

62. Ricardo Romo, "Mexican Workers in the City: Los Angeles, 1915–30," Ph.D. dissertation, University of California at Los Angeles, 1975, cited in Mario Barrera, *Class Segmentation and Internal Colonialism*, unpublished manuscript. Department of Political Science, University of California at San Diego, 1977.

63. Mario García, "Obreros: The Mexican Workers of El Paso, 1900–1920," Ph.D. dissertation, University of California at San Diego, 1975, cited in Barrera, *Class Segmentation and Internal Colonialism*.

a severe shortage of labor and, hence, a renewed demand for Mexican workers. Southwestern employers took advantage of the contingency to transfer recruitment costs to the state. In 1942, an executive agreement between the United States and Mexico initiated the so-called bracero program. Government-paid agents were sent into Mexico and public funds were spent in setting up and expanding the program's operation. Conceived as a wartime expedient, growers managed to extend it repeatedly in the postwar years. In 1951, the program was formalized by Congress as Public Law 78. By 1964, when it was finally terminated, the bracero program had brought close to 5 million workers into the United States. [64]

The rapid expansion of the Argentine economy during the late nineteenth century, which made Argentina one of the world's great agricultural nations, was based almost entirely on peasant labor from Europe. Such labor did not always come spontaneously and often had to be recruited. In 1899, the Argentine Congress was requested to appropriate 11,000,000 pesos to finance passages of European immigrants. In 1903 and again in 1905, agricultural interests complained to the government that the corn crop might rot for lack of harvest labor. Again, the proposed solution was official subsidies to pay passages of Italian and Spanish immigrants.

Grouped in the powerful Sociedad Rural, Argentine landowners also exercised pressure on the government to construct appropriate immigrant reception facilities in Buenos Aires. Congress complied, appropriating 3,000,000 pesos to build a large immigrant hotel, which opened in 1910. Argentine industrialists, associated in the Unión Industrial Argentina, petitioned the government repeatedly to subsidize recruitment of immigrant labor. European workers were urgently needed, first to man skilled industrial posts, but also to provide a mass of unskilled labor with which to counteract growing labor unrest. [65]

Neighboring Chile, being less known and less attractive to European workers, had to make correspondingly greater efforts to recruit them during her period of economic expansion. Migration during this period to Chile was a small fraction of that going to Argentina. To obtain foreign workers who, according to the racial theories of the time were superior to native Chilean labor, the Sociedad de Fomento Fabril subsidized passages for European immigrants and their families during the late nineteenth century. The Sociedad, which grouped Chilean industrialists, repeatedly pressured the government to assume these costs. In 1898, the government began to offer free third-class passage to Chile, free freight for up

64. Julian Samora, Los Mojados: The Wetback Story (Notre Dame, Ind.: University of Notre Dame Press, 1971). See also Jorge Bustamante, "The Historical Context of Undocumented Mexican Immigration to the United States," Aztlán 3(1973): 257–281.

65. Carl Solberg, Immigration and Nationalism, Argentina and Chile, 1890–1914 (Austin: University of Texas Press, 1970).

to two tons of machines and tools, and free transport within Chile from the port of arrival to the immigrant's destination. These provisions were expanded in 1905 to include free passage for families of the immigrants.

Similarly, Chilean mine operators, who formed the Sociedad Nacional de Minería, appealed to the government for help in solving the severe labor shortage of 1905–1908. To pressure the government, the Sociedad de Minería noted that lack of manpower might force a drop in nitrate export, taxes on which provided the bulk of government income. In response, Congress appropriated 2,500,000 pesos to subsidize immigration and agreed to let the mine owners' agents do the selection of immigrant workers in Europe.[66]

To a much greater extent than its neighbors, Paraguay was in need of immigrant workers by the end of the nineteenth century. In this case it was not only a matter of supplementing native labor, but of replacing a population decimated during the war of the Triple Alliance. Immigrants were sought not only as workers but also as colonists for the depopulated interior. Spontaneous immigration to Paraguay was so rare that well into the twentieth century, the census only considered as "immigrants" those who came with free passages paid by the state.

Efforts made by the Paraguayan government included the organization of an Office of Immigration and the expenditure of 400,000 gold pesos between 1881 and 1892 to encourage immigration. The Law of Immigration and Colonization, passed in 1881, provided for free passages from the immigrant's place of origin to his ultimate destination in Paraguay; free entrance into the country of personal belongings, tools, and machinery; exemption from land taxes for 10 years; food for 6 months; and housing for an entire year.[67]

Results of these recruitment efforts were consistently disappointing. Immigration to the River Plate basin as a whole (Table 2.3) was massive, being surpassed only by that to the United States and Canada. Yet, the proportion of immigrants settling in Paraguay was infinitesimal. As seen in Table 2.3, immigration to Paraguay from 1880 to 1920 totaled 22,000, less than 1% of that received by Argentina and less than 10% of that going to Uruguay during the last two decades of the same period.

Thus, active recruitment of migrant labor had to be conducted in many expanding economies not because objective opportunities did not exist, but because insufficient linkages existed to make available populations aware of economic opportunities or to make their physical displacement a straightforward matter. In a critique of orthodox theories of labor immigration, Piore[68] has also emphasized the importance of employer recruitment in determining the size and direction of migrant flows. However, his analysis follows earlier conventional

66. *Ibid.*
67. Lyra Pidoux de Drachemberg, "Inmigración y colonización en el Paraguay, 1870–1970," *Revista Paraguaya de Sociología* 34(September–December 1975): 65–123.
68. Piore, *Birds of Passage*, pp. 19 and ff.

48

TABLE 2.3
Cumulative Immigration to the River Plate Basin, 1870–1920

			Country		
Argentina		Uruguay		Paraguay	
Years	Total	Years	Total	Years	Total
1861–1870	159,570				
1871–1880	420,455				
1881–1890	1,261,477			1881–1890	5635
1891–1900	1,909,903			1891–1900	8695
1901–1910	3,674,004	1901–1910	136,609	1901–1910	16,008
1911–1920	4,878,925	1911–1920	237,675	1911–1920	22,305

Source: Lyra Pidoux de Drachemberg, "Inmigración y colonización en el Paraguay, 1870–1970," *Revista Paraguaya de Sociología* 12 (Sept.–Dec., 1975): 65–123.

views in depicting the process statically. The significance of employer recruitment has changed with the increasing integration of the world economy. Although such activities played a decisive role during the nineteenth and early twentieth century, their frequency and significance have decreased subsequently.

The articulation of capitalism on a world scale has facilitated access to information on economic opportunities to evermore remote areas and has made the movement across long distances easier and more predictable. At present, the normal situation is the *oversupply* of potential migrants to advanced regions and the attempt by governments to regulate the flow. Contemporary labor migrations are for the most part self-transported and self-initiated at no cost to their prospective employers.

Conditions for the Use of Migrant Labor

Vulnerability and the Political Means to Sustain It

In general, the function of migrant labor has not been—as conventional economics suggests—to increase the supply of labor, but rather to increase the supply of *cheap* labor. Immigrant and migrant labor flows have often been encouraged even when a domestic labor surplus exists. As the previously cited case of Argentina and as many examples in the United States suggest, the role of immigrants has frequently been to counteract the organizational efforts of domestic workers and to substitute the latter in areas where labor costs have become high. In the United States, the political impact of European immigration was not

49

radicalizing but deradicalizing, insofar as it undermined the power of militant class organizations.[69] It is thus not surprising that native working-class organization militantly opposed immigration throughout the nineteenth and early twentieth century.

The cheapness of migrant labor is not a built-in feature of the migration process and does not inhere in the personality of migrants, but is dependent on deliberate political manipulation. For the case of immigrant workers in Western Europe, Castells[70] has shown that such manipulation is in turn conditioned by the political vulnerability of immigrants. The very fact of crossing a political border weakens the status of workers vis-à-vis the state. They are thus much more subject to close police supervision and arbitrary decisions by officials and employers. In general, the weaker the legal standing of immigrant workers, the more employers can make use of political threats, including deportation, to obtain compliance.

Political weakness is, of course, a feature more closely associated with immigrants who cross international borders than with domestic migrants. The case of rural–urban migration in underdeveloped countries represents a situation where the overabundance of migratory sources of labor and the very poverty of migrants place them in a position of great vulnerability vis-à-vis urban employers without need of deliberate political manipulation. Yet, even domestic migrants can be made subject to forms of political exclusion. Again, the classic case is South Africa, where the artificial creation of protectorates and native states have converted black workers into immigrants to their own land, subject to the need for legal passes, and readily excludable on necessity.

The following sections describe two processes of deliberate manipulation of immigrant labor that are very different in time and place. The purpose is to illustrate—within the limitations of individual case studies—the general applicability of the point under discussion.

Political Manipulation: The Brazil Coffee Immigrations

The great agricultural immigration to the coffee regions of Brazil took place during the last two decades of the nineteenth century and, as in the cases of Chile and Paraguay, were heavily subsidized by the national government and the state of São Paulo. Active recruitment efforts were conducted in Italy, with the bulk of immigrants coming from the northern region. From 1870 to 1900, a yearly average of 151,539 persons left northern Italy for Brazil as against 86,528 from

---

69. Rosenblum, *Immigrant Workers*. For the more recent case of black migration to northern cities see Edna Bonacich, "Advanced Capitalism and Black/White Relations: A Split Labor Market Interpretation," *American Sociological Review* 41(February 1976): 34–51.

70. Castells, "Immigrant Workers and Class Struggles in Advanced Capitalism: The Western European Experience."

central and southern Italy. Sources of emigration concentrated in the most backward agricultural provinces: Almost half of northern Italian emigration left from the provinces of Veneto and Lombardia, areas where peasants most suffered under quasi-feudal forms of exploitation.[71]

The bulk of this immigration was eventually directed to the large coffee *fazendas* where it took the place of slave labor. The end of slavery in Brazil and the beginning of an active immigration policy were two sides of the same coin, as dictated by the interests of export-oriented landowners. Contrary to the conventional immigration saga, the impact of immigrant labor in Brazil was *not* to bring about a new social and economic order but, by and large, to reinforce the threatened structures of the old.[72]

The point of interest is the series of political decisions adopted by the state that eventually channeled the immigrant flow to its desired role: that of cheap labor for the coffee export sector. Since the colonial period, a policy of immigration existed in Brazil with the purpose of populating the southern regions and counteracting the threat posed by the Spanish. It was essentially a policy of colonization with immigrants grouped in small *núcleos de povoamento*.

The experience with the *núcleos* served as basis for official policy, once the imperial government assumed the costs of organizing and subsidizing immigration. From 1876 to 1890, a total of 14 official colonies for immigrants were established in the state of São Paulo. The provision of labor to *fazenda* owners to substitute slave labor was thus linked by the state with the continuation of a policy of colonization along the lines of the earlier *núcleos de povoamento*.[73]

With this policy, the government attempted to fulfill two goals simultaneously: one to attend to the needs of the *grande lavoura* in the coffee areas; the other to alleviate the growing shortage of agricultural commodities for the domestic market. The strategy was based on the absence of capital by the immigrants and their induced indebtedness for several years, since they had to pay for their lands. In this situation, immigrant colonies were in no condition to integrate themselves into the profitable coffee economy, which required large outlays of capital. They had thus to concentrate on the production of rice, beans, sugar, and other staples for the domestic market.

For the same reason, many official colonies were located in the vicinity of São Paulo so as to have direct access to the areas where demand concentrated. The

71. This section is based on the historical monograph by Jose de Souza Martins, A *Imigração e a Crise do Brasil Agrario*. The three "moments" of immigration which he outlines find general support in the extensive literature on development of the Brazilian coffee export sector. See, for example, Michael M. Hall, "The Origins of Mass Immigration to Brazil," Ph.D. dissertation, Department of History, Columbia University, 1971; and Balán, "Regional Urbanization in Neo-Colonial Countries."

72. de Souza Martins, A *Imigração e a Crise do Brasil Agrario*. Jorge Balán, "Migrações no Desenvolvimento Capitalista Brasileiro," *Estudos CEBRAP* 5, 1973.

73. de Souza Martins, A *Imigração e a Crise do Brasil Agrario*.

official strategy was the apparently reasonable one of converting the immigrant into a "free" worker who would offer himself to the *fazendas* in times of labor demand and who would support himself throughout the rest of the year. Self-support would take the form of raising crops for the local market, thus alleviating the existing shortage.[74]

The dual purpose of official colonies gave them, however, an ambivalent character, which they never satisfactorily overcame. From the point of view of coffee producers, they failed to provide the abundant labor at "reasonable prices" that they required. Part of the problem lay in the location of the colonies, since their distance to the areas of the *grande lavoura* inhibited seasonal migration. More important were the patterns of economic behavior observed among immigrants: Several colonies lapsed into self-sufficiency and, in all cases, the Italian immigrant concentrated on cultivation of his own lands without showing active interest in wage labor.

The Brazilian government and the landowning classes came to learn, from direct experience, the problems anticipated in John Stuart Mill's classic analysis of immigration. For immigrants to be useful to an expanding capitalist economy, the situation had to be arranged so that the means they initially received would *not* be sufficient for their survival. As Mill had already indicated, immigrants had to be prevented from becoming proprietors too soon, since the usual incentives of the free market would not suffice then to attract them to hired labor.

It is at this point where the political basis underlying the uses of immigrant labor became evident. The state ceased to provide the means for the development of autonomous immigrant communities. At the same time, Brazilian scholars and politicians elaborated the work-incentive ideology, which was to justify placement of new immigrants directly into the coffee *fazendas*. According to the most popular version, placement of immigrants in the *fazendas* was the best solution since "after two or three years and if the immigrant family was hard-working and moderate in its habits, it could accumulate sufficient capital to buy and cultivate land for itself."[75] Their work would be more fruitful since, by that time, they would have learned the language and culture and would be able to deal with the natives.

Through this formulation, land proprietorship ceased to be a precondition to become an aspiration for immigrant workers. Land ownership was seen as a legitimate goal for immigrants, but it had to be earned through years of labor and saving. Work in the *fazendas* was offered as the appropriate route, so that chances for upward mobility became directly dependent on the will of the landowner.

Ironically, the old colonies were presented to new immigrants as examples of

---

74. *Ibid.*; Hall, "The Origins of Mass Immigration to Brazil."
75. de Souza Martins, A *Imigração e a Crise de Brasil Agrario*, p. 68.

TABLE 2.4
Illegal Immigrants Located in the United States, 1967–1977

Year	Mexican immigrants	Other immigrants	Total
1967	108,327	53,281	161.608
1968	156,000[a]	60,000[a]	216,000[a]
1969	201,636	81,921	283,557
1970	277,377	67,976	345,353
1971	348,178	71,948	420,126
1972	430,213	75,736	505,949
1973	576,823	79,145	655,968
1974	709,959	78,186	788,145
1975	680,392	86,208	766,600
1976	781,474	94,441	875,915
1977	954,778	87,437	1,042,215

Source: U.S. Immigration and Naturalization Service, Annual Reports for 1967–1977 (Washington, D.C.: U.S. Government Printing Office).
[a] Approximate totals.

what they could attain with the fruits of their labor. Earlier colonies like São Caetano in São Paulo were thus offered as incentives, despite the fact that their members were never without land and never had to pass through the period of wage labor now preached to new immigrants.[76] Through this modification, Italian immigration finally came to fulfill its purpose: substituting slave labor and permitting the expansion of an agriculture-based export economy.

Political Manipulation: Illegal Labor Migration to the United States

Contemporary illegal migration to the United States is a process in which a massive labor flow is covertly permitted so as to fulfill the needs of a large number of rural and urban employers. The number of illegal workers annually entering the United States or already residing in the country has been officially estimated to be in the millions.[77] The only data available so far, are figures of annual apprehensions reported by the U.S. Immigration and Naturalization Service (INS). As shown in Table 2.4, total apprehensions went from 161,608 in 1967 to 1,042,215 in 1977, a 647% increase in a decade. Substantial increases in apprehensions have been registered every year. The only exception is 1975, when

76. Ibid.
77. U. S. Immigration and Naturalization Service, Annual Report 1975 (Washington, D. C.: U. S. Government Printing Office, 1976).

illegal immigration appeared to decrease somewhat in response to a severe recession. The movement recovered in 1976, with apprehensions climbing to a new height.

The overwhelming percentage of Mexicans among illegal immigrants in Table 2.4 is, in part, a function of deployment practices of INS enforcement agencies. The Border Patrol, for example, concentrates its efforts along the Mexican border, neglecting other points of entry. Border crossers thus come to represent an overwhelming proportion of apprehensions, as compared with illegals entering by air or sea. There is widespread agreement, however, that Mexican immigration represents a substantial majority of the current illegal flow.

Although some writers continue to see illegal labor immigration as a phenomenon limited to the rural Southwest, there is increasing evidence that participation of illegal workers in the labor force is not limited to agriculture. A few years ago, INS estimated that one-third of the illegal workers were employed in agriculture; another one-third in other goods-producing industries (meatpacking, auto making, and construction); and one-third in service jobs. A 1975 survey of 628 apprehended illegals found that over 75% were employed in urban blue-collar and service occupations, as opposed to only 19% employed in agriculture.[78]

Another datum showing that illegal migration is not a limited or conjunctural phenomenon is its failure to correlate with the U.S. rate of unemployment. If illegals were at the margins of the labor market—we would expect that the size of the illegal flow would be strongly affected by the rate of domestic unemployment. The data in Table 2.5 show, on the contrary, that illegal immigration, as indexed by number of apprehensions, and U.S. unemployment have only a very weak inverse relationship. From 1970 to 1974, U.S. unemployment remained relatively stable at around 5.4%; during the same period, illegal immigration registered mean annual increases of 23% over the previous year. From 1974 to 1975, unemployment went from 5.6 to 8.5%, a 52% relative increase; in response to this, illegal migration decreased only 4.2%. Modest decreases in the rate of unemployment in 1976 and 1977 have been accompanied by an apparent massive growth of illegal immigration. Apprehensions of illegals surpassed 1,000,000 in 1977, the largest figure since the days of "Operation Wetback" in 1954.[79]

Reasons why massive illegal immigration is permitted in the United States must be sought in the interface between the needs of the competitive sector of capital and the nature of illegal labor. Relative to other countries, especially

78. David S. North and Marion F. Houstoun, *The Characteristics and Role of Aliens in the U. S. Labor Market: An Exploratory Study* (Washington, D. C.: Linton, 1976).

79. Samora, *Los Mojados: The Wetback Story*; Gilbert Cardenas, "United States Immigration Policy Toward Mexico: A Historical Perspective," mimeo, Department of Sociology, University of Texas at Austin, 1976.

TABLE 2.5
Unemployment Rates and Illegal Immigrants Apprehended, 1970–1977[a]

Year	Percentage of U.S. labor force unemployed[a]	Illegal immigrants apprehended[•]	Apprehensions: Percentage change from previous year
1970	4.9	345,353	—
1971	5.9	420,126	+21.6
1972	5.6	505,949	+20.4
1973	4.9	655,968	+29.6
1974	5.6	788,145	+20.2
1975	8.5	766,600	− 2.7
1976	7.7	875,915	+14.5
1977	7.1	1,042,215	+19.0

Sources: U.S. Department of Labor, Employment and Earnings, January 1976 (Washington, D.C.: Bureau of Labor Statistics, Vol. 22, 1976); U.S. Department of Labor, Monthly Labor Review, December 1977; U.S. Immigration and Naturalization Service, Annual Reports, 1970–77 (Washington, D.C.: U.S. Government Printing Office); New York Times, November 24, 1977.

[a] As percentage of the active civilian labor force.

those of the periphery, the American economy is one of high labor costs. This occurs less because of the exhaustion of the domestic labor supply than because of its increasing political organization. A series of labor-promoted legislative measures have resulted in a welfare system that supports the unemployed and maintains a "floor" under the salaries of domestic workers.[80] Other things being equal, high labor costs tend to decrease the rate of profit. This is especially true of small competitive firms, which, unlike those in the monopoly sector, cannot easily pass higher labor costs to consumers.

There are three major strategies used by capital to cope with labor costs. The classic strategy in the United States has been technological innovation through which costs in labor-intensive production are reduced by machinery and new techniques. Monopolistic firms have repeatedly made use of labor-saving technology during this century. A second strategy is the displacement of production to areas of cheaper labor either inside the country or abroad. Some estimates place American foreign investments in industry during the late 1960s at over 20% of domestic manufacturing investment.[81] The rapid industrial development of places such as Korea, Singapore, Taiwan, and the Dominican Republic in recent years has been of this type. Another example of this strategy is that of the Mexican "maquiladoras"—U.S. industries that settle on the Mexican side of the border under a custom-and-tax agreement with the Mexican government and

80. Bonacich, "Advanced Capitalism and Black/White Relations."
81. Pierre Jalee, Imperialism in the Seventies (New York: Third Press, 1973).

produce directly for the American market.[82] Chapter 5 will examine in greater detail this process of internationalization of capital and its consequences for different segments of the American working class.

Not all employers can take advantage, however, of technology and labor reserves in the periphery. Small competitive firms may lack the capital for large-scale technological innovation. Even middle-size enterprises lack the experience, "know-how," and resources to venture themselves into a foreign country. Therefore, important layers of U.S. capital in light industry, services, and agriculture continue to be dependent on finding cheap sources of labor in the local market.

The historical function of immigration has been to provide a source of cheap labor. This function has been dependent, however, on the vulnerability of immigrants and the possibility of ready legal exclusion. Because of a position of legal weakness, immigrant workers have been traditionally used by employers against native labor. In the occasions where immigrants have joined organized labor protests, their "foreignness" has been used as a potent repressive weapon. In these instances, the situation has been defined as a police matter, rather than one involving legitimate class vindications.

Current U.S. immigration law explicitly bars the unregulated entrance of low-skilled workers through a series of occupational selection procedures. As Bach has pointed out,[83] immigration restrictions are part of the "historical bargain" between the state, monopoly capital, and labor, by which the protection of workers in large-scale enterprises was guaranteed in exchange for social stability. The same agreement can be credited with blocking organization of a contract immigrant labor programme, along Western European lines.

The absence of a ready pool of cheap immigrant labor places firms in the competitive sector at a net disadvantage. Collectively, however, competitive capital continues to be politically powerful, being heavily represented in Congress.[84] This forces the state to accommodate its needs somehow, of which cheap labor is paramount. In this situation, the role of illegal immigration is clear. Paradoxically, it is the past triumphs of organized labor that have brought about the emergence of a new class of disenfranchised workers. Illegal workers are even more vulnerable and, hence, more exploitable than those brought in by earlier waves of European immigration.

82. Victor Urquidi and Sofía Mendez Villarreal, "Importancia económica de la zona fronteriza del Norte de México," paper presented at the Conference on Contemporary Dilemmas of the Mexican-United States Border, San Antonio: The Weatherhead Foundation, 1975. María Patricia Fernández Kelly, "Mexican Border Industrialization, Female Labor Force Participation, and Migration," paper presented at the Annual Meeting of the American Sociological Association, San Francisco, September 1978.

83. Robert L. Bach, "Mexican Immigration and the American State," *International Migration Review* 12(Winter 1978): 536–538.

84. James O'Connor, *The Fiscal Crisis of the State* (New York: St. Martin's Press, 1973), chap. 1.

From the point of view of employers, illegal immigration represents a superior alternative to almost all other forms of labor procurement. Because even low wages in the United States are attractive in comparison with those in countries of the periphery, illegal workers can be counted on to accept harsh conditions and perform difficult menial tasks cheaply. Contrary to some assertions, no evidence exists of a "split" market, where illegals are paid less for the same work than domestic workers. Their importance lies instead in holding down the general wage level—for domestic and foreign workers alike—in a number of unskilled occupations.

The logical fit between the labor needs of rural and urban employers and the presence of illegal workers does not suffice by itself, however, to demonstrate the complicity of the state in the process. Our argument is that the present illegal flow represents the *deliberate* political manipulation of labor immigration to satisfy the needs of important sectors of the employer class. Criminalizing labor immigration, a decision originally taken under pressure from domestic trade unions, has in fact turned to the advantage of many employers by furnishing them with a cheaper and more tractable labor force. To support this argument, however, it is necessary to show that intentional actions have been taken by the U.S. government to permit continuation of this covert flow.

Deliberate encouragement by the state of the use of illegal labor involves three conditions: (*a*) that the criminality of illegal entry be maintained so that workers are kept in a situation of vulnerability, but that their employers be made legally immune; (*b*) that the credibility of the threat of deportation be maintained through the action of repressive agencies, but that these agencies do not become so effective as to interfere with the flow of illegal labor; and (*c*) that political authorities in the country where immigrants originate are appeased, but that their efforts to give immigrants legal protection and increase their wages (part of which are always repatriated) be neutralized.

The bracero program was terminated, the new immigration law passed, and illegal immigration emerged as a major source of cheap labor during the Johnson, Nixon, and Ford administrations. Analysis of the history of events during these years show how each of the three conditions was met:

1. The "Texas Proviso," appended to the 1965 immigration law states that "it is a felony to conceal, harbor, or shield from detection" an illegal alien, but that the employment of illegals, "including the practices incidental to it . . . are not deemed to constitute harboring."[85] With this tailor-made statement, employers were specifically exempted from legal responsibility although the criminal character of illegal crossing was upheld. Throughout the 1970s, enterprises in all parts of the country could thus hire and dismiss illegal workers with perfect

85. U. S. Congress, 8 U. S. C., Section 1324, 1952. See Bustamante, "The Historical Context of Undocumented Mexican Immigration to the United States."

impunity. Repeated attempts to repeal the Texas Proviso in recent years have been consistently defeated in Congress.

2. As seen in Table 2.4, hundreds of thousands of illegal immigrants are rounded up and deported every year by the Immigration Service. The threat of capture and deportation is a very real one. At the same time, INS freely admits that those it manages to detain represent only a fraction of the illegal flow.

Detection of illegals is mostly the responsibility of the Border Patrol and the Investigations Division of INS. Deliberate budgetary decisions have kept both agencies chronically understaffed since 1965. Available figures for 1977 put Border Patrol strength at 2013 and the Investigations Division at 924.[86] This force is supposed to guard the 1800-mile open border with Mexico and to root out illegals in the rest of the country.[87] Current estimates thus range from one to three illegal immigrants escaping detection for each one apprehended. A recent study concludes that "the border is so porous that some (illegal aliens) found it possible to spend their weekends in Mexican cities and return to their U.S. place of employment the following Monday."[88]

Several studies have also documented how the Border Patrol itself accommodates the needs of agribusiness along the border. Practices include an emphasis on linewatch duty rather than checks on farms and ranches, by far the most effective means of detection.[89] Patrol raids have been timed to avoid harvest seasons and other periods of peak labor demand when they could seriously hurt local interests. Although exceptions exist, the consensus is that the role of the Border Patrol has been to "regulate" the illegal flow of labor rather than to prevent it.[90]

3. Joint studies conducted by U.S. and Mexican commissions have come to widely different conclusions as to how to deal with illegal immigration. In 1972, and in response to growing agitation on both sides of the border, the presidents of the United States and Mexico appointed a joint commission to study the problem. Final reports were issued in 1973 with entirely different sets of recommendations.

The Mexican Commission argued for reinstatement of the bracero program in some form, so as to transform illegal immigrants into legal contract workers. The manifest reason was to protect the rights of immigrants against exploitation,

86. David S. North, "Illegal Immigration to the United States: A Quintet of Myths," paper presented at the session on Political Economy of Migration, meetings of the American Political Science Association, Washington, D.C., August 1977.

87. *Ibid.*

88. Wayne A. Cornelius, "Mexican Migration to the United States: The View from Rural Sending Communities," mimeo, Department of Political Science, Massachusetts Institute of Technology, 1976, p. 13.

89. Ellwyn R. Stoddard, "A Conceptual Analysis of the 'Alien Invasion.'"

90. Alejandro Portes, "Labor Functions of Illegal Aliens," *Society* 6(September-October 1977): 31–37.

although a more basic one was to increase their wages and, hence, the level of remittances back to Mexico. This recommendation was rejected by the U.S. Commission.[91] Other efforts by the Mexican government to modify the present conditions of labor immigration have met with the same fate. There has been much willingness by U. S. officials to talk about the problem, but they have consistently resisted changing, in any fundamental form, the existing inflow.

Illegal immigration as a means to satisfy labor needs of competitive capital was not a device deliberately created by the U.S. government. Instead, it took advantage of a preexisting labor flow, the bulk of which was created by deliberate recruitment in Mexico in earlier years. By preserving the illegality of the process, the state has managed to meet, simultaneously, the demands of both organized segments of the working class and a politically important sector of capital.

Network Building: The Microstructures of Migration

Structural Forces and Individual Migrants

By focusing on migration as a process external to both the sending and receiving areas, the equilibrium and cumulative-causation perspectives managed to provide an impoverished image of actual events and possible alternatives. Dependency writings tended to depict migration as a straightforward reflection of broader relationships of exploitation and as an irreversible escape from the conditions created by them. Ironically, these critical writings join conventional demography at this point by analyzing migration in terms of two fixed sets of resources: economic opportunities at places of destination and characteristics of places of origin.

This simplified image leads to inferences about the fate of migrants that have been easily proved false. Conventional demographic accounts and those stemming from the dependency perspective do not explain three factual and significant characteristics of migration in general: (a) the survival and frequent growth of peripheral places of out-migration; (b) the survival of migrants in the urban centers; and (c) substantial proportions of return migration and of multiple periodical displacements between two or more regions.

The alternative perspective proposed here envisions migration as part of the routine activities of a single unified economic system. From this perspective, migration appears less as a series of momentous individual decisions to move between separate places, than as a *process* by which workers continuously take advantage of economic opportunities distributed unequally across space. The

91. Cardenas, "United States Immigration Policy toward Mexico."

different nature of these opportunities correspond to the different positions assigned to spatial units in the international division of labor: Opportunities for wage earning are often greater in the center, those for investment and informal economic activity are frequently greater in the periphery.

The best-known migration movements, such as rural–urban migration or massive illegal immigration are thus crests of a process of ebb-and-flow involving many other, less visible currents. More than a single movement from one place to another, migration can be conceptualized as a process of network building. Networks tie-in groups distributed across different places, maximizing their economic opportunities through mutual aid and multiple displacements.

The microstructures thus created not only permit survival of the exploited, but often constitute a significant undercurrent, running counter to dominant structures of exploitation. Migration as a network-building process is not a contemporary phenomenon, nor one restricted to peripheral countries. It is, on the contrary, a constant in spontaneous movements of the laboring class—urban workers and peasants. In his typology of recent European migrations, Tilly associates this process with both circular and chain migrations and, in particular, with the transition from one to the other.[92] Similarly, the MacDonalds' analysis of chain migration as it depopulated southern Italian villages to create the "Little Italys" of North America is based on the networking process.[93] While they characterize this particular flow as based on the unique patterns of familism and dyadic patronage typical of the exporting region, the fact is that the microstructures sustaining migration are a more general phenomenon. The following illustrations refer to two aspects of the network-building process as it occurs today in peripheral countries: its origins in multiple displacements and its interrelationship with the informal sector.

Return Migration: The Case of Huancayo, Peru

Huancayo is the main urban center of the Mantaro Valley region in Peru. It experienced rapid industrial growth, most of it in textiles, in the 1940s. By the end of the 1960s most of the industries had closed down, unable to compete with cheap imports and technologically sophisticated textile production in Lima. Moreover, the local elite progressively lost control of commercial activities in the city and its hinterland since transactions could not be directly conducted with the capital. The city was thus a classic example of a peripheral region progressively deprived of its autonomy by the center.[94] During the last 10 years, however, the

92. Tilly, "Migration in Modern European History."
93. John S. MacDonald and Leatrice D. MacDonald, "Chain Migration, Ethnic Neighborhood Formation, and Social Networks," in *An Urban World*, ed. Charles Tilly (Boston: Little, Brown, 1974), pp. 226–236.
94. Bryan R. Roberts, "The Provincial Urban System and the Process of Dependency," in Portes and Browning eds., *Current Perspectives in Latin American Urban Research*, pp. 99–131.

population of Huancayo has grown rapidly. The average growth rate has been about the same as in Lima. This runs contrary to the prediction of population loss following economic demodernization. The growth has not been solely the result of in-migration from the city's hinterland, but also of the capacity of the city to hold population and attract earlier migrants to Lima. Several thousand textile workers, for example, accepted the loss of their jobs without protest and about 80% of them remained in the region. In addition, Huancayo has received considerable numbers of return migrants from Lima. Approximately 30% of the adult males (excluding those born in Lima) have spent one or more years in Lima. Most of these, like workers staying in Huancayo, are engaged in small-scale enterprises in the areas of commerce, manufacture, repairs, and transport.[95]

Most urban areas in this peripheral region have also gained population during the last 10 years. There are return migrants from Lima in most Mantaro villages and towns; the large majority of adult males were born there, but have migrated elsewhere for at least one year. The migration pattern of return migrants varies, but it is rarely as simple as to include one more place. Some villages appear to channel their migrants toward cotton plantations; others to mines. In each case, these displacements are complicated by additional moves to Huancayo or to Lima.

Incomplete and intergenerational return migrations have also been observed. The author of a recent study of the region, of which the above findings are part, states that "some people begin in a small village, move through the mines to Lima and return not to the village but to the nearest large town. In Jauja, a town of some 14,000 people, some 15 percent of the sample originated in the small villages close by, migrated to the mines or to the coast, and came back to Jauja to retire or to engage in commerce."[96]

Examples of this pattern of multiple displacements and return migration have also been found elsewhere. Recent studies of former illegal immigrants from two rural regions in Mexico suggests that U.S.-bound Mexican workers seldom break their ties with places of origin. The illegal crossing appears to be, on the contrary, a movement jointly planned and articulated with a local network of friends and relatives. There is evidence of a patterned sequence in which periods of illegal work in the U.S. are alternated with periods of residence in Mexico. Money is remitted back to the family and investments are made by or on behalf of the absent worker in areas of origin or those nearby. Recent studies of Dominican illegal immigration to New York reproduce these findings in all its essentials.[97]

95. *Ibid.*
96. *Ibid.*, pp. 122–123.
97. For Mexico, see Cornelius, "Mexican Migration to the United States"; Ina Dinerman, "Patterns of Adaptation among Households of U.S.-Bound Migrants from Michoacan, Mexico," *International Migration Review* 12(Winter 1978): 485–501. For the Dominican Republic, see Vivian Garrison and Carol I. Weiss, "Dominican Family Networks and U. S. Immigration Policy: A Case Study," *International Migration Review* 12(Summer 1979): 264–283.

Although there are few studies of domestic migration that go beyond the usual survey of migrants in places of destination, those that exist suggest the presence of a large proportion of temporary workers among the migrant population of large cities. Their stay appears to be just one step in a series of decisions, constraints, and opportunities.

A final variant is provided by the villagers of Sicaya, in the Mantaro Valley. Many families from this village live in Lima and Huancayo. Many of these migrants are reported to retain land and trade interests in the village. Their place is temporarily filled by migrants from economically less developed villages and from the adjoining department of Huancavelica. In turn, immigrants to Sicaya retain land in their places of origin, recruit others, and attempt to develop small trading activities. Through a series of informal economic relationships, individuals are able to take advantage of differences in levels of "development." The success of these activities depends precisely on the existence of such spatial differences, which can be exploited through personal relationships and individual effort.[98]

The Informal Economy as Means of Survival and Ascent

The "informal sector" can be defined primarily by the absence of routine state regulation. Several authors have noted that government control introduces rigidities in the larger industrial and commercial firms to which smaller informal ones are not subject. The demise of the larger textile firms of Huancayo, for example, did not appear to be solely a consequence of penetration by Lima-based companies, but a consequence also of their inability to compete with the more flexible informal textile production in the city. Workers did not protest the closing of their factories since many of them had the opportunity of becoming small entrepreneurs themselves.[99]

Other characteristics of the informal sector are the substitution of capital by intensive labor, the tendency to segment as enterprises grow, and the heavy reliance on networks of kin and friends. Informal enterprises are generally found in petty manufacturing, services, and transport. Although they operate in the margins of the formal capitalist economy, the structure of peripheral production and state control allows considerable room for maneuvering. The resilience of the informal sector depends on the ability of individuals to find investment opportunities and on their capacity to bypass costs in the fully monetized economy by use of their own labor and that of others.

Though operating at the margins, informal enterprises are not necessarily isolated from each other. A number of interlinkages develop that reinforce their

98. Roberts, "The Provincial Urban System and the Process of Dependency."
99. *Ibid.*

viability. Cheap fares charged by operator-owned buses and the more relaxed rules concerning what can be transported allow, for example, the direct marketing of products by small farmers into the larger urban centers and at distances that would otherwise be prohibitive. Considerable work opportunities are generated by informal enterprises, as in the loading and unloading of trucks, repairing of used machinery, and peddling of products.[100]

In a sense, formal enterprises are the ones that most closely correspond to conditions in the periphery, where a scarcity of capital is coupled with an abundance of cheap labor. Their resilience depends on avoidance of state taxation and regulation and on the use of unpaid labor or labor paid below formal market wages. As will be seen in Chapter 3, however, the existence of the informal sector does not depend on the incapacity of the state to regulate it, but is actually a precondition for the maintenance of a low-wage economy in the periphery.

It is clear that the creation of informal enterprises depends on the emergence of personal relationships for mutual economic assistance and support. How these networks evolve is illustrated by a case study in one of the *colonias proletarias* of Mexico City.[101] A number of families living in one of the capital's shantytowns originated in the same rural region in the state of San Luis Potosi. Men were employed as agricultural laborers living on wages of 10 Mexican pesos (less than 1 dollar) a day for 3–4 months a year. In the 1950s, a group of young men left the region in search of opportunities in Mexico City. After a period of time, two of them found work and settled in a nearby shantytown. Gradually they were able to bring most of their relatives from the original area. A third migrant also settled in the shantytown and brought his relatives. The two groups intermarried and established fictive kinship through *compadrazgo*.

After a period time, one of the migrants was able to find a job as a carpet layer. He gradually trained and found jobs for his kinsmen until 13 of the migrant males from San Luis Potosi were employed in the trade. Their eventual occupational success contrasts with their meager educational achievements: Of 25 heads of families or spouses, 14 were illiterate and 6 had taught themselves basic spelling. Only 2 had had any schooling beyond the fourth grade.

Again, the pattern of mutual assistance and support in job finding is not unique to migration processes in the periphery. The MacDonalds, for example, speak of "chain occupations" as older Italian immigrants in U.S. cities found jobs for newer ones in the industries where they were employed. Similarly,

100. See also Lisa R. Peattie, "Living Poor: A View from the Bottom," paper presented at the Conference on Urban Poverty: A Comparison of the Latin American and United States Experiences, Los Angeles: UCLA School of Architecture and Urban planning, May 1975; Larissa Lomnitz, "Mechanisms of Articulation between Shantytown Settlers and the Urban System," paper presented at the Symposium on Shantytowns, Burg Wartenstein, Austria: The Wenner-Gren Foundation, 1977.

101. Larissa Lomnitz, *Networks and Marginality, Life in a Mexican Shantytown* (New York: Academic Press, 1977).

Anderson's study of the Portuguese in Toronto identifies "networks of contact" as the prime variable leading to occupations and to different levels of occupational success.[102]

The cases of Mexico City, of Huancayo, of villages in the Mantaro Valley and in Jalisco, and of other places document ways in which spatial differences in economic opportunities are combined with the network-building process to permit survival of peripheral populations. Contrary to the usual image, the response of the exploited to conditions created for them by the capitalist system is seldom passive acquiescence. Their effort to manipulate, in turn, these conditions is based on the two resources left in the absence of capital: one's own labor and social bonds of solidarity and mutual support within the working class.

Remote villages in the interior of Mexico and the Dominican Republic survive because of the remittances, investments, and eventual return of illegal workers in the United States. Remote towns and villages in Peru survive because of the economic initiatives of Lima-based migrants. The similarity of both situations is not accidental for they respond to essentially the same structural conditions. These situations attest to an undercurrent of popular economic initiative through which life is made possible within the inequalities and constraints of peripheral capitalism.

Summary

The importance of migration to the question of development in the world system lies in two interrelated characteristics: First, it is a source of labor, one which often plays a fundamental role in capitalist economic expansion; second, it is simultaneously the way exploited classes attempt to cope with the constraints of their situation. As has been shown, such constraints are often deliberately imposed so as to generate labor migration. As was also shown, the advantages of migrant labor for capitalist expansion are not automatic and must frequently be produced through political manipulation. In general, the structure of economic forces in core and periphery tends to be arranged so as to condition migrants to sell their labor in places where needed and at the cheapest possible price. Exceptions, motivated by the occasional clash of interests between landowning and entrepreneurial classes or the temporary measures of a liberal regime, do not substantially modify the general trend.

Workers in peripheral areas frequently attempt, through multiple displacements, to take advantage of a structure of economic opportunities distributed

102. MacDonald and MacDonald, "Chain Migration, Ethnic Neighborhood Formation, and Social Networks," p. 232; Grace M. Anderson, *Networks of Contact: The Portuguese and Toronto* (Waterloo, Ontario: Wilfrid Laurier University Press, 1974).

unequally in space. Since limited opportunities are available through formal channels, such initiatives tend to occur at the interstices. The structure of production under peripheral capitalism, marked by only partial commodification of labor and restricted state control, provides room for informal economic initiatives and, hence, for the possibility of survival.

The phenomenon of migration, therefore, stands at the crossroads between international and domestic inequalities and class exploitation. It is a way through which the exploited contribute to ever-expanding structures of economic domination and, simultaneously, the form in which they react to their constraints. It shows how economic concentration and inequality are perpetuated by the initiatives of both dominant groups *and* their victims. Whereas the case studies previously reviewed are only illustrative, they document the general point that transactions between advanced and backward regions, conducted by people across space, constitute a central problematic and defining feature of the world-system.

3

Unequal Exchange and the Urban Informal Sector

Introduction

A basic characteristic of capital accumulation on a world scale is that it depends on the perpetuation of patterned differences in the conditions of reproduction of the labor force across different political and geographical units. Chapter 2 explored some of the conditions necessary for inducing migration flows from peripheral areas and the utilization of migrant labor in places of destination. The purpose of this chapter is to explore the obverse of this problem: namely, the conditions of reproduction of labor in peripheral areas of the world economy. The existence of vast and persistent differences in the cost of labor between advanced and peripheral countries is a fact consistently documented by the empirical literature on the international economic system.[1] As seen in Chapter 1, this fact is theoretically central for explication of the mechanism of unequal exchange between core and periphery and the concentration of surplus in the centers of the system.[2]

Our concern is not to retrace all the steps of the unequal exchange argument since this has already been done with increasing sophistication in the economic literature. Instead, we will endeavor to correct some factual inaccuracies and limitations of this general argument, as it attempts to explain the conditions for

1. International Labor Office, *Yearbook of Labor Statistics* Vol. 33, Geneva, 1974. The average manufacturing wage in the U.S. is 10 times higher than in the Philippines; 14 times higher than in South Korea; and 24 times higher than India. For additional evidence, see Tables 3.1 and 3.2.
2. Samir Amin, "Accumulation and Development: A Theoretical Model," *Review of African Political Economy* 1(August–November 1974): 9–26; Alain de Janvry and Carlos Garramón, "The Dynamics of Rural Poverty in Latin America," *Journal of Peasant Studies* 5(April, 1977): 206–216; Terence K. Hopkins and Immanuel Wallerstein, "Patterns of Development of the Modern World-System," *Review* 1(Fall, 1977): 111–145; Harry Magdoff, *The Age of Imperialism* (New York: Monthly Review Press, 1969).

the maintenance of a cheap labor economy in peripheral countries. These shortcomings are actually compounded for they involve the arguments of general theorists of capitalist accumulation and dependency, as well as the more specific results of researchers working close to the field. The partial disjunction between theory and research in this area offers the additional opportunity of exploring the bearing of a world-system perspective on a so far neglected topic: the urban class structure and the character of urban poverty in peripheral nations.

Theoretical Review

The dynamics of capitalist expansion on a world scale have been examined in detail in the economic dependency and unequal exchange literature. For purposes of our argument, the recent formulation by de Janvry and Garramón[3] is appropriate. Their statement provides a succinct point of departure to identify limitations in the present state of theory.

For de Janvry and Garramón, there is in the world economy a dual dialectic: the dialectic between production and circulation internal to each sector of the system; and the dialectic between center and periphery. Center economies are characterized as sectorally and socially "articulated." Sectoral articulation involves the existence of linkages between productive sectors. On the supply side, increases in the production of consumption goods stimulates an increase in the demand for capital goods. Such "backward linkages" are singled out by Hirschman and other economists as preconditions for capital formation, technological innovation, and accelerated growth.[4]

Social articulation implies the existence of an objective, albeit contradictory, relationship between profits and real wages. Whereas, from the point of view of individual firms, increases in the wage bill represent a "loss"; from the standpoint of the capitalist class as a whole they are a precondition for the expansion of the market and, hence, the continuation of the accumulation process.

From the demand side, the capacity to consume, according to de Janvry and Garramón, is determined by the returns to labor in the form of wages. This capacity conditions returns to capital, in the form of profits. The organization of production under socially articulated economies implies, first, that labor struggles toward higher wages possess an objective basis of support in the very dynamics of the accumulation process and, second, that the requirement of

3. Alain de Janvry and Carlos Garramón, "Laws of Motion of Capital in the Center-Periphery Structure," *Review of Radical Political Economics*, 9(Summer, 1977): 29–38.
4. Albert D. Hirschman, *The Strategy of Economic Development* (New Haven: Yale University Press, 1958); Hla Myint, *The Economics of the Developing Countries* (New York: Praeger, 1964).

expansion of consumption capacity creates a relentless drive toward proletarianization of the labor force. This presupposes the decomposition of precapitalist modes of production and the full monetization of returns to labor.[5]

De Janvry and Garramón define peripheral economies as sectorally and socially "disarticulated." Sectoral disarticulation implies the absence of backward linkages, either for economies of the "export enclave" type or for those engaged in "import-substitution" industrialization. Industrialization in the periphery occurs under conditions of external dependency for capital goods and technology, so that expansion of industrial production results in direct pressures on the balance of payments.

Social disarticulation implies the absence of an objective relationship between the rate of profits and the level of wages. In export enclave economies, returns to capital are determined by external demand and the capacity to consume is regulated by constraints in the balance of payments. In import-substitution economies, returns to capital are conditioned by the capacity to consume of a restricted market formed by the capitalists themselves and a salaried bureaucratic-managerial "middle" class. Domestic market demand and production capacity are ultimately governed by external demand for exportables, insofar as it affects the balance of payments and constrains the capacity to import capital goods, intermediate inputs, and technology.

Social disarticulation in peripheral economies has two major consequences. First, the absence of an objective requirement for domestic market expansion leads to an unremitting downward pressure on wages. Cheap labor increases returns to capital engaged in import-substitution industrialization, since production is targeted on the high-income market. More important, cheap labor maintains the competitiveness of exports in world markets, including both primary commodities and, increasingly, manufactured consumer goods.[6] Hence, class struggles in the periphery lack the objective basis for compromise that characterizes center economies and tend to polarize into radical workers' movements, on the one hand, and governmental terrorism and repression, on the other.

Second, the absence of an objective requirement for market expansion arrests the drive toward full proletarianization. Peripheral accumulation lacks the contradictory relationship between upward and downward pressures on returns to labor, but substitutes for it the contradictory relationship between the capitalist

5. de Janvry and Garramón, "The Dynamics of Rural Poverty in Latin America"; see also Immanuel Wallerstein, "Rural Economy in Modern World Society," *Studies in Comparative International Development* 12(Spring, 1977): 29–40.
6. Pierre Jalee, *Imperialism in the Seventies* (New York: Third Press, 1973); Jorge Graciarena, "The Basic Needs Strategy as an Option. Its Possibilities in the Latin American Context," *CEPAL REVIEW* (August, 1979): 39–53; Alain de Janvry, "Material Determinants of the World Food Crisis," *Berkeley Journal of Sociology* 21(1976–77): 3–26.

sector as a whole and precapitalist modes of production. The process of disintegration of the rural subsistence sector in the face of capitalist expansion is constrained by the fact that this sector helps reduce payments to labor.[7] It does so by assuming the costs of reproduction of new generations of workers and absorbing those that have become redundant for the capitalist sector. This "subsidy" paid by precapitalist subsistence to capitalist production is translated into wages lower than those that would be required for reproduction under fully proletarianized conditions.[8]

Expansion of money wages in the core as a precondition for continuing accumulation accentuates the tendency of the rate of profit to fall and leads, in turn, to the necessary asymmetric relationship with peripheral economies. Increased consumption in the centers is partially subsidized by extraction of surplus from the periphery. De Janvry and Garramón identify several mechanisms through which international transfers of surplus take place. In the contemporary world-system, these mechanisms do not depend on direct political exactions backed by military force, but are primarily a consequence of the complementary needs of the reproduction of capitalism in center and periphery.

This symbiotic relationship is exemplified by the most transparent mechanism of exploitation—financial imperialism. Center capital is exported as one of the means to combat a secular decline in the rate of profit. Peripheral countries require such capital inputs, both as means to implement import substitution schemes and to alleviate chronic balance of payments difficulties. Returns to core capital take the form of repatriated profits, royalties, transfer payments, and the servicing of the foreign debt.

The less obvious mechanism—unequal exchange—involves the trading of commodities embodying unequal rates of surplus value. Under conditions of social disarticulation in the periphery, real wages paid in the exporting sector are consistently lower than those predominant in the center economies and, hence, the rate of surplus value is higher. Under these conditions, international trade represents a mechanism for the transfer of surplus value, which occurs independent of political demands or financial imperialism. Surplus transfer occurs even with trade at equilibrium production prices being, ultimately, a consequence of the returns to labor under conditions of social articulation and disarticulation.

---

7. de Janvry and Garramón, "The Dynamics of Rural Poverty in Latin America"; Immanuel Wallerstein, William G. Martin, and Torry Dickinson, "Household Structures and Production Processes: Theoretical Concerns, plus data from Southern Africa and Nineteenth Century United States," mimeo, Binghamton, N.Y.: Fernand Braudel Center, State University of New York, 1979.

8. Harold Wolpe, "The Theory of Internal Colonialism: The South African Case," in *Beyond the Sociology of Development*, eds. Ivar Oxaal, Tony Barnett, and David Booth (London: Routledge and Kegan Paul, 1975), pp. 229–252; C. Meillassoux, "From Reproduction to Production," *Economy and Society* I(February 1972): 93–105; de Janvry, "Material Determinants of the World Food Crisis."

TABLE 3.1
Nonagricultural and Manufacturing Sector Wages in Latin American Countries and the
United States

Country[a]	Nonagricultural sector wages ca. 1969 (dollars per week)	Wages in manufacturing ca. 1973 (dollars per hour)
Latin America		
Argentina	15.97[b]	1.16
Brazil	40.71	.74
Colombia	11.58	.19
Dominican Republic	17.66	.45
Ecuador	11.34	.43
El Salvador	—	.45
Guatemala	17.32	.44
Mexico	30.81	1.37
Panama	29.20	.78
Peru	12.38	.78
Venezuela	48.59	1.82
United States	114.61	4.07

Sources: *Statistical Abstract for Latin America, 1970* (Los Angeles: UCLA Latin American Center, 1971), pp. 97, 356; *Statistical Abstract for Latin America, 1977*, pp. 204, 324.
[a] Figures for Chile omitted, because of unreliable exchange rates.
[b] Figure probably affected by an artificially high exchange rate.

Critique

The argument concerning the transfer of surplus from periphery to core and its dependence on wage differentials across regions of the world-economy has been made by a number of authors. Wallerstein states it poignantly:

> If the axial division of labor exists to permit unequal exchange, and unequal exchange is based on differentials in real wages, and if these differentials are not merely wide but widening over time, and if this occurs without the increase of real wages in core-like activities to a point where the accumulation of capital is comprehensively threatened, there must be mechanisms which permit the reduction of money wages in peripheral activities below the level minimally required for the reproduction of the labor-force and yet maintain the labor force in existence.[9]

The extent to which wage differentials for industrial work exist between core and periphery is illustrated by data in Tables 3.1 and 3.2. Table 3.1 compares

9. Immanuel Wallerstein, "Development: Theories, Research Designs, and Empirical Measures," paper presented at the "Thematic Panel on Development," meetings of the American Sociological Association, Boston, August 1979, p. 10.

TABLE 3.2
Comparative Wage Scales for Industrial Work (U.S. dollars per hour, 1975)

Type of labor	Country			
	Brazil	United Kingdom	Germany	United States
Unskilled labor	.24	.96	1.27	3.00
Light assembly	.32	.82	1.40	2.89
Machine operator	.68	1.01	1.50	3.24
Maintenance mechanic	.65	1.42	1.60	3.29
Toolmaker	.81	1.61	1.73	5.03

Source: Adapted from A. Brown and J.P. Ford, *Brazil: Today's Business Opportunity* (London: 1975), p. 124.

U. S. nonagricultural and manufacturing sector wages with those prevailing in Latin America in recent years. U. S. wages exceed the average in Latin America by a factor of 5:1; they double and frequently triple average wages in the relatively advanced countries, such as Argentina, Mexico, and Venezuela. The ratio relative to the more peripheral countries in the region, such as Peru, Ecuador, and Colombia, is close to 10:1.

These wage differentials are not accounted for by major differences in labor productivity. Available studies by the International Labour Office (ILO) and other international organizations do not indicate significantly lower productivity per unit of capital invested in peripheral, as compared with core countries.[10] Table 3.2, for example, presents wage differentials for specific industrial categories at comparable levels of productivity for Brazil and for the United States, United Kingdom, and Germany. The data show that Brazilian wages for unskilled industrial labor are one-fourth of those paid in the United Kingdom, one-fifth of those in Germany, and one-tenth of those in the U. S. At the other extreme, German and British wages for skilled labor more than doubled those in Brazil, whereas American wages exceed Brazilian ones by a factor of 5:1 in these categories.

The mechanism most frequently identified in the accumulation on a world-scale literature for holding down wages in the periphery is preservation of the traditional subsistence sector:

> Functional dualism between modern and traditional sectors thus make it possible to sustain a level of wages below the cost of maintenance and reproduction of the

10. International Labour Office, *Employment, Incomes, and Equality: A Strategy for Increasing Productive Employment in Kenya*, Geneva, 1970; International Labour Office, *Urban Development and Employment in Sao Paulo*, Geneva, 1976; see also John Weeks, "Policies for Expanding Employment in the Informal Urban Sector of Developing Countries," *International Labour Review* 91(January 1975): 1–13; C. Leys, "Interpreting African Underdevelopment: Reflection on the ILO Report on Employment, Incomes, and Equality in Kenya," *African Affairs* 72(1973): 419–429.

labor force—a cost which would determine the minimum wage for a fully proletarianized labor force. Here, wage is only a complement between subsistence
needs of the worker and his family and subsistence production of the traditional
sector.[11]

Similarly, Samin Amir argues that the continuing existence of a labor surplus
and, hence, cheap wages in the periphery is directly linked to rural labor reserves
that constitute the principal element in the labor market. For Rhodesia, Arrighi
shows that the labor surplus actually increased during this century as a consequence of deliberate actions by the state, in particular its "reservations" policy.
For South Africa, Wolpe documents state means by which tribal subsistence
economies were kept in existence as a labor reservoir for the mines and capitalist
agriculture.[12]

The role of the traditional subsistence economy as a mechanism for the
reproduction of the peripheral labor force is, without doubt, fundamental but not
exclusive. Assignment to the traditional subsistence sector of sole or even primary
responsibility for the maintenance of unequal exchange reflects an excessively
simplistic understanding of the modes of labor utilization in peripheral countries. The cases of Rhodesia and South Africa are clear examples of the
mechanism of labor transfer from tribal subsistence to capitalist sectors, but
cannot be overgeneralized to other countries.

Reliance on the modern–traditional economic dualism for explanation of the
phenomenon of unequal exchange leaves the theory open to immediate empirical challenge. The maintenance and expansion of wage differentials between
core and periphery is based on the continuing existence of a sector which is itself
a shrinking component of peripheral economies. It is not difficult to demonstrate
that traditional subsistence enclaves, a distinctly rural phenomenon, have given
way worldwide to rapid urbanization and the expansion of capitalist agriculture.
Even in situations where the *absolute* size of rural subsistence enclaves has not
been altered, it is difficult to explain how a stagnant sector can reproduce and
eventually absorb a continuously expanding urban labor force.

The data in Table 3.3 illustrate the secular trend toward decreasing rural
population and increasing urbanization in Latin America. Although longitudi-
nal data for African countries is less readily available, those presented in Table
3.4 show the same trend toward lesser rural concentration.

11. de Janvry and Garramón, "The Dynamics of Rural Poverty in Latin America," p. 34.
12. Samir Amin, *Unequal Development* (New York: Monthly Review Press, 1976), p. 170;
Giovanni Arrighi, "Labor Supplies in a Historical Perspective: A Study of the Proletarianization of
the African Peasantry in Rhodesia," in *Essays on the Political Economy of Africa*, eds. G. Arrighi and
J. Saul (New York: Monthly Review Press, 1973); Wolpe, "The Theory of Internal Colonialism"; see
also Wallerstein, "Rural Economy in Modern World Society"; and Glaucio Dillon Soares, "The
Web of Exploitation: State and Peasants in Latin America," *Studies in Comparative International
Development* 12(Fall, 1977): 3–24.

TABLE 3.3

Population Defined as Rural and Population in Cities over 20,000 for Latin American Countries, 1930–1970 (percentage)

Country	Rural population[a]				Population in cities over 20,000				
	ca. 1940	ca. 1950	ca. 1960	ca. 1970	ca. 1930	ca. 1940	ca. 1950	ca. 1960	ca. 1970
Argentina	—	40	26	21	38	41	51	55	63
Bolivia	—	74	73	71	13	19	20	18	24
Brazil	69	64	54	44	14	16	21	29	36
Chile	48	40	32	24	32	37	42	53	58
Colombia	—	64	47	45	10	14	21	31	41
Costa Rica	—	67	65	64	13	15	23	24	27
Cuba	54	49	48	47	27	32	34	40	46
Dominican Republic	82	76	70	60	—	7	12	19	27
Ecuador	—	72	64	62	14	17	18	25	32
El Salvador	62	64	61	61	10	12	13	18	27
Guatemala	74	75	66	66	10	10	11	16	17
Haiti	—	88	85	81	6	5	6	7	10
Honduras	—	82	78	74	5	6	8	11	15
Mexico	65	57	49	42	16	18	24	29	35
Nicaragua	—	65	59	52	18	22	15	23	34
Panama	63	64	58	52	25	25	22	33	38
Paraguay	—	65	64	64	13	16	—	23	25
Peru	65	59	53	40	10	13	17	26	32
Uruguay	—	43	28	16	38	37	43	56	60
Venezuela	69	52	37	25	19	28	32	48	56
Latin America	—	63	56	50	17	19	21	29	35

Source: Statistical Abstract for Latin America, 1977 (Los Angeles: UCLA Latin American Center, 1977), pp. 86, 87.

[a] Definition of "rural" varies by country. The most common definitions are nonadministrative centers and population clusters of less than 2500, 2000, or 1500 persons.

TABLE 3.4
Population Defined as Rural and Inhabitants in Cities over 20,000 for African Countries, 1930–1970

Country	Rural population (percentage)[a]				Population in cities over 20,000 (in millions)			
	ca. 1930	ca. 1940	ca. 1950	ca. 1970	ca. 1930	ca. 1940	ca. 1950	ca. 1960
Algeria	78.9	78.0	76.4		.8	1.1	1.3	2.7
Egypt		74.9	69.9	57.1	3.0	4.1	6.3	9.5
Mauritius			65.1	56.1	.1	.1	.1	.2
Morocco		82.1	75.8	64.8	.8	1.2	1.9	2.8
South Africa	74.9	68.6	57.6	52.1	1.8	2.6	3.9	5.7
Tunisia		75.1	73.0	68.0	.3	.5	.7	.9
Zaire (Belgian Congo)			84.2	76.2	.2	.2	.4	1.2

Sources: U.N. Demographic Yearbook, 1952, p. 169; 1955, pp. 185–186; 1972, p. 147. United Nations, Growth of the World's Urban and Rural Population, 1920–2000 (New York: Dept. of Economic and Social Affairs, Population Studies #44, 1969), pp. 99–100.
[a] Definition of "rural" varies by country. The most common are nonadministrative centers and agglomerations of less than 2000.

The existing rural population cannot all be assumed to concentrate in subsistence enclaves; these are found to be an even more rapidly diminishing group in rural areas. Table 3.5 presents changes in the percentage of the labor force represented by the primary sector as a whole and by self-employed and unpaid primary sector workers for six Latin American countries. Over the 1960–1970 decade, both percentages show significant decreases in five countries. In particular, the category of self-employed and unpaid family workers—which most closely approximates the definition of rural subsistence—is shown to be a very rapidly diminishing proportion of the labor force in these countries. The single exception, Uruguay, is a country where the subsistence agricultural sector was an almost nonexistent segment of the labor force to begin with.

Nor is it the case that migrant workers in cities necessarily return to rural places of origin during periods of illness, unemployment, or when reaching old age. The neat theoretical process by which capitalist firms draw labor from subsistence enclaves in periods of high demand and return them there when no longer needed does not correspond to the actual experience in many peripheral countries. The available empirical literature indicates that, although return migration frequently occurs, a large proportion of migrants stay in cities and manage, with time, to firm up their position within the urban economy.

Major studies of urban migration, such as those of Balan, Browning, and Jelin in Monterrey, and Cornelius in Mexico City, document a series of social and political mechanisms used by migrants to shore up their economic position in

TABLE 3.5
Total Primary Sector and Self-Employed and Unpaid Rural Workers
in Latin American Countries, 1960 – 1970
(as percentage of the labor force)

Country	Year	Total primary sector workers	Self-employed and unpaid workers (primary sector)
Brazil	1960	50.9	36.7
	1972	40.2	28.4
Chile	1960	29.9	8.2
	1970	24.4	7.9
Costa Rica	1963	12.6	4.3
	1970	4.8	.9
Ecuador	1962	18.9	8.3
	1968	6.1	2.2
Uruguay	1963	.5	.1
	1970	1.4	.9
Venezuela	1960	32.7	21.1
	1973	19.1	12.0

Source: Statistical Abstract of Latin America, Vol. 18 (Los Angeles: UCLA Latin American Center, 1977), p. 199.

the city and support themselves and their families.[13] The process described by these studies is fundamentally at variance with the image of short-term migration to cities in search of industrial employment, followed by an expected return to rural places of origin.

Similarly, empirical studies of urban poverty by anthropologists such as Mangin, Lomnitz, Leeds, and Peattie show the remarkable consistency with which migrant workers seek rational strategies of adaptation to urban conditions and eventually employ their foothold in the city to bring in relatives and friends from rural areas.[14] An extensive sociological literature on migration to major cities

13. Jorge Balan, Harley Browning, and Elizabeth Jelin, Men in A Developing Society (Austin: Institute of Latin American Studies and University of Texas Press, 1973); Wayne A. Cornelius, Politics and the Migrant Poor in Mexico City (Stanford: Stanford University Press, 1975); see also Alejandro Portes, "Rationality in the Slum," Comparative Studies in Society and History 14(June, 1972): 268–286.

14. William Mangin, "Latin American Squatter Settlements: A Problem and a Solution," Latin American Research Review 2(Summer, 1967): 65–98; Lisa R. Peattie, The View From the Barrio (Ann Arbor: University of Michigan Press, 1968); Anthony Leeds and Elizabeth Leeds, "Brazil and the Myth of Urban Rurality: Urban Experience, Work, and Values in 'Squatments' of Rio de Janeiro and Lima," in City and Country in the Third World, ed. A. J. Field (Cambridge, Mass.: Schenkman, 1969), pp. 229–272; Larissa Lomnitz, Networks and Marginality: Life in a Mexican Shantytown (New York: Academic Press, 1977); Bryan R. Roberts, Organizing Strangers (Austin: University of Texas Press, 1973).

such as Rio de Janeiro and Sao Paulo in Brazil and Buenos Aires in Argentina also fails to show large-scale return migration to the interior of the country.[15]

Finally, recent studies of return migration do not offer evidence that the process occurs in response to the needs of the capitalist economy to expel labor back into the subsistence sector. The best available empirical studies, such as those of Roberts in the Mantaro Valley in Peru and of Arizpe in the Mazahua region of Mexico, indicate that return migration is frequently a self-paced process. Migrants return to invest in land or initiate enterprises on the basis of urban-acquired savings or expertise; those who return merely to live, frequently do so after having amassed sufficient money savings to last for an extensive period.[16]

As indicated in Chapter 2, the survival and growth of isolated rural places in peripheral countries often depends on the networking process by which urban-generated remittances and investments contribute to expand the local economic base. Such processes do not support theoretical accounts of economic dualism or of return migration as a simple response to cyclical downturns in the capitalist sector.

In synthesis, whereas theories of accumulation on a world scale have correctly identified subsistence enclaves and the process of return migration as mechanisms that lower wage levels in the periphery, not all wage labor is reproduced under traditional subsistence arrangements nor do all those who leave this condition in search of money wages return. Additional structural arrangements for controlling returns to labor must exist. Unlike traditional subsistence agriculture, such arrangements should not be based on a declining economic sector, but on one that accompanies the very expansion of the capitalist economy.

Theories of accumulation and dependency that address the issue of migrant labor in cities do identify a second mechanism. This has to do with the classic downward pressure on wages exercised by a reserve army of labor. Peripheral

15. CEBRAP; *São Paulo 1975: Crescimento e Pobreza* (Sao Paulo: Edições Loyola, 1976); James A. Gardner, "Urbanization in Brazil," International Urbanization Survey Report (New York: The Ford Foundation, 1973); Anthony Leeds and Elizabeth Leeds, "Brazil in the 1960s: Favela and Polity," (Austin: Dept. of Anthropology, University of Texas, 1971); Hamilton C. Tolosa, "Macroeconomics of Brazilian Urbanization," *Brazilian Economic Studies* 1(1975): 227–274; Gino Germani, "Social and Political Consequences of Mobility," in *Social Structure and Mobility in Economic Development*, eds. N. J. Smelser and S. M. Lipset (Chicago: Aldine, 1966), pp. 364–394; Adriana Marshall, *El mercado de trabajo en el capitalismo periférico: el caso de Argentina* (Santiago de Chile: PISPAL, 1978); Margot Romano Yalour, Maria M. Chirico, and Edith Soubie, *Clase obrera y migraciones* (Buenos Aires: Editorial del Instituto, 1969).

16. Bryan R. Roberts, "The Provincial Urban System and the Process of Dependency," in *Current Perspectives in Latin American Urban Research*, eds. Alejandro Portes and Harley L. Browning (Austin: Institute of Latin American Studies and University of Texas Press, 1976), pp. 99–131; Lourdes Arizpe, *Migración, etnicismo y cambio económico* (Mexico, D. F.: El Colegio de Mexico, 1978); see also Ina R. Dinerman, "Patterns of Adaptation among Households of U. S.-Bound Migrants from Michoacán, Mexico," *International Migration Review* 12(Winter, 1978): 485–501.

industrialization tends to occur on the basis of capital-intensive technology and, hence, appears to absorb a very limited proportion of the labor expelled from traditional agriculture. For Nun, the gap between the requirements of modern industry and the size of the urban labor surplus is such that it renders the bulk of the "marginal mass" redundant and excluded from any function in the accumulation process.[17]

Dependency writers such as Nun, Quijano, and dos Santos tend to define the relationship between the integrated and "marginal" populations as an urban reproduction of the fundamental dualism between urban capitalist and rural subsistence sectors.[18] The condition of the "marginal mass" is one of disarticulation from the dominant economy and of autonomous attempts at survival through a myriad of interstitial economic activities. But the fact that marginal labor is excessive, even relative to the requirements of the reserve army means that the functions exercised by the latter in capital accumulation are more than fulfilled.

The presence of a vast pool of unemployed and subemployed labor exercises pressure over workers in the capitalist sector and helps depress their incomes below the level that would prevail if such a surplus were not present.[19] This perspective thus envisions the urban economy as a disjointed overlap of a small sector integrated into the networks of world capitalism and a larger one excluded from any participation in modern production or consumption.

The existing empirical evidence does not support the "marginal mass" argument. As Tokman notes, this evidence suggests that technical progress in the formal industrial sector has been followed by wage increases rather than price reductions.[20] Even under the oligopolistic conditions prevailing in many branches of industry in the periphery, the data show that increases in productivity have been partly passed on to labor.

This means that, although payments to labor in the capitalist sector in the periphery are consistently lower than those in the core, they have not been kept at the level of subsistence. Wages in this sector have tended to keep pace with

17. José Nun, "Superpoblación relativa, ejército industrial de reserva y masa marginal," *Revista Latinoamericana de Sociología* 2(1969): 178–235; see also Anibal Quijano, "The Marginal Pole of the Economy and the Marginalized Labor Force," *Economy and Society* 3(1974): 393–428.

18. Quijano, "The Marginal Pole of the Economy and the Marginalized Labor Force"; Miguel Murmis, "Tipos de marginalidad y posicion en el proceso productivo," *Revista Latinoamericana de Sociología* 2(1969): 343–420; Osvaldo Sunkel, *Capitalismo transnacional y desintegración nacional en América Latina* (Buenos Aires: Nueva Visión, 1972).

19. Jorge Graciarena, "The Basic Needs Strategy as an Option"; Nun, "Superpoblacion relativa, ejército industrial de reserva y masa marginal"; Theotonio Dos Santos, "The Structure of Dependence," *American Economic Review* 40(May, 1970): 231–236; Celso Furtado, "The Brazilian 'Model' of Development," in *The Political Economy of Development and Underdevelopment*, ed. C. Wilber (New York: Random House, 1973), pp. 297–306.

20. Victor E. Tokman, "An Exploration into the Nature of Informal–Formal Sector Relationships," *World Development* 6(Sept.–Oct., 1978): 1065–1075.

productivity gains, thus further increasing the gap with the "marginal" labor force.

The relative impermeability of the formal capitalist sector to the presence of the reserve army is attributed by Tokman to the interest of large firms in the stability of their labor force. For this they are willing to pay higher wages.[21] Others, however, identify the causes in effective trade-union activity among formal sector workers and the protective shield provided by labor legislation.[22]

Organized workers in the capitalist urban economy are those to whom minimum wage, overtime, and job security regulations effectively apply. In addition to direct payments in the form of wages, indirect payments provided by the social security system are generally accessible only to employees of the state and workers in formal sector firms. Progressive labor and social security legislation is frequently found in peripheral countries. Its application, however, is restricted to small segments of the labor force.

In a recent study of the social security system of five Latin American nations, Mesa-Lago found that 88% of the total population and 77% of the economically active population were excluded from any coverage under the national social security system.[23] Differential application of labor and social security laws thus have the twin effects of increasing the economic gap between "marginal" and "integrated" sectors of the working class and effectively protecting the latter from the displacement threat posed by the urban "marginal mass."

Hyper-urbanization and the Informal Sector

The characterization of the urban "marginal mass" as an excess reserve army reinforces orthodox demographic descriptions of peripheral cities as cases of "hyper-urbanization" in need of urgent control. Arguments stemming from the dependency and accumulation on a world-scale literature converge at this point with neoclassical formulations; both provide support for statements such as the following:

Causes of widespread unemployment and underemployment in the Third World are now well known. During the 1960s, capital-intensive development strategies in both agriculture and industry failed to generate sufficient employment opportunity

21. *Ibid.*
22. A. Harberger, "On Measuring the Social Opportunity Costs of Labour," *International Labour Review* 103(January–June 1971): 559–579; L. Reynolds, "Wages and Employment in a Labour Surplus Economy," *American Economic Review* 55(1965): 19–39; Carmelo Mesa-Lago, *Social Security in Latin America, Pressure Groups, Stratification and Inequality* (Pittsburgh: University of Pittsburgh Press, 1978), chap. 1.
23. Mesa-Lago, *Social Security in Latin America*, chap. 7.

for all those entering the labor force. As a result, millions have come to survive by crowding into relative unproductive, low-paid service jobs . . . in developing countries, they swell the ranks of growing armies of unemployed or marginally "self-employed" who stay alive by inventing jobs in the interstices of the economy. [24]

As will be seen, this type of assertion is misleading for it ignores a growing body of evidence documenting the interdependence between those who "invent jobs" and firms in the formal economy. The orthodox case for defining rural labor migration into cities as an instance of hyper-urbanization is presented by Bairoch. [25] His monograph provided the theoretical basis for a series of urban labor market studies sponsored by the International Labour Office (ILO).

According to Bairoch, the magnitude of urban growth now taking place in Third World countries is unprecedented and "has led to a degree of urbanization which, relative to the level of development, is excessive, so that it may properly be referred to as 'hyper-urbanization' or 'over-urbanization.' "[26] This trend is said to exercise a harmful influence on economic growth since, in the city, the main consequence of hyper-urbanization is the emergence of a sluggish, "abnormally swollen, overdistended" tertiary sector. [27]

Reactions to the hyper-urbanization arguments led in directions relevant to the general problem of unequal exchange and international differences in returns to labor. The fact that neither traditional subsistence enclaves nor the urban "marginal mass" provides convincing explanations for the inequality of wages in capitalized sectors of core and peripheral countries suggests that the explanation must lie in more novel structures. Such arrangements should accompany the accumulation process, rather than be weakened by it, and should represent an adaptation to the particular political restrictions in the periphery preventing free replacement of urban workers by the reserve army.

The concept of the informal sector was advanced by a series of empirical studies of African and Latin American urban labor markets in reaction to the hyper-urbanization argument. The idea of a dualistic urban economy was already present in Geertz's distinction between the "bazaar" economy and the "firm" economy in Indonesia. [28] The bazaar economy represented both a traditional way of life and a means of absorbing labor surplus. However, Geertz agreed with orthodox economists in depicting the two sectors as antithetical to

24. Elsa Chaney, "The World Economy and Contemporary Migration," *International Migration Review* 13(Summer, 1979): 204.

25. Paul Bairoch, *Urban Unemployment in Developing Countries: The Nature of the Problem and Proposals for its Solution* (Geneva: International Labour Office, 1973).

26. *Ibid*.

27. Bairoch, as cited in Caroline Moser, "Informal Sector or Petty Commodity Production: Dualism or Dependence in Urban Development?" *World Development* 6(Sept.–Oct.): 1048.

28. Clifford Geertz, *Peddlers and Princes: Social Development and Economic Change in Two Indonesian Towns* (Chicago: University of Chicago Press, 1963).

each other and the bazaar economy as a limit to capital accumulation and the expansion of the dynamic firm sector.[29]

The concept of the informal sector was explicitly introduced in a paper by Hart in 1971 on the basis of empirical data from Ghana.[30] It was extensively used in an ILO report on labor market conditions in Kenya[31] and subsequently employed in a series of studies of urbanization in Africa and Latin America. For Moser, the distinct characteristic of Hart's approach, in contrast to earlier dualistic perspectives, was the identification of income-generating activities in the informal sector.[32] Rejecting description of the tertiary sector as an agglomeration of "shoe shiners and sellers of matches," Hart and other researchers portrayed informal activities as a complex, organized, and highly dynamic component of the urban economy.[33]

In retrospect, however, the more significant theoretical innovation of the new literature was the denial that the informal sector comprised an urban extension of traditional subsistence activities and the emphasis on the close articulation of informal labor with firms in the capitalist economy.[34] The informal sector was defined above as formed predominantly by small-scale economic activities conducted outside the state and the state-regulated private sectors. Contrary to stereotypes, such activities do not generally correspond to traditional subsistence production, but embody continuously changing requirements and opportunities in the "modern" economy.

As Roberts notes on the basis of empirical evidence from Peru and Mexico, the informal sector is not "traditional" either in its means of production or its types of activities.[35] Auto- and bus-repair shops represent an important component of the informal sector employing second-hand, but still modern equipment. Informal enterprises are found in intra- and interurban transportation, construction, manufacturing of modern clothes and footwear, and in urban commerce. Production of traditional handicrafts is seldom found, unless it is to provision a lucrative tourist trade.

The nontraditional pursuits engaged by informal sector workers already point to their articulation with the formal economy. It is in this sense that the applica-

29. *Ibid.*

30. Keith Hart, "Informal Income Opportunities and Urban Employment in Ghana," *Journal of Modern African Studies* 11(1973): 61–89.

31. ILO, *Employment, Incomes, and Equality.*

32. Moser, "Informal Sector or Petty Commodity Production."

33. Hart, "Informal Income Opportunities and Urban Employment in Ghana"; John Weeks, "Policies for Expanding Employment in the Informal Urban Sector of Developing Countries"; M. Bienefeld, "The Informal Sector and Peripheral Capitalism: The Case of Tanzania," *Bulletin of the Institute of Development Studies* 6(February, 1975): 53–73.

34. Alejandro Portes, "The Informal Sector and the World Economy: Notes on the Structure of Subsidized Labour," *Bulletin of the Institute of Development Studies* 9(June, 1978): 35–40.

35. Bryan Roberts, *Cities of Peasants, The Political Economy of Urbanization in the Third World* (London: Edward Arnold, 1978), chap. 5.

tion of the label "marginal" to this segment of the labor force reflects a misunderstanding of the structure of urban economies in peripheral countries. Studies in several cities document the extent to which apparently "self-employed" petty manufactures are, in fact, closely linked and dependent on decisions by firms in the formal sector.[36]

As will be seen, the nature of these interlinkages is not exhausted by these kinds of activities, nor is the characterization of informal enterprises as "dependent" for their survival on the formal sector an altogether correct one.

Two preliminary limitations of the concept of informal sector, as presently understood, must be discussed. Both are linked to its origins as a reaction to the notions of "overexpanded tertiary" and "hyper-urbanization." As a residue of that debate, a substantial proportion of the existing literature has become sidetracked into discussion of whether the informal economy is productive or unproductive. Proponents of the traditional tertiarization approach continue to characterize these activities as unproductive; whereas those who would like to see the national state help small entrepreneurs, defend them as highly productive, relative to capital invested.[37]

Such debates are not particularly useful, for the existence of the informal sector is embedded in the global structure of capitalist accumulation of which national states are part. It should come as no surprise that the proportion of the urban "self-employed" covered by state social security hovers around 1% in many countries and does not exceed 25% even in relatively advanced ones like Argentina.[38] State intervention and the effective modification of formal–informal economic relationships would not represent an isolated reform measure, but would lead to a revolutionary transformation of the structure of peripheral accumulation, as presently known.

Second, the informal sector continues to be characterized as interstitial. Tokman, for example, concludes that the future of the informal sector will be involutionary since informal activities present inherent disadvantages compared to formal ones.[39] The generalized view appears to be that informal enterprises

---

36. T. G. McGee, *Hawkers in Hong Kong: A Study of Planning and Policy in a Third World City* (Hong Kong: Centre for Asian Studies, University of Hong Kong, 1973); Chris Gerry, *Petty Producers and the Urban Economy: A Case Study of Dakar* (Geneva: International Labour Office, Urbanization and Employment Research Programme, 1974); Bryan Roberts, "The Provincial Urban System and the Process of Dependency."

37. For description and examples of this debate see Weeks, "Policies for Expanding Employment in the Informal Urban Sector of Developing Countries"; Tokman, "An Exploration into the Nature of Informal–Formal Sector Relationships"; and D. Mazumdar, "The Urban Informal Sector," World Bank Staff Working Paper #211, Washington, D.C., 1975.

38. Carmelo Mesa-Lago, *Social Security in Latin America, Pressure Groups, Stratification and Equality*, Tables 7-6 and 7-7.

39. Tokman, "An Exploration into the Nature of Informal–Formal Sector Relationships"; see also V. Tokman, "Informal–Formal Sector Interrelationships," *CEPAL REVIEW* (Jan.–June, 1978): 99–134.

exist in those areas considered unprofitable by foreign or domestic large-scale capital, but that the natural expansion of the market will eventually lead to their displacement. Such assertions are made despite evidence that the number of "self-employed"[40] represents a constant, if not growing, proportion of the labor force in many cities, and despite research documenting the continuous emergence of informal enterprises in new and previously unsuspected areas.[41]

Definitions of the informal sector as interstitial represent another instance of misapplication of the model of development of core countries to conditions in the periphery. Such definitions are based on a static conceptualization of the informal economy as formed by those enterprises now in existence. Such activities might well disappear, but will give rise to new ones. The empirical evidence points to the capacity of the informal sector to constitute and reconstitute itself in response to changing conditions in the "modern" economy.

Recent official data from Colombia, for example, estimates that employment in the informal sector comprises 45% of total urban employment and generated 40% of all new employment in cities between 1974–1978. The category of "self-employed" represented 23.4% of the urban labor force in 1971 and increased to 25.1% in 1978. The category of unpaid family worker, also associated with the informal sector, remained stable during this period. Together, self-employed and unpaid family workers represented 60% of all new employment in commerce.

Industries with fewer than 10 workers are termed "informal" in Colombia since they are not generally subject to labor legislation and workers are not protected by social security systems. In 1971, informal enterprises generated 42.3% of all industrial employment; in 1974, the proportion increased to 46.7%. Between these years, informal sector jobs represented 58.6% of total new industrial employment in Colombia. These and similar figures have led scholars and even official agencies to reject predictions of the demise of the informal economy in response to the growth of capitalism and to regard informal enterprise as a stable component of the national economy.[42]

40. As discussed previously, the term is inappropriate. Many apparently self-employed workers are actually disguised wage workers for firms in the formal sector. For an analysis of the different varieties of labor subsumed under "self-employment" see Ray Bromley and Chris Gerry, "Who are the Casual Poor," in *Causal Work and Poverty in Third World Cities*, eds. Bromley and Gerry (New York: John Wiley, 1979), pp. 3–23.

41. Roberts, *Cities of Peasants, The Political Economy of Urbanization in the Third World*, chap. 5; Luiz Antonio Machado da Silva, *Mercados Metropolitanos de Trabalho Manual e Marginalidade*. M.A. thesis, Social Anthropology Programme of the National Museum, Rio de Janeiro, 1971; Anthony Leeds, "Housing-Settlement Types, Arrangements for Living, Proletarianization, and the Social Structure of the City," in *Latin American Urban Research Vol. 4*, eds. Wayne A. Cornelius and Felicity M. Trueblood (Beverly Hills: Sage Publications, 1974), pp. 67–99; Peattie, *The View from the Barrio*.

42. Mauricio Romero, "Nuevas perspectivas ocupacionales y cambios en la estrategia de reproducción de la fuerza de trabajo," mimeo, ILO Technical Mission to the Ministry of Labor and Social Security, Bogota, 1980.

The Informal Sector and Peripheral Accumulation

In Chapter 2, informal activities were defined as an important mechanism through which peripheral workers could turn migration to advantage by maximizing opportunities distributed unequally in space. It is indeed in this light that most writings on the informal sector have viewed such activities: as means by which the poor can take care of themselves within the constraints of peripheral economies. It is now time to consider the obverse of this picture. The informal sector has significance not only as an aggregation of *individual* means for survival, but also as a *structural* feature of the process of peripheral accumulation.

To do so, we must examine the basic requirements of high surplus labor extraction *along with* the constraints impeding the application of classical strategies for achieving this purpose in contemporary peripheral economies. The theoretical argument advanced by de Janvry and Garramón depicts peripheral economies as ones of high surplus labor extraction, this being, in turn, a precondition for the operation of unequal exchange. High surplus labor extraction depends on an unmitigated downward pressure on wages, which is made possible by the condition of social disarticulation between production and consumption in these economies.

The logical thrust of this argument leads to the expectation of a direct drive against returns to labor, including enforcement of subsistence-level wages, absence of the "indirect" wage represented by social security benefits,[43] and free replacement of employed workers by the reserve army. Empirically, however, such conditions do not hold. Instead, we find the proletariat connected with key sectors of the export trade, import-substitution industries, public utilities, and transportation to be consistently protected by a complex system of labor contracts and labor legislation. Such a system maintains formal sector wages considerably above subsistence and safeguards this segment of the working class against arbitrary dismissals and competition from the marginal mass.

Under conditions of social disarticulation, the existence of such protective system represents a political constraint on capital forced by the mobilization and struggle of strategically located sectors of the working class. Its structural effect is to neutralize the most obvious means to ensure conditions of high surplus labor extraction. Such means are precisely those that accumulation on world-scale theories have assumed to operate.

Maintenance of a cheap labor economy in the periphery is not impeded, however, by the political power and derived advantages of the organized segment of the working class. Structural alternatives to the reduction of payments and

---

43. C. Meillassoux, "From Reproduction to Production"; Wallerstein, "Rural Economy in World-Society"; Arghiri Emmanuel, *Unequal Exchange: A Study of the Imperialism of Trade* (New York: Modern Reader, 1972).

indirect benefits for this segment must, however, fulfill one of two conditions: (*a*) to decrease the costs of reproduction of labor employed by the capitalist sector; and (*b*) to decrease the relative size of this segment of the labor force.

The level of wages paid by the capitalist sector and the level of demand by organized workers is fixed, at any particular point, in relation to the costs of subsistence defined in both biological and normative terms. The official minimum wage in many peripheral countries represents a more or less manipulated attempt to approximate these costs of subsistence.[44] Reduction of average reproduction costs, as indexed by the minimum wage or a similar statistic, represents an indirect means to control the level of labor demands and, hence, the final wage-structure. Yet, such reduction could scarcely occur if means of consumption for a peripheral working class were restricted to commodities purchased in the market.

The available economic data show that, under conditions of increasing interpenetration and technological dependence, average costs of consumption on the basis of formal market goods and services are not substantially less in the periphery. Oligopolistic control of markets in fact enables multinational subsidiaries to charge prices above core-market levels for basic goods, such as medicines.[45] Unrestricted speculation can drive the price of necessities, such as housing, to levels equal or higher than those predominant in core countries.[46]

Thus, reduction in costs of reproduction for the fully proletarianized segment of the working class must occur through extramarket means. For a predominantly urban labor force, such means cannot be limited to rural subsistence, but must be located in the city itself. Through them, the apparent paradox of formal sector wages significantly higher than bare subsistence *and* simultaneously lower than wages for similar work in core economies can be accomplished.

Nor is this difference enough, for the costs of labor of organized workers are still higher and, hence, returns to capital lower than what would be possible with free access to the surplus labor force. Under these conditions, firms in the periphery generally seek to maintain the number of workers protected by labor

44. See, for example, Edmar Bacha, *Os Mitos de Uma Decada* (Rio de Janeiro: Paz e Terra, 1976), chap. 2; Werner Baer, "La reciente experiencia brasileña: una interpretación," *Revista Paraguaya de Sociología* 34(Sept.–Dec. 1975): 7–39.

45. Gary Gereffi, "Drug Firms and Dependency in Mexico: the Case of the Steroid Hormone Industry," *International Organization* 32(Winter, 1978): 237–286; Constantine Vaitsos, *Intercountry Income Distribution and Transnational Enterprises* (London: Oxford University Press, 1974), chap. 4.

46. See, for example, Wayne A. Cornelius, "The Impact of Cityward Migration on Urban Land and Housing Markets," paper delivered at the Conference on the Urban Impact of Internal Migration, University of North Carolina at Chapel Hill, September 1975; Jorge E. Hardoy, Raul O. Basaldua, and Oscar Moreno, *Política de la tierra urbana y mecanismos para su regulación en América del Sur* (Buenos Aires: Editorial del Instituto, 1968); Luis Aureliano Gama de Andrade, "Politica urbana no Brasil: o paradigma, a organização e a política," *Estudos CEBRAP* 18(Oct.–Dec., 1976): 119–147.

contracts and legislation at a minimum. For temporary and unskilled tasks, they attempt to bypass formal hiring procedures reaching directly into the unorganized labor pool. Through this mechanism, surplus labor and surplus value extraction can be maximized, even while maintaining a formally "privileged" segment of the labor force.

The informal sector has been defined on the basis of a number of characteristics.[47] From the point of view of this analysis, the crucial ones are two: (a) informal sector activities generally employ unpaid family labor; (b) when paid labor is employed, it is generally at wages below the official minimum with no social security protection.

Informal sector activities result therefore in an output of goods and services at prices lower than those that could be offered under formal production arrangements. Although the most obvious interpretation of this price "edge" is that it permits the survival of informal enterprises, the most important aspect is that it maximizes surplus extraction by reducing labor reproduction costs for firms in the formal sector.

At this point, a distinction must be made between the informal sector and the concept of petty commodity production. Petty commodity production is part of the classic Marxist analysis of different modes of production and their mutual articulation. This analysis would define contemporary urban economies of the periphery as formed by a capitalist sector, deeply integrated into the international system, and a variety of precapitalist modes each transformed in its relation with the dominant one.[48]

For explanation of the present dynamics of peripheral accumulation, the concept of petty commodity production is, however, of limited value. The crucial problem is not that it leads to the wrong conclusions, but that it fails to encompass the process in its totality. This limitation has two aspects. First, the concept suggests either preexisting modes of production, transformed by the arrival of capitalism, or transitional ones, giving way in time to fully commodified relations. As the preceding discussion and following examples show, informal sector activities are neither traditional nor transitional but very "modern" features of the system of capitalist accumulation and, as such, continuously reproduced by the operations of this system. Second, the concept of informal sector includes, but is not exhausted by that of petty commodity production. As Wallerstein and his associates have noted, the concept of "in-come,"

47. For a review of definitions of the informal sector see Moser, "Informal Sector or Petty Commodity Production"; for a discussion of the relationship of the term with that of "marginality" see Portes, "The Informal Sector and the World Economy."
48. Bienefeld, "The Informal Sector and Peripheral Capitalism: The Case of Tanzania"; similar images are presented in Ernest Mandel, *Late Capitalism* (London: NLD, 1975), chap. 2 and Dos Santos, "The Structure of Dependence."

from the standpoint of individual households, encompasses a variety of strategies including formal sector wages, the proceeds from the market sale of goods (petty commodity production), and others as well.[49]

Additional strategies for gaining access to means of consumption include (a) direct subsistence production by household members; (b) rents (from use of land, housing, animals, or money); (c) transfer payments (gifts, alms, and other "free" subsidies); and (d) wages earned in informal firms.

The activities of the petty producer in manufacturing and marketing thus represent only one of the strategies by which means of consumption "come-in" individual households. All these informal strategies possess an inner coherence, not only from the point of view of individual households, but from that of the economic system as well.

As defined here, the concept of informal sector thus encompasses *all* income-producing activities outside formal sector wages and social security payments. To a greater extent than the concept of petty commodity production, it enables us to examine the interplay between such multiple activities and their impact on the reproduction and costs of urban labor.

Reproduction of the Working Class

The presence of the urban informal sector makes possible a condition of high surplus labor extraction by compensating for concessions made to the organized segment of the working class with the continuing exploitation of unorganized informal workers. Stated formally: The amount of surplus value, V, is the difference between total wages paid, W, and the total exchange value produced by employed labor, T. The difference between W and the cost of subsistence, S, defined in biological and social normative terms, can be generally attributed to past working-class organization and the resulting labor contracts and protective legislation.

These protective covenants and the strengthening of working-class organizations tend to increase the difference, D, further, between subsistence and average wave levels. For capitalist firms, the means to maintain and even expand V while yielding to increases in D is to push S to a minimum. This is not done directly by the firm, but by the organization of the entire economy.

Two values of S might be distinguished. S_1 represents the theoretical cost of subsistence, if the full value of necessities had to be purchased as commodities in

49. Wallerstein, Martin, and Dickinson, "Household Structures and Production Processes," p. 2.

the market. S_2 represents the actual costs of subsistence, including household-produced goods and services and those acquired through informal channels. The size of the gap between S_2 and S_1 is fundamentally different between core and peripheral economies. Whereas even in advanced countries S_2 and S_1 do not coincide, the distance is much larger in the periphery.

Stated differently, the portion of D represented by the distance between S_1 and S_2 is the quantity of surplus labor extracted from informal sector workers. Although such labor may not directly produce surplus value, it affects the relative level of W and hence the rate of surplus value in the formal sector. It permits an average level of wages in formal firms that is above subsistence while being, at the same time, a fraction of those predominant in the centers. In this manner, the labor of unpaid family and informal workers eventually finds its way into the coffers of large industrial corporations and finance houses.

The next sections illustrate this argument by examining the actual modes of articulation of the informal and formal economies as documented by recent research. Examples are divided according to what appear to be the three major "in-come" producing strategies of urban working-class households outside the formal economy: (a) subsistence and networking activities; (b) petty commodity production and trade; and (c) informal land occupation.

Subsistence Networks

Household subsistence activities include the production of goods, such as foodstuffs and services. Though more limited than in the countryside, food production in the city is not insignificant. It includes animal products such as eggs, milk, and meat and vegetable crops. In his study of Guatemala City shantytowns, Roberts noted the quantity of animals kept even in the most densely populated areas. Some residents not only raised poultry and pigs for their own consumption, but had enough to sell in the market.[50]

An identical story is told by Birbeck in his study of garbage-dump pickers in Cali. Birbeck found garbage picking to be a highly organized informal enterprise and one where workers would use the refuse to feed animals at home, both for consumption and sale.[51]

A consistent finding of studies dealing with urban squatter settlements is the opposition of inhabitants to be relocated into government projects where animal raising and gardening are impossible. Ray reported this trend among Caracas squatters relocated into multistory "superblocks." Identical opposition to resettlement plans was found by Mangin in Lima, Portes in Santiago de Chile, and

50. Roberts, *Cities of Peasants, The Political Economy of Urbanization in the Third World*, p. 112.

51. Chris Birbeck, "Self-employed Proletarians in an Informal Factory: The Case of Cali's Garbage Dump," *World Development* 6(Sept.–Oct., 1978): 1173–1185.

Leeds and Potengy Grabois in the favelas of Rio de Janeiro.[52] In each case, what appeared to outside officials as a marginal economic activity was regarded by the settlers as a primary source of livelihood.

Urban subsistence activities are not limited to direct production of food, but to its procurement through channels that bypass costs in the formal marketing system. The unpaid labor of unemployed family members is frequently used for that purpose. A study by Luz Joly in Panama outlines the existence of informal networks through which village products, such as pork meat (*puercos brujos*) and vegetables, are channeled directly into the squatter settlements of Panama City. By avoiding costly government inspection procedures, urban families involved in the networks can acquire these products at considerable savings relative to formal market prices.[53]

Similar mechanisms for informal transportation and distribution of village products into urban working-class areas are reported in studies of Lima's squatter settlements by Mangin and Roberts and of Santo Domingo by Cortén.[54] The unpaid labor input of kin and friends appears to be a prerequisite for efficient access to village production and the consequent lowering of prices.

A third important subsistence activity is housing construction. Unlike their counterparts in core economies, a significant proportion of workers in the periphery build their own houses. In most instances, this is housing erected after the spontaneous or organized occupation of vacant land or after purchase of a small lot in one of the "pirate" subdivisions encircling peripheral cities.[55]

More recently, governments and international agencies, such as the World Bank, have sponsored "sites-and-services" programs in which squatters are given access to an urbanized lot and credit for the purchase of construction materials.[56] Evaluations of some extensive sites-and-services programs, such as those conducted by the Salvadoran Housing Foundation and the "Operación Sitio" pro-

52. Talton F. Ray, *The Politics of the Barrios of Venezuela* (Berkeley: University of California Press, 1969); Mangin, "Latin American Squatter Settlements"; Portes, "Rationality in the Slum"; Elizabeth Leeds, *Forms of "Squatment" Political Organization: The Politics of Control in Brazil*, M.A. thesis, Dept. of Political Science, University of Texas at Austin, 1972; Giselia Potengy Grabois, *Em Busca da Integração: A Política de Remoção de Favelas no Rio de Janeiro*. M.A. thesis, Social Anthropology programme of the National Museum, Rio de Janeiro, 1973.

53. Luz Graciella Joly, Ph.D. dissertation in progress, Department of Anthropology, University of Florida (personal communication).

54. Mangin, "Latin American Squatter Settlements"; Roberts, "The Provincial Urban System and the Process of Dependency"; Andre Cortén, "Como vive la otra mitad de Santo Domingo: estudio de dualismo estructural," *Caribbean Studies* 4(1965): 3–19.

55. Alejandro Portes and John Walton, *Urban Latin America* (Austin: University of Texas Press, 1976), chap. 2; Roberts, *Cities of Peasants, The Political Economy of Urbanization in the Third World*, chap. 6.

56. The rationale for such programs has been most vigorously defended in front of the international agencies by John F. C. Turner, see his, *Housing by People* (London: Marion Boyars, 1976); also J. Turner and R. Fichter, *Freedom to Build* (New York: Collier, 1972); for a recent critique see Rod Burgess, "Petty Commodity Housing or Dweller Control? A Critique of John Turner's Views on Housing Policy," *World Development* 6(Sept.–Oct, 1978): 1105–1133.

gram in Chile, indicate that urban squatters generally prefer this type of program to those involving the purchase of a government house or apartment.[57]

Reasons for this preference involve the lower costs of purchasing a lot and the opportunity to tailor home construction to family needs, including the conduct of other subsistence activities. At the start, a temporary shack may be built in the back of the lot, while construction materials are bought and accumulated. Construction proceeds as resources and time permit and involves the labor of family members, other kin, and neighbors. Studies by Mangin, Cornelius, Turner, Collier, Leeds and others consistently report that the quality and appearance of communities built through such self-help schemes very quickly surpass those of government projects for the same income groups.[58]

The theoretical importance of self-built housing in peripheral cities is not limited to the fact that it solves the housing problem for the poor. Rather, its significance is that it solves a crucial problem for capital insofar as the latter requires the *in situ* reproduction of a low-wage urban labor force. Wages paid to workers in the formal sector are generally insufficient to permit access to the "regulated" land and housing markets characterized, in most large cities, by unbridled speculation.[59]

Stated differently, the cost of providing shelter to all members of the urban working class through conventional market channels would require a quantum increase in wages or, alternatively, massive state subsidies. Self-built housing is cheaper than any comparable form, including low-cost government projects, because there is a large input of labor by the worker himself, his kin, and his friends.

By permitting workers to engage in a traditional form of subsistence activity—house building—in squatter settlements or encouraging them to do so in new sites-and-services projects, the formal sector capitalizes on vast amounts of unpaid labor. Such labor allows the continuation of wage scales bearing no relation to the level of rents in the regulated housing market. To a greater extent

57. For the Salvadorean programme, see Luis de Sebastian and Research Team of the Central American University, *Investigación evaluativa de los programas habitacionales y de desarrollo de la comunidad de la Fundación Salvadoreña de Desarrollo y Vivienda Mínima* (San Salvador: Universidad Centroamericana, 1976); for the Chilean programme, see Alejandro Portes, *Cuatro poblaciones: informe preliminar sobre situación y aspiraciones de grupos marginados en el Gran Santiago*, Monograph Report, Land Tenure Center, Santiago, 1969.

58. Mangin, "Latin American Squatter Settlements"; Cornelius, "The Impact of Cityward Migration on Urban Land and Housing Markets"; John F. C. Turner, "Uncontrolled Urban Settlements: Problems and Policies," *International Social Development Review* 1(1968): 107–130; David Collier, *Squatters and Oligarchs: Authoritarian Rule and Policy Change in Peru* (Baltimore: Johns Hopkins University Press, 1976); Anthony Leeds, "The Significant Variables Determining the Character of Squatter Settlements," *América Latina* 12(July–Sept., 1969): 44–86; C. A. Frankenhoff, "Elements of an Economic Model for Slums in a Developing Economy," *Economic Development and Cultural Change* 16(1967): 27–35.

59. Portes and Walton, *Urban Latin America*; Jorge E. Hardoy, *Las ciudades en América Latina* (Buenos Aires: Paidos, 1972), chap. 2.

than food production, part of the cost of a crucial element of reproduction—a place to live—is thus shifted into the informal economy.

Subsistence activities are not, however, conducted in isolation. In the preceding chapter, the concept of social networks was introduced as a key mechanism for the survival of workers in peripheral economies. The work of Lomnitz in Mexico City remains the most exhaustive account of this survival strategy involving the pooling of resources and information and a constant exchange of credit and other favors.[60] Food production and procurement, housing construction, as well as information on job openings and small loans, are among the items exchanged within such networks.

Social networks increase the efficiency of urban subsistence activities (as well as of others in the informal economy) and maximize the number benefiting from them. For example, a 1977 study of 5 squatter settlements in Santo Domingo found that 27.8% of family heads had no stable income and that an additional 38.3% earned less than the minimum wage of 4 pesos per day. The author, Duarte, observed that the survival of such workers and their families depended on the organization of subsistence and income-sharing activities by the extended family and its social networks: "The great instability of the family head demands participation by all other members in sub-occupations, which together combine into a minimum level of subsistence."[61]

As with the broader concept of the informal sector, the importance of social networks is not limited to their function for individual survival. Networks act as an effective social security system, supplementing formal benefits to employed workers, channeling the labor of others into informal pursuits, and providing for basic needs of the sick and elderly. By facilitating subsistence production and other informal activities, networks lower costs of reproduction relative to what they would be in a fully monetized market economy. Thus, mechanisms of survival—signaling the rationality of workers under the scarcity conditions of peripheral cities—ultimately benefit capitalist firms that appropriate them in the form of lower wages.

Petty Commodity Production and Trade

The reproduction of a peripheral urban working class takes place largely within the confines of the neighborhood—*barrio* or squatter settlement. Aside from subsistence activities carried out by the extended family and its networks, many goods and services are purchased from other informal enterprises in the

60. Larissa Lomnitz, "Migration and Network in Latin America" in Portes and Browning, eds., *Current Perspectives in Latin American Urban Research*, pp. 133–150; Larissa Lomnitz, *Networks and Marginality, Life in a Mexican Shantytown* (New York: Academic Press, 1977).

61. Isis Duarte, "Marginalidad urbana en Santo Domingo," paper presented to the First Congress of Dominican Sociology, Santo Domingo, Nov. 1978, p. 43.

immediate area. The raising of pigs. poultry, and vegetables in the settlement is not only a subsistence activity, but one that permits the sale of these products to others at competitive prices. Similarly, the informal networks tying the urban settlements to rural village food production, not only subsidize the consumption of those directly involved, but also provide the basis for a thriving trade.

In Bogota, domestic animals are sold to subsidize major household purchases, such as clothing, furniture, or electric products. They can also be sacrificed for homemade food products sold in the shantytowns or city streets. Other basic necessities—such as clothing and footwear—are also frequently supplied by informal production. In the suburb of Soweto, South Africa, a thriving informal industry turns old car tires into shoes; these shoes sell for R2.50 and last about 5 years. Comparable shop-retailed shoes in South Africa cost R20 and last for 2 years.[62]

Studies by Roberts in Peru and Peattie in Colombia document the proliferation of informal services of all sorts in working-class settlements.[63] Such services include repair work on cars, appliances, and furniture; alterations and repair of clothing and shoes; local transportation; basic medical attention and child care; washing and ironing; hairdressing; and many others. Informal services are cheaper and are frequently used, not only by inhabitants of the settlements, but by others in higher-income areas of the city. The consumption of basic and not-so-basic services by wage workers in the capitalist sector seldom occurs through formal market channels, but is generally oriented toward informal sources of supply. Cheaper services provided by the informal sector multiply the consumption "yield" represented by formal-sector wages.

In addition to the direct production of goods and services, informal enterprises are commonly found in the distribution of manufactured goods. Together with animal and vegetable raising, petty commerce is perhaps the most frequent informal economic activity in working-class settlements. Petty commerce is conducted by front-room stores—*colmados, bodegas, ventorrillos, mercados, cantinas,* and so forth—or by street traders. In her study of 5 squatter settlements in Santo Domingo, Duarte reports one small store or bar for every 20 households.[64] In Cali, Bromley notes the wide proliferation of street trading, a daily average of 9500 vendors among "licensed" ones alone.[65]

62. David Webster, "The Political Economy of Survival," Work in Progress, University of Witwatersrand, (Nov. 10, 1979): 57–64.

63. Roberts, "The Provincial Urban System and the Process of Dependency"; Lisa R. Peattie, "Living Poor: A View From the Bottom," Proceedings of the Colloquium on Urban Poverty: A Comparison of the Latin American and the U.S. Experience, Los Angeles: UCLA School of Architecture and Urban Planning, May, 1974.

64. Duarte, "Marginalidad urbana en Santo Domingo."

65. Ray Bromley, "Organization, Regulation, and Exploitation in the So-Called 'Urban Informal Sector': The Street Traders of Cali, Colombia," World Development 6(Sept.–Oct. 1978): 1161–1171.

The relevance of petty commerce to the problem of reproduction of the urban working class is somewhat different from that of petty commodity production. The latter tends to lower costs by avoiding state regulation and employing unpaid or minimally paid labor. Although petty commerce is also labor-intensive, the economies of scale of large retailing chains tend to reduce any competitive edge of informal enterprises in this area. The result is that prices charged for manufactured goods by small stores and street traders are equal and frequently higher than those found in supermarkets.[66]

The contribution of petty commerce to the reproduction of the urban working class, which is simultaneously the reason for its existence, hinges on three aspects: (*a*) the volume of sales; (*b*) spatial location; and (*c*) the widespread use of credit.

As noted by Bromley in Cali and Peattie in Bogota, informal commerce is characterized by breaking bulk and selling the goods in very small quantities, not available in large retail stores.[67] Consumption patterns of wage workers in peripheral cities are characterized by frequent and small-quantity purchase of goods, in contrast with the less frequent and more substantial acquisitions of higher-income groups.[68] This working-class pattern is tied to a situation where money income is itself received in small amounts and at irregular intervals

Second, the relative isolation of working-class areas, frequently situated in the urban fringe, creates major transportation obstacles for purchasing goods in centrally located retail stores. Lower prices charged by formal retailers are often offset by transportation costs and by the time invested in these trips. In his study of formal–informal commerce in Santiago, Tokman found that small neighborhood stores were frequently quite able to compete, despite charging higher prices. Their crucial advantage was physical proximity.[69]

Put differently, labor-intensive petty commerce facilitates access to consumption by wage workers in squatter settlements and other fringe areas. Although prices charged for manufactured goods are higher on the surface, they still represent a net subsidy relative to their real costs in the formal retail sector.

Third, petty commerce, especially small stores operate through the granting of informal credit to customers. The system—known in parts of the Caribbean and Central America as "coger fiao"—involves interest-free credit for small purchases of food and other goods. Only regular customers are granted credit and this serves to tie individuals to a particular store. On the other hand, the "fiao"

66. Victor Tokman, "Competition between the Informal and Formal Sector in Retailing: The Case of Santiago," *World Development* 6(Sept.–Oct., 1978): 1187–1198; Guillermo Geisse, "La desigualdad de los ingresos: punto de partida del círculo de la pobreza urbana," paper presented at the Seminar on New Directions of Urban Research, University of Texas at Austin, May 1974.
67. Bromley, "Organization, Regulation, and Exploitation in the So-Called 'Urban Informal Sector'"; Peattie, "Living Poor."
68. Tokman, "Competition between the Informal and Formal Sector in Retailing."
69. *Ibid.*

system is uniquely tailored to a demand based on a small and irregular money income.

A study of Medellin's settlements by Molina found a heavy preference by those in charge of daily shopping (usually women) for local small stores. The reason given was the availability of credit. In the case of Medellin, prices charged by these stores for goods included in the *canasta familiar* were not found to be higher than those in large supermarkets; this was attributed to the willingness of petty merchants to maintain profit margins at a minimum.[70]

The enforced loyalty of customers is compensated by the risk of nonpayment and the costs of interest-free loans absorbed by the store. The informal credit system permits access to consumption to sectors of the working class that would otherwise be denied it. This "subsidy" to the reproduction of wage labor occurs at no cost to the formal sector, for the costs and risks are borne by informal merchants.

The lives of wage workers in the state and private capitalist sector in peripheral countries are conditioned at every step by their relationships with the informal economy. Though these workers are also consumers of formal sector goods, this frequently occurs through the channels of local petty trade. In addition, a significant proportion of their needs are satisfied directly by informal production sources. The relative cheapness of these goods and services is what enables wage workers to meet basic needs and even save, within the constraints of a meager wage. Their savings may, in turn, initiate other family-based informal enterprises in direct production or trade.

Informal Land Occupation

A substantial proportion of the urban working class in peripheral countries lives in officially nonexistent neighborhoods. Hundreds of such "pirate" or "parachute" settlements surround the perimeter of large cities. The population living in such areas ranges from an estimated 25% in cities like Rio, Lima, and Santiago to 40% in Caracas and Cali and over 50% in Recife and provincial Peruvian cities.[71]

The subsistence production of housing by the urban working class can obviously not occur without access to land. The urban land market in capitalist peripheral countries is governed less by need than by use of land prices as a safeguard against inflation and as a profitable and secure investment. Speculative prices brought about by rapid urban growth are seldom regulated, much less seriously taxed by governments. The landowning class can thus appropriate

---

70. Humberto Molina, "Una estrategia para el desarrollo urbano," *Revista de Extensión Cultural*, Universidad Nacional de Colombia-Medellin #7, n.d. For similar data on the Dominican Republic, see Duarte, "Marginalidad Urbana en Santo Domingo."
71. Portes and Walton, *Urban Latin America*, chap. 2.

values produced by an expanding urban economy without any significant investments or improvements of the land.[72]

Studies of the urban land market in Latin America register increases of 400% in central city prices in Caracas over a 10-year period; 800% in Cali, Colombia in 3 years; and 6000% in residential areas of Mexico City over two decades.[73] Unbridled speculation and the absence or inadequacy of government subsidies bars the urban working class from access to normal market channels for land acquisition.

This situation has resulted in the emergence of informal means for land acquisition in every major peripheral city. Whereas the specific strategies vary, the final result is the constitution of working-class communities, often numbering in the tens of thousands, which stand in violation of private property laws and are, in turn, officially unrecognized by the state. There are three major informal strategies for land acquisition:

1. *"Spontaneous" settlements* are formed gradually in illegally occupied land. The emergence of these settlements is not dependent on deliberate collective decisions. Instead, settlements grow by accretion, with a few families setting up residence at the start. If not expelled, they are soon joined by others until the entire area is occupied. The absence of any prior planning results in a haphazard layout of alleys and houses. The pressing need for housing leads to high densities and to the construction of precarious two- and three-story structures. This pattern is common in the *favelas* of Rio de Janeiro and is also found in the *villas miseria* of Buenos Aires and *barriadas* of Lima.[74]

2. *Land invasions* are the result of prior deliberate organization by a group of homeless families, sometimes with outside political or economic support. Lots are allocated to each family in advance, the entire site being surveyed prior to the invasion. The actual land occupation is planned to maximize external support and to contain repression by the police.

Invasions usually involve large number of participants, a pattern designed to call attention to the plight of the invaders. Land invasions are the most drastic and frequently the most dangerous strategy for urban land acquisitions. They represent the dominant form in Lima's *barriadas* and were common among Santiago's *poblaciones* before the 1973 military coup. In Colombia, they are dominant in Cali, Medellin, and Barranquilla. They have also been reported in Asian cities.[75]

72. *Ibid.*; Hardoy, *Las ciudades en América Latina*, chap. 4.
73. Hardoy *et al.*, Politica de la Tierra Urbana."
74. Portes and Walton, *Urban Latin America*, chap. 2; Potengy Grabois, En Busca da Integração; Leeds, "Forms of 'Squatment' Political Organization."
75. Collier, *Squatters and Oligarchs*; Mangin, "Latin American Squatter Settlements"; Cornelius, *Politics and the Migrant Poor*; Alejandro Portes, "The Urban Slum in Chile: Types and Correlates," *Land Economics* 47(August, 1971): 235–248; T. G. McGee, *The South East Asian City* (London: G. Bell, 1967).

3. *Clandestine subdivisions* are established by landowners who sell cheap lots to poor families. The buying and selling of clandestine lots constitutes an informal extension of the formal pattern of land speculation for profit. Owners are able to offer comparatively low prices by failing to meet minimal public regulations on the size of lots and the provision of services. Buyers receive bare land and a dubious title without access to water, electricity, transportation, or social services.

Clandestine or "pirate" subdivisions are the dominant form in Bogota. They are frequent in the southern periphery and are found in the hillsides surrounding the city and beyond the river Bogota, subject to periodic flooding. "Pirate" urbanizers are not usually landowners, but middlemen who acquire land from old proprietors of the *sabana* and sell it through informal contracts. Lot sizes of 72 m² sell at present for between U. S. $10–30 per square meter, without water, sewage, or electricity. Clandestine settlements also exist in Chile under the name *loteos brujos* and appear to be the dominant form in Mexico City and San Salvador.[76]

The emergence of illegal forms of land occupation has been conventionally regarded as a symptom of the breakdown of the urban order. Scholars and journalists sounded the alarm early about the "festering sores" and "political timebombs" represented by illegal settlements.[77] Those sympathetic with the plight of the settlers did not differ greatly in substantive interpretation. They viewed illegal occupation, and especially organized land invasions, as a logical outcome of the contradictions of peripheral capitalism and a serious threat to the dominant order.[78]

Contrary to these interpretations, recent studies have clarified the character of illegal settlements as a stable component of the structure of peripheral urban economies. Not only has the phenomenon existed for decades without posing any visible challenge to the dominant classes, but these classes have been known

76. Ramiro Cardona, *Dos barrios de invasión* (Bogotá: Asociación Colombiana de Facultades de Medicina, Boletin #21, 1968); CENAPROV, "Esquema para investigación sobre el problema habitacional en Colombia," Report to the IX National Assembly of Central Pro-Vivienda, Bogotá, October 1979. Portes and Walton, *Urban Latin America*, chap. 2; Susan Eckstein, *The Poverty of Revolution, the State and the Urban Poor in Mexico* (Princeton: Princeton University Press, 1977), chap. 2.

77. Representative examples of this alarmist literature are found in Tad Szulc, *Winds of Revolution: Latin America Today and Tomorrow* (New York: Praeger, 1965); Barbara Ward, *"The Uses of Prosperity," Saturday Review* (August 29, 1964): 191–192; Karl Schmitt and David Burks, *Evolution or Chaos: Dynamics of Latin American Government and Politics* (New York: Prager, 1963); and Marshall B. Clinard, "Urbanization, Urbanism, and Deviant Behavior in Puerto Rico," in *Social Change and Public Policy*, Social Science Research Center (San Juan: University of Puerto Rico, 1968), p. 29.

78. See Daniel Goldrich, "Political Organization and the Politicization of the Poblador," *Comparative Political Studies* 3(July, 1970): 176–202.

to promote land invasions and organize clandestine settlements in many occasions. The work of Collier, in particular, has traced the origins of illegal settlements to routine political bargaining at the level of the state and to the interests of dominant classes.[79]

Illegal occupation generally occurs in land of little speculation value. Invasions might be permitted or encouraged as a means of gaining political support for the government party. Finally, owners whose title to a particular site is dubious might encourage its partial occupation by poor families as a way of creating an instant popular constituency with which to pressure their claims on the government.[80]

Still, Collier's analysis of the relationships linking illegal settlements with the dominant classes is incomplete. By focusing exclusively on the political bargaining process, these relationships are regarded as a "game" between squatters and oligarchs whose interests are frequently convergent. The nature of this articulation is, however, more complex and transcends the goals of particular landowners, the schemes of the party in control of the state, or the requirements of urban renewal plans.

The basic shortcoming of an exclusively political analysis is that, whereas subsistence and petty production activities conducted in illegal settlements are defined as part of the informal economy, the very formation of the settlements is not. This prevents understanding that illegal land occupation stems from the same structural causes as other informal activities and, in addition, provides the physical basis for them.

Illegal land occupation results from wage scales bearing no relationship to the market price of land. Squatter and other illegal settlements represent a subsidy to the reproduction of the urban working class outside formal capitalist relations. Access to land enables the worker and his family to engage in the direct subsistence activities of home building and food production. More generally, the constitution of the settlement brings together workers employed in the formal economy and those employed in informal petty production and trade.

The settlement, as a social community, is the context wherein networks of exchange and mutual support are created. It is also in this context where the articulation of money wages with informal sources of supply permit the simultaneous reproduction of the different segments of the working class. Subsidized illegal settlements and the gamut of informal economic activities based on them are ultimately appropriated by capital in the form of lower wages. Squatter settlements and land invasions do not represent an abnormality or a contradiction in peripheral economies, but are, instead, an intrinsic component of the process of capitalist accumulation, as it occurs in them.

79. Collier, *Squatters and Oligarchs*.
80. *Ibid.*, chap. 1.

Constraints on the Expansion of the Working Class

The reduction in costs of subsistence for the segment of the working class employed in formal capitalist enterprises is not the only means of ensuring high surplus value extraction. As mentioned previously, the wage scales and social security benefits of this segment represent, under conditions of social disarticulation in the periphery, a political constraint on capital. Firms seek to further reduce labor costs by avoiding expansion of their organized work force and reaching down directly into the pool of informal sector workers. Through this strategy, minimum wage, health, social security, protection against arbitrary dismissal, and other clauses of labor legislation can be avoided.

Economists have frequently noted the slow absorption of labor by the manufacturing sector of peripheral countries. In Mexico, one of the most heavily industrialized peripheral nations, the manufacturing sector absorbs roughly one-fifth of the economically active population, having increased its share by only 5% since the early days of the Revolution.[81] The general explanation given is that peripheral industrialization is based on imported capital-intensive technology, which demands little labor.

A neglected factor in this explanation is the increasingly apparent use of informal sector workers by formal enterprises to perform labor intensive or seasonal work. Manufacturers limit expansion of their organized labor force by the use of intermediaries that carry out the stipulated tasks with unorganized informal workers. Widespread use of this strategy, a fact not registered by official statistics can have a significant impact on the rate of labor absorption by the "modern" sector.

The purpose of this last section is to document some of the mechanisms through which this strategy is implemented. These can be divided into two broad categories: (*a*) use of informal labor for commodity production; and, (*b*) use of informal labor to facilitate commodity circulation.

Informal Production

Maquila in Mexico City denotes a put-out arrangement through which production is farmed out by large- and medium-size firms to informal entrepreneurs. The arrangement is particularly common in the garment and footwear industries. The informal broker receives the material, such as leather or ready-cut cloth, and is responsible for delivering a certain number of competently finished units by a certain date. For this, he receives a fixed sum out of which he pays his workers.[82]

81. Susan Eckstein, *The Poverty of Revolution, the State and the Urban Poor in Mexico*, chap. 1.
82. Larissa Lomnitz, "Mechanisms of Articulation between Shantytown Settlers and the Urban System," paper presented at the Symposium on Shantytowns, Gloggnitz, Austria: The Wenner-Gren Foundation, July, 1977.

Workers in these informal production arrangements generally work at home. In the garment industry, *maquila* workers are mostly women. They generally furnish their own sewing machines and are paid a piece rate:

A blouse which retails for 120 pesos costs the merchant 60 pesos, plus the cost of the material which he has given ready-cut to the broker. The broker pays a seamstress 15 or 20 pesos and keeps the rest for himself.[83]

Lomnitz, who furnishes this example, notes that the piece rate is lower than the minimum wage with no social security benefits of any type included. Further, a fixed number of units must be delivered by a certain date. To accomplish this, the seamstress requires the assistance of her children, mother, neighbors, or other members of her network. Such extra labor goes unpaid. Finally, mistakes in production, such as damaged material or imperfectly finished garments, are deducted from her wages. According to her estimate, there were 25,000 seamstresses in Mexico City in 1975 working 16 to 18 hours a day without minimum wages or any social security protection.

Along the same lines, Schmukler outlines the development of the Argentine clothing industry from the earlier division between large-scale "store" production and handmade clothing to attempts in the 1940s to standardize products through the factory system. Minimum wage and social legislation during these years led entrepreneurs to rechannel production toward the informal sector. A few large enterprises producing standardized items for the mass market continue operating factories. However, these enterprises, as well as medium and small ones, depend on middlemen and informal workshops to handle the more labor-intensive, cyclical, and specialized types of production.[84]

Advantages of informal production include, first, cheaper cost per unit since workers subremunerate their own labor and that of kin and paid help. More important, informal production adapts to seasonal demand, permitting formal enterprises to hire and dismiss labor at will while avoiding unemployment compensation.

Workers in *maquila* and similar arrangements are often referred to as "self-employed." They have been described in the literature as informal entrepreneurs themselves. The appearance of self-employment and independence conceals the fact that their labor duplicates and frequently competes with that of organized workers. Informal production is concealed wage-labor production, where lesser productivity due to lower or no capital investment is more than compensated by the very low returns to labor. A basic characteristic of this form of production is

---

83. *Ibid.*, p. 22.
84. Beatriz Schmukler, "Diversidad de formas de las relaciones capitalistas en la industria Argentina" in *El subempleo en América Latina*, eds. V. Tokman and E. Klein (Buenos Aires: El Cid Editores, 1979), pp. 309–351.

the piece-rate system. Workers are paid by the unit and assume the full costs of work hazards and errors of production.

A second example is provided by Birbeck's recent study of the garbage recycling industry in Cali. Recuperated materials—such as paper, bottles, scrap metal, and bone—obtained by the garbage pickers in the public dump, are bought by industrial consumers at considerable savings from the original raw materials. Waste paper, for example, is acquired by the industry at a third of the costs of pulp. A single dump produces something like 7 to 10 tons of paper, 2 tons of cloth, 2 tons of bottles, 1 ton of tin, and .5 ton of bone per day, all destined for industrial consumption.[85]

The piece-rate system in this case consists of a price per unit of weight. The price is arbitrarily fixed by the industries and varies with demand. This price is not what the pickers receive since they sell to informal brokers who resell, in turn, to larger dealers or directly to the industries:

> Because of the nature of their relationship with the industrial market for recuperated materials, the garbage pickers in effect work for the factories but are not employed by them. They are little more than casual industrial outworkers, yet with the illusion of being self-employed.[86]

The advantages that formal industries derive from this system are not limited to lower prices for recycled materials but include, as a primary consideration, free access to a flexible supply of labor. This is reflected in the various attempts to rent "garbage rights" in Cali from the public service enterprise. Although the fixed rents are rather low, industries balk at the requirement that pickers be provided with work clothing and medical care. This would mean recognizing these workers as part of the formal labor force and, hence, giving up all the advantages derived from their "self-employment."

A final example of informal production is the system of "chain subcontracting" in the construction industry. Construction firms in peripheral cities frequently bypass formal hiring procedures by making use of informal arrangements with labor brokers. Characteristics of the job to be done, the date of delivery, and the price are arranged between the firm and the informal entrepreneur. The latter brings in his own men, supervises their work, and pays them at his discretion.

In Dakar, Gerry found a system of multiple subcontracting in which jobs arranged by large labor brokers were in turn handed down to small, informal entrepreneurs. The more intervening levels between the firm and the worker, the lower the wages received by the latter.[87]

---

85. Birbeck, "Self-employed Proletarians in an Informal Factory."
86. *Ibid.*, p. 1174.
87. Chris Gerry, "Petty Production and Capitalist Production in Dakar: The Crisis of the Self-Employed," *World Development* 6(Sept.–Oct., 1978): 1147–1160.

Informal construction work is not a case of concealed wage-labor since there is no illusion of self-employment among the workers. They are temporary workers hired and paid by an informal boss rather than directly by the firm. For Mexico City, Lomnitz has described a clientelistic system in which construction engineers in the formal sector develop a set of informal linkages with a group of skilled foremen or *maestros* whom they carry from job to job. The engineer is the *patron* for his *maestros* since he provides them with work in exchange for their loyalty. To reach the status of *maestro*, a workman must not only be skilled at his task but must develop a sufficiently wide network to mobilize large numbers of men on short notice. Such networks do not encompass urban shantytowns only, but reach all the way to distant rural villages. [88]

In Bogota, the construction industry employs from 50,000 to 75,000 workers. Small construction firms do not have their own workers, but subcontract all work to informal entrepreneurs. Larger firms may keep their own plant of *maestros*, *oficiales*, and *ayudantes*. This personnel seldom exceeds 20% of all workers employed at a given time, its main task being to supervise work done by the subcontractors. [89]

For construction firms, the key advantage of this system does not lie in the cost of labor, but in the flexibility of hiring and dismissing workers on short notice. *Maestros* are well aware of the wages paid to organized skilled workers and of the legally required employers' contribution for social security and taxes. They may bill the firm for these costs and pocket the difference between them and the minimum wages paid to workers.

Lomnitz cites the case of a steel-reinforcing foreman who, in times of peak construction activity in Mexico City, captained a crew of 300 to 400 workers and earned up to U. S. $3200 per week. For formal sector firms, such earnings are a relatively low price for avoiding incorporation of workers into the organized segment of the working class and the attendant legal obligations.

Informal Circulation

Street traders and hawkers are a familiar sight in large peripheral cities. After years of neglect, official agencies have seized on this and related activities as examples of a vigorous, self-reliant, and efficient small sector operating parallel to large-scale enterprises. In reality, a substantial proportion of petty traders are little more than disguised piece-rate workers for formal sector firms. Their activities furnish an efficient means for the circulation of both national and imported products in the domestic market.

A common example is newspaper vending. Newspapers sell at a fixed price

88. Lomnitz, "Mechanisms of Articulation between Shantytown Settlers and the Urban System."
89. Data gathered by the author in interviews with construction industry executives in Bogota, January 1980.

with a fixed profit margin per unit. Vendors might buy directly from the company and realize the full profit, say 15%, in each newspaper or buy from intermediaries who keep part of the margin. Many vendors are children who sell part-time and alternate this work with other activities:

> The relationship between newspaper company and street trader is designed to maintain the image of independence on the part of the street trader and to protect the newspaper company against the higher distribution costs that would be incurred by the use of wage-workers, who would have to be at least 15 years old, given long-term contracts, paid the national minimum wage, and given all the benefits specified as resposibilities of the employer.[90]

In Lima, large ice cream factories, chocolate factories, and bakeries sell much of their production through street sellers paid a fixed commission. Ice cream vendors, for instance, are given refrigerated barrows by the company, which stipulates the price per unit and the margin of profit. Small and medium leather and clothing factories also commercialize much of their production through street traders; this is done either directly or through wholesalers.[91]

Street selling, in appearance one of the most spontaneous and autonomous informal sector activities, is actually a well-organized business controlled by firms in the formal sector. Workers not only lack social security protection, but their earnings—in the form of commissions and profit margins—seldom exceed the level of subsistence. In Lima, 40% of the estimated 150,000 street traders in 1972 earned less than the minimum salary; another 43% earned between one and one-and-a-half minimum salaries.[92]

In his study of Cali, Bromley distinguished two major types of street selling:

1. *Commission sellers* deal in the products of one or a few firms which specify the retail price and the margin of profit which may be kept by the trader. The company might lend its sellers equipment, such as street stands or barrows, and help them obtain the necessary licenses on condition that they deal only in their products and sell at stipulated prices. In addition to newspapers, soft drinks, ice cream, and many food products are sold on commision by petty traders.

2. *Dependent selling* involves an arrangement between a wholesaler of one or more products and a group of informal retailers. The latter are dependent on the wholesaler for access to the products, for necessary equipment—such as refrigerators, vans, and barrows—and for credit. The merchandise is usually acquired on credit and paid at an interest. The system insures low profit margins for the informal traders and their continuing dependence on the wholesaler. It is in

90. Bromley, "Organization, Regulation and Explanation in the So-Called 'Urban Informal Sector,'" p. 1165–1166.
91. Alois Möller, "Los vendedores ambulantes en Lima," pp. 415–471.
92. *Ibid.*, p. 438.

the interest of formal sector merchants to increase the number of dependent traders under their control since this would expand profits both from sales and from interests on commodity loans.[93]

Stores in shantytowns and other working-class settlements are part of the system of dependent informal trade. Their subordination to wholesalers permits a number of additional demands, increasing formal profit margins. Duarte describes three such mechanisms common in the Dominican Republic: (a) higher prices for informal retailers; (b) higher interests on commodity loans; and (c) billing for goods never delivered. In Lima, produce wholesalers also overcharge for goods delivered or force petty merchants to accept overripe fruits and vegetables. Those who protest run the risk of being blacklisted and denied access to goods.[94]

Even without such exactions, the system of informal retail networks has definite advantages for formal-sector firms relative to the expansion of the stable commercial work force. Like informal production workers, street traders and shantytown merchants work without any social security protection and entirely at the discretion of the large companies. Their wages—disguised as commissions or minimal profit margins—are considerably below those received by organized and protected sales personnel.

Informal trade therefore furnishes a labor-intensive, cheap instrument for commodity circulation in peripheral economies. By channeling goods through a network of apparently self-employed traders, import houses, and industries producing for the domestic market limit the expansion of the organized work force and reduce costs of circulation, increasing their profitability.

Conclusion

The class structure of peripheral urban economies can be described in terms of four broad categories:

1. Domestic and foreign capital owners, senior executives, and state managers
2. Salaried professionals and technicians in public and private employment
3. Clerical and manual wage labor in public enterprises and private industry and services
4. Casual wage labor, disguised wage labor, and self-employment in petty production and trade

---

93. Bromley, "Organization, Regulation and Exploitation in the So-Called 'Urban Informal Sector,'" pp. 1165–1166.

94. Duarte, "Marginalidad urbana en Santo Domingo," p. 40. Moller, "Los vendedores ambulantes en Lima," p. 423.

The first three classes comprise the formal sector. The interests of the first class are, however, structurally opposite to those of the other two. Class 1 members are dependent—directly or indirectly—on the rate of surplus value. Although for some this may be tied to expansion of the internal market, the structure of sectorally disarticulated peripheral economies leads to the dominance of the export sector. This translates in turn into a consistent drive against the portion of the product going as salaries and wages to Classes 2 and 3.

The organization and political mobilization of these classes counteract the interests of capital and prevent their monetary returns from reaching the minimum possible under a "free" labor market. In this situation, the preservation of the share of the product going as profits to Class 1 requires a reduction of the costs of consumption for the other two classes, a reduction of their size relative to the available unorganized labor, or both.

Depending on the specific situation, the relationship between the urban classes is one in which Class 1—the owners—uses Class 4 against the intermediate classes, or one in which Class 1 allows Classes 2 and 3 to exploit Class 4, thereby cheapening their costs of reproduction and reducing upward pressures on wages. In whatever version, the fundamental point is that the informal sector subsidizes part of the costs of formal capitalist enterprises, enabling them to enforce comparatively low wages on their own labor.

The reliance on family subsistence activities for the reproduction of the work force is not a new phenomenon in the history of capitalism. Nor is it the employment of unorganized and vulnerable labor in "putting-out" and similar arrangements. Those familiar with the early history of capitalism in Europe and the not-so-old rise of industrialism in the United States could point out to a wealth of similar examples. The fundamental difference and the reason why our analysis of the informal economy has not been assimilated into the abundant literature on similar European experiences is that the two phenomena took place at separate moments in the development of the world economy.

Putting-out and informal labor exploitation, the existence of vast layers of semiproletarianized labor accompanied the autonomous expansion of industrialism in the centers. They gradually gave way to full proletarianization as the system was transformed by the rise of finance capital and imperialism. Indeed, the capacity of the central economies to bring their working classes into fully commodified relations was, in part, dependent on their reach abroad and the exploitation of peripheral labor.

It is impossible to assimilate the informal economy as it exists today in peripheral countries to the earlier "transitional" stage of advanced capitalism, for the present situation is the deliberate and continuously reproduced consequence of a new worldwide structure of accumulation. Thus, informal enterprise is not a vestigial presence, a lag from precapitalist times, but rather a very modern and expanding creation. It is an integral component of peripheral capitalist economies and its development is mandated by the conditions in which these economies are incorporated into the contemporary world-system.

Because the context is different from that of the "transitional" stage in Europe and the United States, there is no reason to expect that the informal sector will disappear through gradual "involution" and every reason to anticipate that it will continue to exist and expand. The continuously increasing relative gap in wage levels between core and peripheral workers at comparable levels of productivity requires it. The constantly expanding gap between formal sector (Classes 2 and 3) and informal sector living conditions within the periphery and the increasing number of informal enterprises and of the urban "self-employed" provide evidence of it. Such has been the experience of the last decades despite orthodox economic theory and its adherents. Conditions can change, but they will not do so to reproduce, mirrorlike, the particular evolution of nineteenth-century European capitalism. The system itself has changed.

Two final clarifications of our argument must be made: First, the distinction between manual workers in the formal and informal sectors refers to the separation between types of labor and not between physical individuals. Workers frequently alternate between periods of formal and informal employment and the same individual may simultaneously hold jobs in both sectors. The attributes of formal and informal employment and the interrelationships between them must, therefore, be understood as characteristics of the economic structure and not of physically separate groups. Second, the preceding analysis of peripheral classes indicates that the informal sector's subsidy to consumption is not limited to Class 3 workers. The same applies, though less directly, to salaried technicians and professionals. Empirical evidence on this point is more tenuous, although recent reports on informal labor markets in Lagos and Dakar in Africa and Cali and Santo Domingo in Latin America coincide in observing that "cheap informal services allow the petty bourgeoisie to sustain a seignorial life style, relatively distinct from the consumption of services in core countries."[95] Handmade household furniture and utensils, house-to-house deliveries, auto repairs, gardeners and cooks, nurses and maids are among the many channels through which the urban salaried class avails itself of cheap informal labor for its own reproduction.

In a recent speech, the secretary of ECLA (United Nations' Economic Commission for Latin America) reported that a third of the total economic production for the region is concentrated in three gigantic cities: Buenos Aires, São Paulo, and Mexico City. He went on to say that more than 50% of the people living in these cities survived "in unacceptable conditions of extreme poverty."[96]

95. Duarte, "Marginalidad urbana en Santo Domingo," p. 42; see also Bromley, "Organization, Regulation and Exploitation in the So-Called 'Urban Informal Sector'"; Webster, "The Political Economy of Survival"; and Gerry, "Petty Production and Capitalist Production in Dakar."
96. Reported in *Latin America Weekly Report*, (November 16, 1979): 36.

The complaint and the ensuing call to improve this situation represent little more than rhetoric at this point, for the structure of production and accumulation in these cities is based, to a large extent, precisely on the activities of those living under "unacceptable conditions." Meeting basic and perhaps not-so-basic needs of workers in the organized formal sector is a process dependent on the labor of other workers whose basic needs are either not met or met outside the money economy.

Direct subsidies to reproduction by informal to formal-sector labor are also indirect subsidies to core-nation capital and, hence, means to defend the rate of profit on a world scale. The concrete forms that this transfer takes range from low-price raw materials and foodstuffs to an increasing flow of cheap manufactures. Paralleling the mechanisms of rural subsistence enclaves, but in a far more diversified and complex manner, firms are thus able to exploit not only the work energy of their own workers in the periphery, but those of their kin, neighbors, and friends as well.

4

Ideologies of Inequality and Their Transformation in the Periphery: The Case of Latin America

Introduction

The ideas that men form about the conditions of their existence constitute a fundamental element of social structure. Not only do they reflect the material substratum of the social order, but they contribute to render it legitimate and stable. The Marxist critique of ideas since the last century has uncovered the roots of mental constructions in the objective conditions of material life and social organization. Although ideas in general remain of interest to some, sociological analysis has progressively focused on one particular type. This comprises those integrated systems of religious, philosophical, or scientific ideas designed to provide a coherent interpretation of the universe and of man's place within it. In particular, attention has focused on the issue of how these various systems contribute to explain the reality of exploitation and inequality and the bearing that these explanations have on the continuation of this situation.

Such systems are called *ideologies*. The term possesses a pejorative connotation dating back to its origin in the eighteenth century. Destutt De Tracy, the creator of the term, was himself dismissed by Napoleon as an ideologist.[1] The same meaning is apparent in contemporary "end of ideology" writings.[2] The scientific study of ideology is devoid of this connotation, however, for it defines such systems as integral components of the social order. As such, the object of the analysis is not to denounce mental constructions as ideological, but rather to

---

1. L. N. Moskvichov, *The End of Ideology Theory: Illusions and Reality* (Moscow: Progress Publishers, 1974), pp. 62 and ff.

2. See for example Edward Shils, "The End of Ideology," *Encounter 5*, (November, 1955): 53; Daniel Bell, *The End of Ideology: On the Exhaustion of Political Ideas in the Fifties* (Glencoe, Ill.: The Free Press, 1960); and John Kenneth Galbraith, *The New Industrial State* (Boston: Houghton Mifflin, 1967).

understand their social roots and their articulation with other elements of social structure.

Seen from this perspective, the study of ideology has proceeded since the nineteenth century in two main directions. One is the critique of philosophical systems that tended to view ideas as immanent and independent of material reality. Marx's attack on "ideologists" did not concern so much the content of particular doctrines, as the insistence of Hegelian philosophers in regarding such systems as elements of immanent mental development.[3] This critical tradition continues to our day with the attack on theories that regard "value orientations" as primary foundations of the social order.[4]

The second and more substantive line of inquiry consists of studies of the articulation of ideologies with concrete politicoeconomic systems.[5] Such efforts have also continued to our day including, among others, studies of the rise of positivism in Western Europe and analyses of ideologies of racial inequality worldwide.[6] Studies of ideology are typically historical and tend to analyze its interaction with the material base as a process *internal* to a certain politically bounded unit such as a nation-state (Germany), an empire (China), or a conglomerate of economically interrelated nations (Western Europe).

Having examined international labor migration and the uses of informal labor to sustain the unequal exchange mechanism, we turn now to the complementary problem of the ideas employed to legitimize these and other arrangements of exploitation in the periphery. As with capital and labor, the circulation of ideas has become accelerated and extended with the expansion of the world-system. This has brought about a growing, although seldom noted convergence in the ideological notions legitimizing inequality in both center and periphery.

The question of ideology does not represent a problem for the world-system perspective, but rather a misutilization of its analytic possibilities. Studies of ideology are conducted, for the most part, exclusively within a national

---

3. Karl Marx, "Contribution to the Critique of Hegel's Philosophy of Right." in *Marx and Engels on Religion*, ed. R. Niebuhr (Moscow: Foreign Languages Publishing House, 1957), pp. 59–68; Karl Marx and Friedrich Engels, *The German Ideology* (New York: International Publishers, 1939).

4. C. Wright Mills, *The Sociological Imagination* (New York: Oxford University Press, 1959).

5. Weber's studies of world religions in precapitalist societies are well-known examples: Max Weber, *The Sociology of Religion*, trans. Ephraim Fischoff (Boston: Beacon Press, 1963); Max Weber, "The Social Psychology of the World Religions." in *From Max Weber: Essays in Sociology*, eds. Hans H. Gerth and C. Wright Mills (New York: Oxford University Press, 1958), pp. 267–301; Reinhard Bendix, *Max Weber, an Intellectual Portrait* (Garden City, N. Y.: Doubleday, 1962), part II.

6. H. Stuart Hughes, *Consciousness and Society, The Reorientation of European Social Thought 1890–1930* (New York: Vintage Books, 1958); Moskvichov, *The End of Ideology Theory*; James A. Geschwender, *Racial Stratification in America* (Dubuque, Iowa.: Wm. C. Brown Company, 1978); Michael Hechter, *Internal Colonialism, The Celtic Fringe in British National Development, 1536–1966* (Berkeley: University of California Press, 1975), parts I and II.

framework in which the procession of ideas and doctrines is explained by reference to the changing views of intellectuals and the "schools" they create. At best,
these studies trace shifts in the dominant ideology to changes in the internal class
structure, with little more than perfunctory attention to the external variable.[7]

In this chapter, we thus make two analytic shifts. First, we move from the
analysis of structures, political and economic, to that of the ideological
superstructure. Second, we alter the direction of analysis and, instead of examining how specific labor processes affect worldwide structures, we explore how the
world-system context influences seemingly domestic phenomena.

A world-system perspective represents a significant contribution to the three
fundamental aspects in the study of ideology: (a) the origins of the dominant
system of ideas; (b) the nature of the social conditions it is called on to explain;
and (c) the causes of its eventual demise and substitution by an alternative
interpretation. In the case of peripheral countries, the first aspect is linked to
the increasing influence and even hegemony of imported ideas accompanying the
increasing incorporation of the nation into the world economy. Similarly,
the second aspect relates to the fact that ideologies of inequality in the periphery
must not only explain the reality of domestic inequality among its social classes,
but must also reconcile national populations with the overwhelming reality of
external subordination.

Finally, the third aspect relates to the impossibility of explaining ideological
transformation in an entire region, comprising several nation-states, on the basis
of simultaneous changes in their internal class structures. The internal variable
remains fundamental, but is not sufficient in the case of peripheral countries, to
account for widespread shifts in ideological systems of legitimation.

The sequence of dominant ideologies in Latin America is examined in this
chapter as a case study of the interplay among world processes, domestic class
structures, and ideology. Because little has been written on the topic from this
perspective, we cannot concentrate exclusively on the contemporary situation,
nor examine in detail the many national variants. In keeping with the goals
previously outlined, this chapter is organized as a general sketch of the history of
ideologies in the region. The story that we are about to tell has been told before,
but not from this perspective and not with the same implications. The analysis
thus sacrifices detail in favor of casting light on that aspect that the numerous
national studies of ideology have neglected: the interpenetration and influence of
the world economy on domestic systems of legitimation.

Our approach to ideological transformation in Latin America is based on two
propositions:

---

7. See, for example, Thomas E. Skidmore, *Preto no branco, raça e nacionalidade no
pensamiento brasileiro* (Rio de Janeiro: Paz e Terra, 1976); Carl Solberg, *Immigration and
Nationalism, Argentina and Chile, 1890–1914* (Austin: University of Texas Press, 1980).

1. The *content* of ideologies in a peripheral area depends, to a large extent, on its changing mode of incorporation into the world-system and, in particular, on the core power which exercises hegemony over it.
2. The *strength* of ideological systems of legitimation varies inversely with the complexity of the class structure and the spatial concentration of the working class.

Since complexity and concentration have increased in the periphery, the hold of ideology over its working classes has experienced a consistent decline.

We identify three "moments" in the history of ideology in Latin America corresponding to broad shifts in the content of dominant ideas and in their strength as systems of legitimation. A fourth moment, the contemporary one, mixes elements of at least two earlier ones, although it is still in process of transformation.

Patrimonialism

What is Latin America today was incorporated into the mercantilist world as colonies of Spain and Portugal. Both utilized the new colonies primarily as sources of raw materials. Spain, in particular, made use of vast amounts of bullion from the viceroyalties of Peru and New Spain to finance its European imperial strategy.[8] The gradual decline of the Iberic powers forced them to rely on political measures to maintain a colonial commercial monopoly, increasingly challenged by the emerging core nations. The contradiction between the economic interests of the creole landowning class in trade with the European core economies and the political mechanisms designed to prevent it culminated in the independence struggles during the early nineteenth century.[9]

Taking advantage of the Napoleonic occupation of Spain, major countries in the region declared and successfully defended their independence. These movements brought to an end three centuries of absolutist rule by Spain and, in a less regimented form, by Portugal. Up to that moment, political domination by the metropolis paralleled its ideological hegemony over colonial society.

8. Immanuel Wallerstein, *The Modern World-System, Capitalist Agriculture and the Origins of the European World-Economy in the Sixteenth Century* (New York: Academic Press, 1974), chap. 2; Richard M. Morse, "The Heritage of Latin America," in *The Founding of New Societies*, ed. Louis Hartz (New York: Harcourt, Brace and World, 1964), pp. 123–177.

9. Tulio Halperin Donghi, *Historia contemporánea de América Latina* (Madrid: Alianza Editorial, 1970); see also Peggy Korn, "The Problem of the Roots of Revolution: Society and Intellectual Ferment in Mexico on the Eve of Independence," in *Latin American History: Select Problems*, ed. Frederick B. Pike (New York: Harcourt, Brace, and World, 1969), pp. 100–132. Morse, "The Heritage of Latin America."

The explanation of inequality in the Spanish and Portuguese colonies in the Americas found its early popular roots in the medieval Catholic theodicy of salvation and its intellectual ones in the scholastic political philosophy articulated by Spanish theologians of the sixteenth century. The structural situation that these ideologies were called on to explain was one characterized by a class structure where white *peninsulares* monopolized wealth and power and where Indians and other nonwhites bore the burden of physical labor.

The patrimonial ideology was brought to the Americas by religious orders arriving in the wake of military conquest. Jesuits, Dominicans, and Franciscans were the major ones and, though they often differed in detail, the basic ideas of natural law and a hierarchical social order were common to all. Many of these men sincerely believed that the title of "Emperor of the Indies" bestowed by Pope Alexander VI on the Spanish kings had the sole purpose of furthering evangelization of the infidels.[10] Material greed and exploitation of the Indians were deplored and denounced as contrary to the true purpose of the Conquest.

The scholastic heritage underlying the new ideology never conceived of society as the result of a deliberate compact among men. Civil society was rather a permanent aspect of a divinely ordained natural order. For Francisco de Vitoria, *prima* professor of theology at Salamanca, "the source and origin of communities was not an invention of man, nor may they be considered as something artificial, but that which comes from nature itself."[11]

Suarezian political philosophy had no difficulty in translating the dominant religious sentiment into a philosophy of the state. According to Suárez, natural sovereignty is vested by God in the people, but the latter lack capacity to put it to effective use. The people then *alienate*, not delegate, power to the prince on a permanent and unconditional basis. Whereas the collectivity is, in principle, prior and superior to the prince, the latter becomes the effective and absolute source of authority. The prince is morally bound by his own law. Judgment of his conduct is not, however, the prerogative of men, but of God.[12] Through this series of delegations, divine authority was transformed into terrestial power and the absolute rule of kings legitimized.

The same principle of natural hierarchy was applied to the rule of the Spaniards over native Indians. Natural law commanded the perfect to rule over the imperfect, the wise over the ignorant. For Fray Juan Gines de Sepulveda, "these barbarians are obligated to accept the rule of the Spaniards according to

10. John L. Phelan, "The Problem of Conflicting Spanish Imperial Ideologies in the Sixteenth Century," in Pike, ed., *Latin American History* pp. 40–64.

11. Francisco de Vitoria, "De Vitoria" in *El pensamiento político hispanoamericano* (Buenos Aires: Ediciones de Palma, 1967), p. 30.

12. Morse, "The Heritage of Latin America"; see also James Lockhart, "The Social History of Colonial Spanish America: Evolution and Potential," *Latin American Research Review* 7 (1972): 6–46.

natural law. For them it ought to be more advantageous than for the Spaniards, since virtue, humanity, and the true religion are more valuable than gold and silver."[13]

The image of a hierarchical society patterned after the order of heaven permeated every writing on conditions in the New World. Differences were to emerge between those who, like Sepulveda, advocated the doctrine of a just war against the infidels and those who defended a more humane treatment. The two positions came into open conflict in the Debates of Valladolid (1550–1551), called to advise the crown on Indian policy. Sepulveda's views were based on the Augustinian doctrine that denied all personal rights to those outside the Christian faith. The contrary position was eloquently argued by Bartolome de Las Casas. As his teacher de Vitoria had done, Las Casas endeavored to replace Augustinian doctrine with a Thomistic view, which simultaneously articulated a juridical justification of the Conquest and defended the fundamental rights of the Indians.[14]

The two competing theological positions did not simply represent themselves, but gave expression to increasingly divergent interests within the framework of Spanish colonization. Sepulveda defended, in the ideological language of the time, the interests of Spanish colonists in free access to the native supply of labor. Las Casas expressed the long-term Hapsburg interest in the preservation of resources of the empire, in particular its population. Whereas the taxation system gave the king a share of immediate production, his concern with the long-term preservation and expansion of the available labor force conflicted with the colonists' dreams of rapid enrichment.[15]

Not surprisingly, the doctrine of humane treatment prevailed in the crown's official policy. A series of decrees declaring the Indians vassals of the king and protecting their personal and property rights were issued by the Hapsburgs during the sixteenth century. Assignment of Indian labor to Spanish colonists, known initially as *repartimiento* was transformed into the *encomienda*, which, as Gibson[16] notes, signified a relationship of entrustment rather than allocation. Repeated proof of abuses committed by *encomenderos* led to abolition of the institution.

The "New Laws" of 1542–1543 issued by Charles I contained numerous provisions for the defense of the natives, including absolute prohibition of slavery. In one noteworthy passage, the king orders cessation of the fishing of pearls

13. Juan Gines de Sepúlveda, "Sepúlveda" in J. L. Phelan, "The Problem of Conflicting Spanish Imperial Ideologies in the Sixteenth Century," p. 51.

14. *Ibid.*

15. *Ibid.*; Halperin Donghi, *Historia contemporánea de América Latina*; Woodrow Borah, "Colonial Institutions and Contemporary Latin America," *Hispanic American Historical Review* 43 (1963): 371–379.

16. Charles Gibson, "The Problem of the Impact of Spanish Culture on the Indigenous American Population," in Pike, ed., *Latin American History*, pp. 66–98.

when it endangers the lives of Indians and blacks for "as is logical, we estimate their lives much more than the interests from the pearls."[17]

Spanish patrimonialism was ultimately inspired by the social order of the European manorial economy. Stable relationships of support emerged between lord and serf, both bound by a common interest in the preservation of a self-enclosed economic unit. The manor produced for subsistence. Equally important, it brought together dominant and subordinate individuals who shared the same language, religion, and culture and who could thus claim membership in the same community.

In the context of Spanish and Portuguese America, this patrimonial habit of mind was superimposed on a social order where Europeans were almost exclusively occupied in conquest, commerce, and religion, and in which the direct producers were men of the nonwhite races. No common social bond existed in this situation to alleviate the reality of exploitation.

More important, colonial production was not organized for subsistence, but for the market. Whereas the organization of the labor force—slavery and the encomienda—differed from the wage labor system, production was still for profit, reverting to subsistence only when effective demand slackened.[18] Capitalist agriculture provisioned the mines and emerging cities of the Spanish and Portuguese empires; a few selected products also found their way into the international market: sugar from Cuba and Northeast Brazil, cocoa from Venezuela and Ecuador, indigo from Central America, hides from the River Platte.

It was, however, the exploitation of precious metals that constituted the primary reason for existence of the colonies and the basis of their wealth. The mines of Mexico and Alto Peru gave economic foundations to two viceroyalties. Discovery of gold in Minas Gerais, triggered a migrant flow from Portugal and the rest of Brazil, which displaced the center of political hegemony in the colony from the sugar-producing northeast to the central southern region.[19]

The integration of the American colonies into the mercantilist networks of trade, the opportunities for profit in mining, and the provisioning of mines and towns did not leave much room for the observance of traditional rights under medieval patrimonialism. Royal prohibitions and the ceaseless denunciations of missionaries did not prevent ruthless exploitation of the available labor force by

17. Antonio Muro Orejon, *Las leyes nuevas, 1542–43 reproducción de los ejemplares existentes en la sección del patronato del archivo general de Indias* (Sevilla: Escuela de Estudios Hispanoamericanos de la Universidad de Sevilla, 1945), p. 11.

18. On this point see Paula Beiguelman, "The Destruction of Modern Slavery: A Theoretical Issue," *Review II* (Summer 1978): 71–80; also James Lockhart, "Encomienda and Hacienda: The Evolution of the Great Estate in the Spanish Indies," *Hispanic American Historical Review* 49 (August 1969): 411–429.

19. Halperin Donghi, *Historia contemporánea de América Latina;* Jorge E. Hardoy "Two Thousand Years of Latin American Urbanization," in *Urbanization in Latin America: Approaches and Issues,* ed. J. E. Hardoy (Garden City, N.Y.: Anchor Books, 1975), pp. 3–56.

Spanish colonists. The extent of this exploitation led to the demographic collapse of the seventeenth century. Fifty years after the conquest, the Caribbean island population had been annihilated; 100 years after, the native population of Mexico had been reduced by 90%.[20]

Paradoxically, the gap between an economic order based on enslavement of native labor and the Catholic ideology of natural rights served the legitimation needs of colonial society well. The crown's official endorsement of the natural law doctrine—although ineffective in rationalizing the exploitation of the available labor force—gave credence to the ultimate justness of the Conquest and the view that its many excesses were products of individual greed.

High functionaries of the crown, such as *oidores* of the royal courts, frequently joined in deploring the excesses of the colonists and condemning these actions as violations of the king's express will.[21] To the last, men like Bartolomé de Las Casas continued to believe in the ultimate benevolence of Spanish imperialism and to attribute the deaths by the thousands of the native population to the avarice of individual colonists. Against them, he inveighed with words that ring true to our day:

> The *encomienda* or *repartimiento* was the most cruel sort of tyranny that can be imagined, and it is most worthy of infernal damnation. . . . The wretched tyrannical Spanish *encomenderos* worked the Indians night and day in the mines and in other personal services. They collected unbelievable tributes. The *encomenderos* forced the Indians to carry burdens on their backs for a hundred and two hundred leagues, as if they were less than beasts. . . . And I solemnly affirm, as God is my witness, that so long as these *encomiendas* remain, all the authority of the kings . . . will not be enough to prevent all the Indians from perishing.[22]

The political and economic domination exercised by Spain and Portugal over their colonies coincided with their ideological hegemony. Aside from protests, such as these, inserted into the dominant ideology and indirectly supporting it, no articulate challenge to the established interpretation of society gained any significant support. Revolts, no doubt, took place, often in response to the desperation of the oppressed, but they did not embody any new and persuasive counterideology. As Morse has noted, "the rebellions that took place often claimed as their raison d'être, violations of the very principles of natural law and personal rights laid down by the Crown."[23]

The patrimonial ideology that permeated three centuries of colonial rule in

---

20. Halperin Donghi, *Historia contemporánea de América Latina*.
21. For an account of official complaints in Peru, see Guillermo Lohman Villena, *El corregidor de indios en el Perú bajo los Austrias* (Madrid: Ediciones de Cultura Hispanica, 1957).
22. Bartolomé de las Casas, "Las Casas" in Phelan, "The Problem of Conflicting Spanish Imperial Ideologies in the Sixteenth Century," p. 57.
23. Morse, "The Heritage of Latin America," p. 158.

Latin America can be seen as an instance of a first moment of legitimation in which the strength of the belief system was at its highest for its premises were identified with reality itself. For these 300 years, vast inequalities between the classes and the ruthless exploitation of Indians and then blacks existed without an articulate ideological challenge. The dispersion of Indian and blacks in mines, *haciendas*, and plantations and their disorganization did not provide fertile grounds for such a challenge. Until the moment in which Napoleonic troops took Ferdinand VII of Spain into custody in 1808, the authority of the patrimonial ruler and the concepts of natural law and natural hierarchy had been fundamental pillars on which colonial production and society rested.

Positivism

The natural law tradition and the underlying Catholic world view had other consequences that were to outlast its role as a system of legitimation. Because it viewed man less as builder of his own destiny than as part of an organic design, it did not need to defame the subject races in order to justify their situation. Whereas "white" was always associated with "better" or "superior," the nonwhite races were also viewed as having a position in society as integral part of God's plan. Their subordination was in the natural order of things and needed not be blamed on prior faults or vices.

This tolerance was to be lost with the advent of the scientific ideologies of the nineteenth century. The first half of this century was, for Latin America, a period of political and economic uncertainty. With the exception of Brazil, independence decapitated patrimonial authority, leaving the new republics in vain search for alternative sources of political stability.[24] The attempt to construct a federation on lands from the old viceroyalties of Peru and Nueva Granada failed, even when backed by the prestige of Bolivar. Farther north, the conservative dream of empire under Agustin de Iturbide collapsed, leading to the secession of the Central American provinces. The Central American Federation, in turn, split into five pocket republics.[25]

The fundamental characteristic of these times is the transition from insertion into mercantilist networks of trade by route of Spain and Portugal to a direct articulation with the emerging capitalist world economy. In many ways, England was the direct inheritor of Spain in Latin America, taking over and directly benefiting from established channels of commerce. Although domination was

24. *Ibid.*; Borah, "Colonial Institutions and Contemporary Latin America."
25. Halperin Donghi, *Historia Contemporánea de América Latina*; see also Edelberto Torres Rivas, "Poder nacional y sociedad dependiente: Notas sobre las clases y el estado en Centro-américa," *Revista Paraguaya de sociología* 29 (January–April, 1974): 179–210.

less politically overt, it often approached the old condition of monopoly. Merchants from Liverpool replaced merchants from Cadiz, taking over the richest and the most prestigious parts of local commerce everywhere. Fifty years after independence, English surnames abounded in the local aristocracies of Buenos Aires and Valparaiso.[26]

This British hegemony, at times challenged by France or the United States, did not bring the expected abundance of capital. During the first half of the nineteenth century, neither England nor any other European power made significant investments in Latin America. What the industrial powers looked for in the newly independent republics were, above all, markets. Sale of surplus industrial goods was promoted by influential British consuls and by the never-ending appetite of local aristocracies for things European. Most of these imports had to be paid for in metallic.

Latin America thus became a conglomerate of "export-enclave" economies. The exhaustion of the gold mines meant that sources of foreign exchange and the most important economic activities concentrated in production of raw materials and agricultural commodities. The rural and mining economy continued to be based, as in colonial times, on the labor of the nonwhite races: Indians in Mexico and throughout the Andean region; blacks in Brazil, Venezuela, Colombia, parts of Central America, and the Peruvian coast.[27]

Landowners thus had a vested interest in preventing the extension of the legal rights gained by political independence to the subject races. Venezuelan landowners continued to resist the abolition of slavery even after the end of the slave trade and freedom for the offsprings of slaves (*libertad de vientres*) had been decreed. Brazil imported more slaves during the first half of the nineteenth century than at any point before in history. The hegemonic sugar interests of the Brazilian northeast led a tenacious struggle against British efforts to end slavery and the trade. It was not until 1888 that the Emperor D. Pedro formally proclaimed the abolition of slavery.[28]

Independent Latin America thus reoriented its external trade toward the new world centers, Britain and France, while simultaneously preserving a domestic structure of production based on the old colonial class and race divisions. The attack on the colonial Iberic powers and on the Catholic ideology that

---

26. Halperin Donghi, *Historia Contemporánea de América Latina*; Gino Germani, "Hacia una democracia de masas." in *Argentina, sociedad de masas*, eds. Torcuato S. di Tella, Gino Germani, and Jorge Graciarena (Buenos Aires: Eudeba, 1965), pp. 206–227.

27. On capitalist agriculture and the exploitation of the Indian, the classic statement is that of Mariategui: See Jose Carlos Mariategui, "The Problem of the Indian." in *Seven Interpretive Essays on Peruvian Reality* (trans. M. Urquidi), J. C. Mariategui (Austin: University of Texas Press, 1971), pp. 22–30; see also Fernando H. Cardoso and Enzo Faletto, *Dependencia y desarrollo en América Latina* (Mexico D. F.: Siglo Veintiuno, 1969).

28. Skidmore, *Preto no branco, raça e nacionalidade no pensamiento brasileiro*; Halperin Donghi, *Historia Contemporánea de América Latina*.

legitimized them meant that a different ideology had to be found to interpret inequality under the new conditions.[29]

This renewed ideological offensive, coinciding roughly with the second half of the nineteenth century, was based on the widespread adoption of positivism.[30] European positivism had an inclusiveness and a compelling moral character that made it a suitable replacement for Catholic patrimonialism. For the dominant classes, it was not difficult to apprehend the legitimation potential of a system that in the name of science and progress enjoined the elites to keep a tight rein on the ignorant masses: "Judging the mass of the population 'unprepared' for full participation in society, [elites] found in the authoritarian dimension of positivism a model of modernization which explained and justified their combined hold on power."[31]

Of the many different doctrines and philosophies that Latin America received from Europe during the nineteenth century, it was undoubtedly positivism that most closely reflected local class conditions. As Leopoldo Zea stated:

> Positivism could just have been an academic philosophy; a philosophy to be discussed by those who entered it, rather than the philosophy adopted by a nation. . . . The governing party required a new order, an order based on ideological principles which were not those of the defeated conservatives. Positivism was successful as a doctrine placed at the service of the winning class because its members were ideologically predisposed toward it.[32]

The conquest by positivism of the ideological field paved the way for the subsequent adoption of scientific theories of evolution. The introduction of evolutionism reproduced in Latin America the contradiction between European racial theories of the time: On the one hand, humanitarian doctrines justified the abolition of slavery, a decision taken and directly benefiting the core British economy; on the other, British and French philosophers elaborated the theories of white supremacy that legitimized European imperialism in Africa and Asia.[33]

In Latin America, this ideological contradiction adopted peculiar forms. Abolitionists were, for the most part, simultaneous defenders of the theories of Spencer and Gobineau. The liberation of the black race was thus frequently justified, not in the name of its advancement, but in the name of its eventual extinction. During the wars of independence, conscription of freed slaves had

29. Leopoldo Zea, *El positivismo en México* (Mexico, D.F.: Ediciones Studium, 1953), chap. 3; Gonzalo Izquierdo, *Un estudio de las ideologías chilenas, la sociedad de agricultura en el siglo XIX* (Santiago: Imprenta Técnica, 1968).
30. Zea, *El positivismo en México*.
31. Skidmore, *Preto no branco, raça e nacionalidade no pensamiento brasileiro*, p. 29.
32. Zea, *El positivismo en México*, p. 81.
33. Geschwender, *Racial Stratification in America*; Beiguelman, "The Destruction of Modern Slavery"; Thomas E. Skidmore, "The Death of Brazilian Slavery," in Pike, ed., *Latin American History*, pp. 134–171.

already been defended as a way of ensuring that blacks would contribute their quota of the dead, thus maintaining the racial balance. It was the argument used, at least once, by Simon Bolivar. Brazilian intellectuals, such as Joaquin Nabuco, fighting to rid the country of a pernicious slavery system, accepted, nevertheless, the innate inferiority of blacks and the need to "whiten" Brazil through European immigration.[34]

The ideological contradiction between abolition, on the one hand, and racial inequality, on the other, did not stand on its own, but gave expression to conflicting interests between fractions of the dominant class. Those interests most closely identified with British commercial capital naturally spoused the cause of abolition; whereas those linked to the plantation system in sugar, cotton, or coffee logically defended the status quo. For the abolitionist fraction, however, the end of slavery did not signify racial equality, but rather the modernization of modes of surplus labor extraction in agricultural production.[35]

The theories of racial inequality that became official dogma by the end of the nineteenth century had several intellectual origins. Social historians, such as Carlyle and Arnold, reflecting on the vigor of European imperialism, proposed a phenotypic scale where white men, especially the Nordic and Anglo-Saxon varieties, would occupy the apex. These writers attempted to reconstruct history as a series of victories and conquests by the Aryan race in its progress toward world supremacy.[36]

A second current stemmed from the attempt to translate Darwinian evolutionism into the nascent field of sociology. Spencer[37] conceived of society as an organic and evolving being governed by the biological principle of adaptation. The theory gave scientific legitimacy to the de facto supremacy of European nations and endorsed again a racial-ethnic hierarchy culminating in European man.

The hegemony exercised by these theories on Latin American social thought paralleled the political and economic subordination of the region to the new European centers. They also fitted well the obvious reality of racial inequality and exploitation of the nonwhite races throughout the region. Thus, like the class structure itself, Latin American social thought of the *fin-de-siècle* became

34. Halperin Donghi, *Historia contemporánea de América Latina*, p. 138; Joaquim Nabuco, *O abolicionismo*, (London, 1883), as cited in T. E. Skidmore, *Preto no branco, raça e nacionalidade no pensamiento brasileiro*.

35. Jorge Balán, "Regional Urbanization under Primary Sector Expansion in Neo-Colonial Countries," in *Current Perspectives in Latin American Urban Research*, A. Portes and H. L. Browning (Austin: Institute of Latin American Studies and University of Texas Press, 1976) pp. 151–179; Jose de Souza Martins, *A Imigração e a Crise do Brasil Agrario* (São Paulo: Livraria Pioneira, 1973).

36. Emory S. Bogardus, *The Development of Social Thought* (New York: Longmans, Green, 1960), chaps. 16, 20; see also Hughes, *Consciousness and Society*.

37. Herbert Spencer, *Principles of Sociology* (New York: Appleton, 1914); Bogardus, *The Development of Social Thought*, chap. 20.

uniformly racist. Racist were the self-deprecatory arguments to explain the reality of Latin American backwardness and racist was the self-satisfied assurance with which the black and the Indian were confined to the toiling classes.

Evolutionism thus replaced the Catholic doctrine of natural hierarchy as the dominant interpretation of inequality. The cleavage between the races—identified in Latin America with that between the classes—did not flow any longer from a divine and natural design, but was the consequence of the biological superiority of some and the inferiority of others. In 1888, Luis Carranza rejected the view that the lowly state of Peruvian Indians was the result of harsh treatment, finding the reason, instead, in the psychological aberrations of the "singular and curious" Indian race.[38]

A few years later, his compatriot, Alejandro Deustua found the misfortunes of Peru caused by "the Indian race, which has reached the point of psychic dissolution and which, because of the biological rigidity of its beings, which have definitely ended their evolutionary cycle, has not been able to transmit to the mestizo peoples the virtues that it exhibited in its period of progress."[39] Identical views about the Indians were voiced in Mexico and, with reference to the blacks and mulattos, in Brazil, Venezuela, and Cuba.

Unlike Catholic patrimonialism, however, the doctrine of evolutionism did not achieve complete ideological monopoly. By the end of the nineteenth century, dominant landowning and commercial classes already faced articulate opposition from displaced interests and from an emerging urban proletariat. Whereas the reactionary opposition found ideological expression in the vestiges of Catholic patrimonialism, the emergent urban classes articulated their interest into one or another version of recent socialist theories.

Positivism and evolutionism can thus be seen as instances of a second moment of ideological legitimation. Despite repeated attempts, which paralleled those of their counterparts in core European nations, dominant classes never succeeded in gaining universal acceptance for the new "scientific" doctrines. As did the bourgeoisie of the centers, Latin American landowners and merchants attempted to portray themselves as the "universal" class and its interests as identical with those of society. Nowhere was this more evident than after the victory of liberalism in Mexico:

> Once the bourgeoisie had triumphed, it attempted to justify its victory through persuasion. It pretended that the state was what it had promised: a servant of the entire society; it offered respect for all ideas and affected not to support any in

38. Luis Carranza, *Artículos publicados por Luis Carranza*, Lima, 1888, as cited in "The Problem of Identity and National Destiny in Peru and Argentina," in Pike, ed., *Latin American History*, p. 180.
39. Alejandro O. Deustua, "The Indian as a Machine," translated from *La cultura nacional* (Lima: Empresa Editora El Callao), cited in Pike, *Latin American History*, pp. 66–68.

particular. However, reality proved otherwise. The state would be nothing but the instrument at the service of the bourgeoisie.... This is what the Mexican bourgeoisie did: to identify its own interests with those of others, while avoid giving offense to those ideas which still had a hold over the masses.[40]

Although failing to regain the ideological hegemony of colonial times, the Latin American bourgeoisie still adhered to the principles of its own legitimacy. The new "scientific" ideology obviously gave expression to the general interest of the dominant class, but, in addition, it held a solid grip on its own world views. Evidence of this is provided by the willingness of that class to accept the less than flattering implications of the doctrine of white supremacy. As seen previously, European proponents of a racial hierarchy did not hesitate to place themselves at the top. Mediterranean whites were relegated to a lesser category: intermediate between the creative Nordics and Anglo-Saxons and the "hopeless" Negroids and Mongoloids.

Nineteenth century Latin American social thought not only accepted that position, but dwelt with almost masochistic insistence on it. Argentine, Brazilian, Chilean, and Mexican writers repeatedly deplored the inferior heritage left to them by their forebears. They showed continued preoccupation with the debilitating consequence of miscegenation, especially when the white blood that still existed was of inferior genetic origin:

> Under [Spanish] colonial influences, intelligence atrophied and the practical spirit of work and economy disappeared, along with the concern for political rights. All that remained were absurd ideals, aggressiveness, hallucinatory fanaticism... such was the spirit of the race to which the conquerors belonged. Such was the spirit that they imparted to the blood of our creoles.[41]

In Latin America, this ideological conviction was reflected in the strong impulse given to European immigration, preferably from the northern countries, as a way of "whitening" miscegenated populations and revitalizing the elite. European immigration was preferred even when other alternatives made better economic sense. Faced with abolition of slavery, Brazilian coffee planters contemplated importation of Chinese workers for a while. Chinese labor would have been cheaper, but racial considerations dictated the final choice in favor of Italian immigrants.[42] In Chile, despite a relative abundance of native labor, industrialists and landowners repeatedly pressured the government to subsidize passages for European workers, said to have "superior" qualities.[43]

Positivism and evolutionism were dominant in Latin America for a period of

40. Leopoldo Zea, *El positivismo en México*, p. 105.
41. Alejandro O. Deustua, "The Spaniard and his Inimical Legacy," Lima, 1894, as cited in *Latin American History*, Pike, p. 200.
42. See de Souza Martins, *A Imigração e a Crise do Brasil Agrario*.
43. See Carl Solberg, *Immigration and Nationalism, Argentina and Chile, 1890–1914*.

roughly nine decades until the interlude between the world wars. This period-icization is subject to many variations among specific countries. By the 1930s, however, the decline of British hegemony and the rise of new world powers co-incided with the end of the dominance exercised by the theories of evolution. Changes in the world-system and the internal class situation again determined an urgent search for new sources of legitimacy.

Marginality

The ideological impasse of the 1930s and 1940s was marked by a confused, but fierce competition among conflicting factions. Characteristic of its continu-ing role as periphery, Latin America reflected the agitated state and the cata-clysmic events affecting the world powers. The dominant economic reality dur-ing this period was the Depression. It loosened the once promising ties with the economic centers and spelled the definite decline of Great Britain as the hegemonic power. The increasing gravitation of North American capital was felt throughout the region, especially in the traditional "zone of influence" around the Caribbean.[44]

All core nations were much too concerned, however, with the debacle of their own economies to think of rescuing the lesser regions. Cast adrift of the old neocolonial ties, Latin American countries were forced into economic self-reliance while simultaneously experiencing the full force of conflicting interna-tional tensions. It was a period of incipient import-substitution industrialization and of deliberate state intervention in the economy to ease the effects of the crisis.[45]

In the ideological plane, the spread of European socialism and especially the emergence of the Soviet Union had a profound impact on the labor movement. At the opposite extreme, corporatist models propagated by the new fascist regimes appealed to Latin American dictators who saw in them a belated justification of their own authoritarian policies. Military officers and sectors of the middle class also viewed corporatism as an appropriate means to put an end to the growing unrest from below.[46]

Economic attempts at self-reliance in Latin America coexisted in time with

44. For the specific case of Argentina, see Aldo Ferrer, *La economía Argentina, Las etapas de su desarrollo y problemas actuales* (Buenos Aires: Fondo de Cultura Económica, 1972); for Chile, Anibal Pinto Santa Cruz, *Chile: un caso de desarrollo frustrado* (Santiago: Editorial Universitaria, 1962); for Brazil, Manuel Correia de Andrade, "Os anos trinta no Brasil," *Comunicaçoes* PIMES #12 (Recife: Universidade Federal de Pernambuco, 1976).
45. Halperin Donghi, *Historia contemporánea de América Latina*.
46. de Andrade, "Os anos trinta no Brasil"; see also Guillermo O'Donnell, "Modernización y golpes militares: Teoría, comparación y el caso argentino," *Desarrollo Económico* 47 (October–December, 1972): 519–566.

the first attempts at revindication of the native past. The directions of this new current, however, varied. The exaltation of the Indian and rejection of European things were the trademarks of populist and socialist movements. The two nations that could lay claim to the two great pre-Hispanic civilizations—Mexico and Peru—were, unsurprisingly, the cradles of the most vigorous *indigenista* movements. The APRA in Peru and the Party of the Mexican Revolution resurrected Inca and Aztec symbols and revived nativist sentiments as means to sustain mass mobilization.[47]

Glorification of the Iberic heritage was, on the other hand, the preserve of the right. With Spanish domination safely behind one century of independence, the *hispanicista* movement could evoke the glories of empire and reaffirm the qualities of the Spanish race. It also noted the many common points between the Spanish patrimonial heritage and the new corporatist ideas. The model of an organic and vertical society, of preordained places under a paternalistic state had a familiar Mediterranean ring appealing to the dominant classes after the demise of evolutionary theory. In Brazil, Getulio Vargas patterned his *Estado Novo* after the corporatist model and flirted with the Axis powers until American pressure forced him into line. In Argentina, the overthrow of Hipolito Irigoyen signaled the end of effective democracy. The military government under General Uriburu initiated reorganization of the country along quasi-corporatist lines.[48]

World War II and its aftermath brought about major changes, marked by the consolidation of U. S. hegemony in the region and the strengthening of Pan-Americanism as its political tool. After a brief spell of economic autonomy and nationally led industrialization, major Latin American nations fell under a new form of economic domination. Contrary to Britain, U. S. capitalism based its economic well-being during the period on its own internal market. Thus, U. S. interest in Latin America was less as a market than as a source of cheap foodstuffs and raw materials.[49]

47. For Mexico see Susan Eckstein, *The Poverty of Revolution, the State and the Urban Poor in Mexico* (Princeton: Princeton University Press, 1977); Manuel Moreno Sanchez, *Crisis política de Mexico* (Mexico, D. F.: Editorial Extemporáneos, 1971); Octavio Paz, "Mexico: la ultima década," Hackett Memorial Lecture, University of Texas at Austin, 1969. For Peru, see Mariategui, *Seven Interpretive Essays on Peruvian Reality*; François Bourricaud, *Poder y sociedad en el Perú contemporáneo* (Buenos Aires: Sur, 1967); David Collier, *Squatters and Oligarchs: Authoritarian Rule and Policy Change in Peru* (Baltimore: The Johns Hopkins University Press, 1976).

48. For Brazil, see de Andrade, "Os anos trinta no Brasil"; Thomas E. Skidmore, "Politics and Economic Policy Making in Authoritarian Brazil, 1937–71," in *Authoritarian Brazil, Origins, Policies, and Future,* ed. Alfred Stepan (New Haven: Yale University Press, 1973), pp. 3–46. For Argentina, O'Donnell, "Modernización y golpes militaires"; Halperin Donghi, *Historia contemporánea de América Latina*; Thomas E. Skidmore, "A Case Study in Comparative Public Policy: The Economic Dimensions of Populism in Argentina and Brazil," Washington, D. C.: Latin American Program of the Wilson Center, Working Papers #3, 1977.

49. Halperin Donghi, *Historia contemporánea de América Latina*; Cardoso and Faletto, *Dependencia y desarollo en América Latina*; Celso Furtado, "U.S. Hegemony and the Future of Latin America," in *Latin American Radicalism*, Irving L. Horowitz, J. de Castro, and John Gerassi (New York: Vintage Books, 1969), pp. 61–74.

Internally, the dominant event of the postwar period was the acceleration of the massive displacement of population toward the cities. The turn-of-the-century racism was directed against groups that were, for the most part, dispersed throughout vast rural regions. These groups now streamed toward cities in search of economic advantage. The well-documented demographic movement was accompanied by increased political mobilization.

The class structure of major Latin American countries changed during this period to accommodate a visible and increasingly mobilized urban working class. Instability and conflict in the two preceding decades had alerted this urban proletariat to the significance and potential benefits of political action. Not surprisingly, the most successful political form of the period appeared to be populism. Cultivated by Peron in Argentina and Odria in Peru, populism alternatively threatened the dominant classes and appeared as the only viable alternative to socialism.[50]

Socialism and populist parties asserted that the poor did not deserve their situation and blamed local and foreign capitalists for existing inequalities. At the other extreme, corporatist doctrines provided a coherent interpretation of inequality, but were discredited by their association with the defeated fascist states. Mobilization of the working class and its increasing concentration in cities made it necessary for the Latin American dominant classes to find a new basis of legitimacy.

Scanning the intellectual horizon of the 1950s in Latin America, one major systematic effort at relegitimation of the class structure is found. The ideological history of Latin America at this time parallels the history of its changing mode of incorporation into the world economy. Just as patrimonialism and positivism found their origins in the philosophies then dominant in the metropolis, the new ideology was to be based on the contemporary social thought of the new hegemonic power.

With the decline of evolutionism, North American social science had turned toward an emphasis on cultural processes. Whereas the earlier explanatory models were discredited, the original question was not. U. S. scholars still asked what propelled Western Europe and the United States into an advanced industrial civilization unparalleled in the history of mankind. The answer was found in cultural values and derivative normative patterns. A narrow interpretation of Max Weber singled out the Calvinist ethic as the cultural "motor" that had helped bring about the miracle of modern capitalism.

Culturalist social science explained inequality by noting that the subordinate

50. For Argentina, see Germani, "Hacia una democracia de massas"; Kalman H. Silvert, "Peronism in Argentina: A Rightist Reaction to the Social Problem of Latin America," in Pike, ed., *Latin American History*, pp. 340–390; O'Donnell, "Modernización y golpes militares"; Skidmore, "A Case Study in Comparative Public Policy." For Peru, Collier, *Squatters and Oligarchs*; Bourricaud, *Poder y Sociedad en el Péru Contemporáneo*; Abraham F. Lowenthal, "Peru's Ambiguous Revolution," *Foreign Affairs* (July 1974): 799–817.

classes and countries lacked certain ideational themes that the dominant ones had. The list of the missing traits is long and still expanding: universalism, achievement orientation, empathy, modernity, and so forth. The significance of culturalism as an ideology of inequality was that it absolved anew the dominant classes from responsibility for the situation, which was imputed to the ethical or psychological shortcomings of the exploited.

To label a person, community, or nation "traditional" is somewhat less offensive than to label them "racially inferior," but the placement of responsibility for inequality on the shoulders of the victims remains unaltered. Although "tradition" does not carry the stigma of permanence of nonwhiteness, it is still sufficiently durable to justify a stable system of exploitation. Simultaneously, the 1950s and early 1960s in Latin America registered the emergence of Christian Democratic parties in many countries. Christian Democracy was an import from postwar Europe. In Latin America, it represented an attempt by urban-based commercial and industrial interests to respond to the new challenges from below. Early Christian Democratic doctrine was a blend of papal social encyclicals—pious and unconvincing documents that preached social justice in the name of Christian charity. They were weak in systematic social analysis and, what was more important, failed to explain existing class inequality.

The convergence between the political force represented by Christian Democracy and culturalist North American social science produced a new ideology in Latin America. Its reformist call was echoed in the Alliance for Progress and the platforms of Christian democratic and other "progressive" parties throughout the region. Its most systematic form was developed, however, by a group of Catholic scholars under the leadership of European Jesuits. The recognized intellectual leader of the group was Roger Vekemans, a Belgian Jesuit who arrived in Chile with the specific mission of intellectually buttressing the Christian Democratic party. He and other Jesuits headquartered at the Centro Bellarmino in Santiago and began publishing the magazine *Mensaje*, which was to become a potent ideological force during the 1960s.[51]

The mixture of Catholic doctrine and North American social science that *Mensaje* developed was labeled the theory of "marginality." As an interpretation of inequality, it represented a blend of the culturalist argument of value inferiority with a mild reproach to dominant classes for having neglected the poor. Vast inequalities existed because the masses were not integrated into the normal economic, social, and political structures of the society. This occurred for two reasons: (*a*) the marginal population lacked certain cultural resources and values

51. *Mensaje* is still published in Chile, although its ideological impact is much reduced; during the early 1960s, "Special Numbers" of the magazine were widely read in Latin America and had a profound impact on Christian Democratic thought. See for example, *Mensaje*, "Revolución en América Latina," #115, December 1962; and *Mensaje*, "Reformas revolucionarias en América Latina," #123, October 1963.

for participating in modern society; (b) the society itself had neglected them, creating serious barriers to their effective participation.[52]

Following the North American model, marginality still assigned primary responsibility for inequality, however, to the cultural inferiority of the poor. The influence of the culturalist theme of tradition and modernity was explicitly acknowledged: "Those who do not belong or do not participate are not only non-modern, under any definition of modernity, but are traditional since they represent the current projection of earlier pre-Columbian and pre-industrial situations."[53]

The newness of the theory and its "scientific" ring attracted national and international attention. Marginality was adopted as the official viewpoint on poverty of Christian Democratic parties. With the arrival of the Christian Democrats to power in Chile in 1964, marginality was elevated to state doctrine. A government agency was created with the explicit purpose of "promoting" the marginal masses so that they could take their place in society.[54]

The writings emanating from the Centro Bellarmino also found a receptive ear in the developed countries. The theory of marginality and the reform programme it proposed, supported—in timing and content—the Alliance for Progress. The Catholic theoreticians in Santiago gave sense and justification to the emerging alliance between the Latin American industrial and commercial classes and the expanding interests of the United States in the region. The new themes of tradition and modernity, marginality and integration, appeared to fill the ideological vacuum left by the demise of racial theories of inequality and to provide a reasonable alternative to socialist counterideologies.

Despite its intellectual elegance, the influence of marginality theory was, however, short-lived. Later studies have shown that the major actors in its emergence were part of a consciously designed effort to halt the political advance of communism in Latin America.[55] To the persistent questioning of inequality by a mobilized urban proletariat, the Catholic theorists responded with an ideological "package" that negated class struggle although proposing a mild program of reform.

But marginality never became the true ideology of the dominant classes. In no instance, did the latter deviate from the pursuit of class interests to seriously implement the program of reform advocated by the new ideology. In this situation, marginality became an exclusively instrumental doctrine, produced and

52. See Roger Vekemans and Ismael Silva Fuenzalida, "El Concepto de marginalidad," in DESAL, *Marginalidad en América Latina: un ensayo de diagnóstico* (Barcelona: Herder, 1969), pp. 15–63. Also Roger Vekemans and Ramon Venegas, "Marginalidad y promoción popular," *Mensaje* 149 (June 1967): 218.

53. Vekemans and Silva Fuenzalida, "El Concepto de marginalidad," p. 59.

54. Vekemans and Venegas, "Marginalidad y promoción popular."

55. David Mutchler, *The Church as a Political Factor in Latin America* (New York: Praeger, 1971).

diffused among the masses through "popular promotion" and community action programmes. The theory and its practical corollaries came to represent a third moment of ideology in Latin America: the bifurcation of ideological beliefs and the sponsoring by the dominant class of a commissioned intellectual product for consumption by the masses.

The demise of marginality as an ideology of inequality was due to its transparent character as an instrument of social control. In the absence of vigorous implementation by the class whose position it legitimized, the new ideology could not withstand the sustained drift toward consciousness and militance among the working classes. The fabric of the material order lay exposed to all and this inevitably led to class mobilization and class struggle.

Nowhere was the failure more evident than in the applied programs inspired by marginality. Once in the field, popular *promotores* paid by these programs found that they had very little to promote. In the absence of active support by foreign and local capital, the attempted redefinition of inequality in terms of abstract needs for integration and value change could not gain credibility. Concrete needs for employment, higher incomes, and housing kept showing through the thin web of ideology. Time and again, those to be "promoted" showed themselves to be far more adept at coping with the realities of peripheral economies than their would-be saviors.[56]

With the arrival of the Allende government in Chile, the largest popular promotion program vanished without trace of popular concern. In other countries, community development programs became incorporated into the bureaucracies of older ministries. The era of Alliance-supported community action and Christian Democratic popular promotion came to an end without having changed the conditions of exploitation or significantly altered its definition in any country.

Developmentalism

The authoritarian regimes that have come to power during the last two decades in major Latin American countries can be defined as attempts to cope with the crisis of legitimacy of the class structure and put an end to the threat of working-class mobilization. They also correspond to a changing mode of

56. Alejandro Portes, "Rationality in the Slum: An essay on Interpretive Sociology," *Comparative Studies in Society and History* 14 (June 1972): 268–286; also Larissa Lomnitz, *Networks and Marginality, Life in a Mexican Shantytown* (New York: Academic Press, 1977); and Janice E. Perlman, *The Myth of Marginality, Urban Poverty and Politics in Rio de Janeiro* (Berkeley: University of California Press, 1976).

incorporation in the world system as "advanced" peripheral countries became platforms for the production and export of manufactures on the basis of cheap labor. The historical context preceding the advent of these bureaucratic-authoritarian regimes is one marked by repeated and increasingly successful challenges by populist and socialist movements to the class structure.[57]

The advent and consolidation of the Cuban revolution was the opening and perhaps most important of these events. It was followed by the electoral victory of populist Janio Quadros in Brazil and the increasing leftist militance of his successor Joao Goulart. The powerful Christian Democratic party was defeated at the polls by a coalition of the Marxist parties and Salvador Allende became president of Chile in 1970. After 18 years of exile and persecution in Argentina, Peronism returned to power in the wake of an overwhelming popular vote.[58] Interspersed among these major events were the organization and growth of powerful urban and rural guerrilla movements that succeeded in mobilizing important sectors of the population. Although ultimately unsuccessful, armed movements like the Tupamaros in Uruguay, the Movimiento Izquierda Revolucionaria (Revolutionary Leftist Movement, MIR) in Venezuela, and the Revolutionary Armed Forces (FAR) in Guatemala, seriously challenged for extended periods the military forces of the national governments.[59]

Faced with a crisis of legitimacy that produced repeated electoral victories for the parties of the left, national ruling classes supported by hegemonic multinational interests turned toward the military. Military governments abolished democratic institutions seeking, simultaneously, to disable the existing structures of class mobilization and demand making. These regimes, initiated with the Brazilian coup of 1964, pursued two ideological goals: "security" or the preservation of the class order against working-class protests and organized subversion; "development" or acceleration of peripheral capitalist accumulation.[60]

The pursuit of "development" meant, in essence, a readjustment of the pro-

57. Guillermo O'Donnell, "Reflections on the Patterns of Change in the Bureaucratic-Authoritarian State," *Latin American Research Review* 13 (Spring 1978): 3–38.

58. *Ibid.*; also Guillermo O'Donnell, "Estado e alianças na Argentina, 1956–76," in *O estado na America Latina*, ed. Paulo Sergio Pinheiro (Sao Paulo: Co-edições CEDEC/Paz e terra, 1977), pp. 17–57. For Chile, see Arturo Valenzuela, *The Breakdown of Democratic Regimes, Chile* (Baltimore: Johns Hopkins University Press, 1978). For Brazil, Glaucio A. Dillon Soares, "After the Miracle," *Luso-Brazilian Review* 15 (Winter 1978): 278–301.

59. See Antonio Mercader and Jorge de Vera, *Tupamaros, estrategia y acción* (Montevideo: Editorial Alfa, 1969); Alberto Fuentes Mohr, *Secuestro y prisión, dos caras de la violencia en Guatemala* (San Jose: Editorial Universitaria Centroamericana, 1971); Regis Debray, "Latin America: Some Problems of Revolutionary Strategy," in Horowitz *et al.*, eds., *Latin American Radicalism* pp. 499–531; Ernesto Guevara, "Message to the Tricontinental," in Horowitz *et al.*, eds., *Latin American Radicalism*, pp. 621–646.

60. Soares, "After the Miracle"; O'Donnell, "Reflections on the Patterns of Change in the Bureaucratic-Authoritarian State."

ductive structures of Latin American countries to take advantage of new opportunities for the production and export of manufactures.[61] Countries like Brazil, Mexico, and Argentina, already well in the road toward import-substitution industrialization, attempted to carve a new position in the international division of labor as industrial exporters. This shift, however, was not the consequence of autonomous decision making, but corresponded to changed conditions in the centers. The latter had begun to divest themselves of labor-intensive production, while reserving the areas of high technology.

The competitive edge of Latin American countries was and is an abundant pool of low-wage labor—skilled and unskilled. As just seen, cheap labor in the periphery is sustained by the interpenetration of formal and informal economic structures, but is simultaneously threatened by the organized segment of the proletariat. Aside from the immediate political danger they posed, working-class unions and parties seriously began to threaten this competitive edge. The destruction of working-class organization was necessary to guarantee to local and multinational firms the full use of the existing reservoir of labor. As O'Donnell states:

> The Bureaucratic-Authoritarian state is a system of exclusion of the popular sector, based on the reaction of dominant sectors and classes to the political and economic crisis to which populism and its successors led. In turn, such exclusion is the requisite for attaining and guaranteeing "social order" and economic stability; these constitute necessary conditions to attract domestic investments and international capital and, thus, to provide continuity for a new impulse toward the deepening of the productive structure.[62]

The doctrine of developmentalism has thus been adopted by authoritarian regimes in Latin America as the official ideology of inequality. This doctrine bypasses earlier ideological emphasis on the origins of inequality to affirm that, no matter what the causes of poverty are, it will not be overcome until certain measures are taken. A true solution to poverty and a gradual reduction of inequality must flow out of economic development. In order for this to occur, existing inequalities must be maintained and even expanded so as to facilitate concentration of income in the hands of the capitalist class and stimulate investment. After investment and production reach a certain level, their self-propelled

61. On this point see Pierre Jalee, *Imperialism in the Seventies* (New York: Third Press, 1973); O'Donnell, "Estado e alianças na Argentina, 1956–76"; Peter Evans and Gari Gereffi, "Foreign Investment and Dependent Development: Comparing Brazil and Mexico," mimeo., Harvard University Center for International Affairs, n.d.; and Andre G. Frank, "Unequal Accumulation: Intermediate, Semi-Peripheral, and Sub-Imperialist Economies," *Review* 2 (Winter 1979): 281–350.
62. O'Donnell, "Reflections on the Patterns of Change in the Bureaucratic-Authoritarian State," pp. 13–15.

dynamism will benefit the majority of the population by "filtering down" in the form of employment demand and higher wages.

The fallacies of this approach to national development have been examined at length in the economic literature.[63] What is of interest here is that, in its ideological form, developmentalism again places the brunt of sacrifices to be borne for the common good on the shoulders of the masses. For this reason, both the dominant domestic and multinational classes have strongly supported this interpretation. Thus, like positivism, the new ideology finds its most ardent defenders among the groups whose position it legitimizes. The parallel is not surprising since both positivism and the new ideology are compelling justifications of privilege—both arguing that concentration of wealth will result in the greatest benefit to society in the long run.

It is not the case that authoritarian regimes do not perceive a need for a measure of popular legitimacy. Exclusive reliance on repression is costly and does not convey the image of political stability required to stimulate foreign investment. Most attempts to show concern for the needs of masses have been, however, ineffective. In a typical speech in São Paulo, the former president of Brazil affirmed that "to give housing, to give water, to give health, to provide adequate sewage systems is an integral part of human rights." He went on to assert that "our social program is essentially a human rights program, though many do not wish to recognize the fact."[64]

These pronouncements were made during ceremonies initiating a new program of basic sanitation in São Paulo. Although São Paulo is the wealthiest city in Brazil, close to 80% of houses in the urban periphery do not have access to sewers and 54% do not have running water. Most of these houses are located in one of the approximately 5000 clandestine subdivisions situated along 26,000 officially nonexisting streets.[65] The "human rights" plan inaugurated with that speech is targeted on the central city, thus leaving most of the working-class suburbs in the same condition as they were before.

Developmentalism has not been an effective instrument of legitimation among the majority of the population. First, unlike earlier interpretations of inequality, developmentalism is explicitly tied to a temporal dimension. Imposition of sacrifices and growing economic inequality are justifed in the name of "filtering down" effects to take place in the near future. To the extent that these

---

63. See Soares, "After the Miracle"; Edmar Bacha, *Os mitos de uma Decada* (Rio de Janeiro: Paz e Terra, 1976); Alejandro Portes, "Housing Policy, Urban Poverty, and the State," *Latin American Research Review* 14 (Summer 1979): 3–24.

64. "Geisel Acha que Direitos Incluem Assistencia a Povo," *Jornal do Brasil*, August, 13, 1977.

65. Jose Alvaro Moises and Verena Martinez-Alier, "A revolta dos suburbanos," in CEDEC, *Contradições urbanas e movimentos sociais* (São Paulo: Co-edições CEDEC/Paz e Terra, 1977), pp. 13–63.

effects fail to occur,[66] the original interpretation becomes discredited. This pushes the regime toward renewed reliance on repression as the only source of stability.

Second, economic policies pursued by authoritarian regimes tend to fragment the internal solidarity of its own class base. The pursuit of economic orthodoxy, demanded by international agencies and foreign banks as a prerequisite for renewed investment capital, requires the lifting of protectionist measures. Deprived of state protection, domestic enterprises must fend for themselves against powerful and increasingly numerous multinational companies. Segments of the national bourgeoisie, which at the start of the military regime were the most ardent supporters of repression against the working class, find themselves squeezed out by the free-trade policies and denationalization of the economy required by the developmentalist model.[67]

Unless state policy shifts in the direction of nationalism, part of the domestic bourgeoisie is forced to forge a new alliance with its former class enemies against *entreguismo* to foreign capital. The ideological justification of this alliance takes the form of nationalism, a demand for return of political democracy, and a concerted attack on developmentalism.[68]

The dual challenge of working-class militance and the disaffection of part of the domestic bourgeoisie means that the scope of influence of developmentalist ideology does not extend beyond the circle of its own proponents. Attempts to coopt the masses through provision of welfare and other social services are feeble and frequently diverted to the benefit of higher-income groups.[69] Thus, to the extent that ideologies not merely reflect but affect the class structure, the authoritarian regimes now dominant in Latin America represent unstable solutions. In the absence of extensive economic redistribution, something that the logic of peripheral capitalist accumulation rules out, chances for these regimes to reestablish mass legitimacy appear remote.

Conclusion

Ideology has been defined as "a system of beliefs that presents value-judgments as empirical truths in order to justify, with or without conscious

66. Bacha, Os Mitos de uma Decada; Eckstein, The Poverty of Revolution, the State and the Urban Poor in Mexico; Portes, "Housing Policy Urban Poverty, and the State"; Paz, "Mexico: la ultima década"; Fernando H. Cardoso, "Associated Dependent Development: Theoretical and Practical Implications." in Authoritarian Brazil, Origins Policies, and Future, ed. Stepan, pp. 142–176.

67. O'Donnell, "Reflections on the Patterns of Change in the Bureaucratic-Authoritarian State."

68. Ibid.; Cardoso, "Associated Dependent Development."

69. Perlman, The Myth of Marginality, Urban Poverty and Politics in Rio de Janeiro; Portes, "Housing Policy, Urban Policy, and the State."

intent, a particular socioeconomic group's claim to material and prestigial rewards."[70] Theories of ideology have tended to concentrate on two aspects: (a) the origins and content of a system of ideas; and (b) its effectiveness as a means of legitimation among the subordinate groups and/or the elite itself. In order to link the results of our review of Latin American ideologies with the theoretical literature in this area, it is necessary to examine some of its common contemporary assumptions.

Concerning the origins of ideology, critical studies since Marx and Engels have successfully debunked the notion of ideas as immanent products of the mind following an independent evolution. The opposite extreme is more apparent at present, as later scholars came to define ideology as a byproduct of material interests and a faithful reflection of the class structure. Mannheim, for instance, came to postulate a deterministic relationship between ideas and the underlying structure of class interests. For him, ideology and utopia represented biased forms of thought conditioned, at every step, by the material concerns of different groups.[71]

This position incurs a basic contradiction for an ideology that is a transparent mirror of the class structure is no ideology at all. Systems of ideas derive their capacity for legitimation out of their professed divorce from the here-and-now and their aspirations to a higher plane. To accomplish their purpose fully, ideas must be accepted, by dominant and subordinate classes alike, as part of a reality above everyday interests and conflicts.[72]

A corollary of the view of ideology as a reflection of the class structure is the automatic imputation of its origins to the dominant classes. Ideology then becomes a commissioned product subordinate to and modified at will by those in positions of power. In actual fact, however, these classes have seldom been able to create or freely choose the ideological principles most closely adapted to their interests, not to alter them once institutionalized. The prize of legitimate privilege has been, in many historical instances, the undertaking by the elite of enterprises which run directly contrary to their short-run interests.[73]

The conditioning by the class situation of ideologies of inequality seldom goes beyond the setting of "structural possibilities."[74] The origins and content of a dominant system of legitimation generally depend on factors external to the

---

70. Walter Metzger, "Ideology and the Intellectual: A Study of Thorstein Veblen," *Philosophy and Science* 16 (April 1949): 125.

71. Karl Mannheim, *Ideology and Utopia* (New York: Harcourt, Brace, and World, 1936), part II.

72. Max Weber, "The Social Psychology of the World Religions."

73. Georges Sorel, *Reflections on Violence*, trans. T. E. Hulmes (New York: The Free Press, 1950), chap. 1; Moskvichov, *The End of Ideology Theory*.

74. The expression is used by F. H. Cardoso in the introduction to his study of entrepreneurial ideologies; see F. H. Cardoso, *Ideologias de la burguesia industrial en sociedades dependientes* (Mexico, D. F.: Siglo Veintiuno Editores, 1976).

classes which directly benefit from it. Hence, the ideological "tone" of a particular period is never a matter of unilateral decision by the ruling class; it is rather a process in which the content of existing intellectual systems is apprehended, their legitimizing potential explored, and their major tenets gradually reinterpreted to fit the class structure.

In the case of Latin America, the content of dominant ideologies has been decisively influenced by its incorporation first as colonies of a mercantilist world and then as periphery of the capitalist world economy. Since colonial days, ruling classes in Latin America have lacked the option of developing autochthonous systems of legitimation. In agreement with their subordinate position in the world economy, their role has been confined, in almost all instances, to adapting a received intellectual product to local conditions.

Our analysis has not shown how the circulation of ideas actually occurs in the world-system, nor how it interpenetrates, in concrete detail, with the mechanisms of economic domination managed by the centers. Our review has highlighted, however, the close correspondence between the nature of external subordination to which Latin America has been subject and the content of its internally dominant ideologies. In particular, we have noted the historical correlation between shifts in the power exercising hegemony over the region and major changes in the interpretation and justification of class inequality: In every instance, the fundamental ideas on which the legitimacy of the class structure have been based correspond to those then dominant in the hegemonic power.

But if the content of ideology has been subject to decisive external influences, its strength as a vehicle of legitimation has been closely dependent on internal events and, specifically, on changes in the class structure. The effect of ideology on social structure has itself being the subject of considerable debate. It is within this context that our results acquire their relevance.

The theory of ideology has progressively abandoned the view of these systems as epiphenomena and moved on to recognize their independent causal effect on the social structure. As Cardoso states, "ideology is neither the immediate transcription of the conditions of social existence, nor the realm of pure illusion; it cannot be discarded as false consciousness, nor can it be accepted as the substantive expression of a mode of social relations."[75]

It is by now generally accepted that the most useful perspective on ideology is neither as prime mover nor as historical byproduct, but as a component of the social order in which relationships with the material base are both continuous and reciprocal. The problem, however, is that effects of ideology on the class structure are not constant, but vary with different historical periods. A main point of reference on this issue is Gramsci's analysis of legitimation and social change under European capitalism.

75. *Ibid.*, p. 46.

Gramsci distinguished between "leading" and "dominant" classes in that the former possessed the ability to maintain "traditional" (religious, folk) beliefs among the masses. This was opposed to a situation of pure domination in which the masses detached themselves from past mythologies and came to act rationally on the basis of economic interests, thus forcing an increase in coercion.[76] Gramsci's distinction thus focused on the relative effectiveness of legitimizing ideologies and the loss suffered by the dominant class when they had to be substituted by force or material cooptation.

An additional distinction, not contemplated in Gramsci's analysis, is that between types of "dominant" class. The central difference here is whether this class adheres or not to the principles of its own legitimacy. Qualitatively different outcomes can be expected from a situation in which dominant classes identify ideology with reality itself and from one in which they regard it exclusively as an instrumental product. This difference underlies Sorel's treatment of the "myth" and its impact on European class structure. For him, an ideologically imbued class, such as the early industrial bourgeoisie, represented a far more resilient and dynamic force in society than one which had lost all faith and relied on cooptation and the instrumental use of ideas.[77]

In Latin America, the passage from a "leading" to a "dominant" class is exemplified by the transition from the patrimonial ideology of the Iberic countries to the new lay religion of positivism. The difference between the two moments of legitimation lies in the termination of the virtual monopoly exercised by earlier doctrines and the beginnings of a measure of pluralism. Positivism and the ensuing theories of race carried conviction, however, with Latin American ruling classes. They showed themselves willing, on repeated occasions, to undertake policies dictated by ideological precepts rather than economic need.

The passage from one type of dominant class to another and the definitive loss of the myth of hegemony in Latin America corresponded to the advent of marginality theory. This third moment of ideology was characterized by increasing political unrest and the use by dominant classes of every possible means to control mass protest. Ideology was one such means, but the notions of tradition and modernity, marginality and integration never became part of the actual world view of elites. These notions did not succeed in shrouding the increasingly transparent reality of material interests and conflict for either dominant or subordinate classes.

The transformation of ideologies of inequality in Latin America has thus been marked by decreasing strength of the successive systems of legitimation. This has

---

76. Antonio Gramsci, *Selections from the Prison Notebooks*, trans. Q. Hoare and G. Nowell (New York: International Publishers, 1971), pp. 206–276.

77. Sorel, *Reflections on Violence*, chap. 2; see also the detailed discussion of Sorel's ideas in H. Stuart Hughes, *Consciousness and Society*, chap. 3.

not been the result of any evolutionary necessity, but a direct consequence of the growth and complexity of the class structure. The ideological monopoly exercised by doctrines of natural law was not due to their intrinsic persuasiveness, but to the closure of colonial society and the simplicity of its mode of production. In this context, the direct producers—alien, for the most part, to Western European civilization—were dispersed through mines and plantations and subject to different forms of enslavement; dominant classes were relatively homogenous both in economic interests and worldly outlooks.

Challenges to positivist ideology during the nineteenth and early twentieth centuries were, in turn, traceable to the increasing segmentation of the dominant class, including the displacement of previously hegemonic sectors, and the first signs of emergence of an urban proletariat. Such trends were to continue during the twentieth century and give rise, in time, to strong populist and socialist movements.

The growth and militance of the parties of the left and the inability of traditional conservative and liberal parties (associated, respectively, with patrimonial and positivist ideas) to stem the tide, prompted the emergence of a "third" alternative. This failed attempt at relegitimation drew on Latin America's Catholic heritage, posing itself as its new reformed version. For theoretical support, it adapted the social thought then fashionable in the new hegemonic power, the United States.

The advent of contemporary authoritarian regimes and the associated developmentalist ideology represent a convergence of powerful external and internal forces. The requirements of global accumulation have redefined Latin America away from its traditional roles as a market and, increasingly, into that of a source of cheap industrial labor. The availability and stability of a cheap labor force is incompatible with the increasing mobilization and political organization of the working class.

Internally, dominant classes faced the need of stemming the tide from below and achieving some kind of ideological reaffirmation of their position. The new faith on economic orthodoxy and its promise of developmental "miracles" seemed to fulfill this need. Some segments of domestic entrepreneurs have found their enthusiasm for military repression and laissez faire economics tempered by the threat of multinational takeover. However, the new ideology continues to find ardent support among state managers, military officers, and the stronger segments of national capital. For these, developmentalism provides a thoroughly persuasive justification of privilege, which renders their collective interest identical with national salvation.

Unlike positivism, the ideological moment most similar to the present one, developmentalism, faces continuous and severe challenges. By the end of the twentieth century, refurbished explanations of privilege cannot be forced on a dispersed and weak working class, but on one that has been brought into cities,

134

exposed to industrial discipline, and to the significance of political organization. Thus, the apparent stability under military repression and economic orthodoxy conceals an unabated trend toward polarization of the class structure.

The present stage of instability and repression in Latin America has yet to run its course. Its significance lies in its correspondence with the moment of ideological disintegration anticipated by several theorists and the reaction of external and domestic hegemonic interests. What the present stage will show is the extent to which organized force can endure as the sustaining principle of a class order that, with the exception of the very few, has lost its legitimacy. As in the past, the outcome will depend on the interplay between external constraints and domestic forces. Whereas the political struggles will occur within the confines of nation-states, the form which they adopt and their long-term effects will not be divorced from the international system and Latin America's mode of incorporation in it.

5

The Internationalization of Capital and Class Structures in the Advanced Countries: The United States Case

Introduction

Over the course of the last 150 years sociological theory has traveled in a curious circle. As a new discipline emerging in the 1830s, sociology was compelled by a desire to understand the "great transformation." Classical theorists such as Saint Simon, Marx, Durkheim, Weber, Spencer, Schumpeter, Veblen, and many others were fundamentally concerned with the problems of industrialization and the modern state. Yet, this master theme virtually disappeared from the sociological writings of the first half of the twentieth century, particularly in the United States. Academic sociology "essentially severed social theory from the concerns which originally . . . inspired all of the most prominent social thinkers—the nature of the transformation that destroyed 'traditional' society and created a new 'modern' order."[1]

In a limited way this theme was reintroduced with the rediscovery of the traditional and underdeveloped nations after World War II (and, significantly, during the Cold War). Social scientists took up the study of these backward regions, focusing on their internal problems with the aid of evolutionary metaphors borrowed from classical theory and grafted on to fashionable functionalist percepts. This was a time of heady endeavors to internationalize social science—to gain status in the effort to "help," to participate in the broad mission of the Point Four Program *cum* Alliance for Progress. Few developmentalists doubted that this was the "springtime of freedom" for the less developed countries. Misgivings about the nature and mixed blessings of progress in classical theory, had they ever been heeded, were easily forgotten. The halcyon days were brief, however.

1. Anthony Giddens, *The Class Structure of the Advanced Societies* (New York: Barnes and Noble, 1973), p. 17.

This work was soon challenged by a "second decade" of development studies that repudiated societal evolution and differentiation, stressing instead the Third World experience of the "development of underdevelopment"—its dependence and exploitation at the hands of the metropolitan countries. More realistic than its predecessors, dependency theory nevertheless painted a homogeneous portrait of metropolitan dominance visited upon an acquiescent set of satellites.[2]

Classical theory was drawn on only selectively in Marx and Lenin. Recently this has begun to change in promising ways. Dependency theory has reformed itself merging easily with new approaches based on processes of unequal exchange and accumulation in a world economic system.[3]

As we suggested in the Introduction, even these new approaches have developed along nonintersecting planes—the low road of area studies and the high road of somewhat disembodied global systems. Yet, in each case, despite a sophisticated theoretical perspective, this recent work has failed in one key respect to come full circle and realize its own methodological dictum. If the essential premise of dependency and world-systems analyses is that development is a global process, and if this requires, in part, a closer examination of how the neocolonial practices of the core nations have contributed to the underdevelopment of the periphery, it also requires that equal attention be given the structural transformations of the advanced societies that stem from their interdependent participation in the Third World and the global economy.

> The present phase of World history, the emergence of civilizations and peoples long held in subjugation, renders particularly acute the emendation of Marxism to cover the structures peculiar to these societies and to the struggles in which they are now engaged. The depiction of the latter of course, entails a refinement of the political sociology of the advanced societies to include the colonial and imperialist phenomena *which may now constitute important elements of the internal functioning of the advanced states.*[4]

Of course, there are some important exceptions to the neglect of this "side" of the global equation. Marx was intermittently concerned with India regarding the domestic consequences of colonialism for Britain.[5] Recently Magdoff[6] has sought to demonstrate the heavy dependence of the U.S. economy on its invest-

2. Ivan Oxaal, Tony Barnett, and David Booth, *Beyond the Sociology of Development: Economy and Society in Latin America and Africa* (London: Routledge and Kegan Paul, 1975).

3. *e.g.*, Samir Amin, *Accumulation on a World Scale: A Critique of the Theory of Underdevelopment* (New York: Monthly Review, 1974); Arghiri Emmanuel, *Unequal Exchange: A Study of the Imperialism of Trade* (New York: Modern Reader, 1972); Immanuel Wallerstein, *The Modern World-System I: Capitalist Agriculture and the Origins of the European World-Economy in the Sixteenth Century* (New York: Academic Press, 1974).

4. Norman Birnbaum, *Toward a Critical Sociology* (New York: Oxford University Press, 1971), pp. 108–109, emphasis added.

5. V. G. Kiernan, *Marxism and Imperialism* (London: Edward Arnold, 1974), chap. 5.

6. Harry Magdoff, *The Age of Imperialism* (New York: Monthly Review, 1969).

ments and sales abroad. Yet, to demonstrate these linkages is only a first step toward understanding how the global economy affects the social organization of advanced nations in as much detail as we do for the underdeveloped countries. It should be understood that in arguing for this next step toward the completion of a world-system methodology, no special criticism is being leveled at the approach. On the contrary, although such criticism is sometimes warranted and necessary, this perspective offers a great deal more promise than alternatives that continue to restrict their analyses to national societies or disembodied imperialism.

Turning our attention to the characteristic features of the advanced societies, recent social theory is usefully summarized in two contrasting models. No one seems to doubt that the post-war period is a historical watershed, yet portraits of it diverge radically. Perhaps the most widely received notion is that the highly developed countries have entered upon the stage of a "post-industrial society [that] emphasizes the centrality of theoretical knowledge as the axis around which new technology, economic growth and the stratification of society will be organized."[7]

In postindustrial society the fulcrum of the economy shifts from manufacturing to the tertiary sector of commerce and services, the semiskilled and engineering occupations are replaced by the professional and technical, technical skill comes to rival property as a basis of power, and the university replaces the business enterprise as the primary institution.

Alternatively, and drawing inferences from some of the same changes, it is suggested that the advanced societies have moved to the stage of "late capitalism [which] far from representing a 'post-industrial society,' thus appears as the period in which all branches of the economy are fully industrialized for the first time."[8] Late capitalism follows on the era of monopoly capitalism and is made possible by the "third technological revolution" in which machines now produce raw materials and foodstuffs, automate industry, and invade the realm of circulation. The hallmark of late capitalism is the international concentration and centralization of capital and the organizational form of big capital is the multinational corporation. From the standpoint of social structure these changes extend universally the polarization of social classes.

Although we make no pretense that these two theories can be "tested" here, they help frame the analysis that follows and sensitize us to the key interpretive issues. To anticipate in a broad sense our detailed conclusions, the postindustrial model fails to understand changes in the global economy thus spuriously interpreting intranational developments, whereas the late capitalism approach—typically rendered in purely economic terms—takes on a more tangible and social structural aspect here.

---

7. Daniel Bell, *The Coming of Post-Industrial Society: A Venture Towards Social Forecasting* (New York: Basic Books, 1973), p. 112.

8. Ernest Mandel, *Late Capitalism* (London: NLB, 1975), p. 191, first German edition published in 1972.

The purpose of this chapter is to analyze how the class structure of the United States is transformed by participation in a global economy based increasingly on the internationalization of capital.[9] In this discussion the graceless term "internationalization of capital" is used deliberately to distinguish our concerns from more restricted issues such as the imperialist involvement of the advanced countries in Third World economies and the worldwide operations of multinational companies. Important as these are, they constitute only a portion (and sometimes a small one, as in the case of direct investment in poor countries) of the *cross-penetration* of international capital in the form of royalty and licensing fees, consulting services, deposits in foreign banks, investments in Eurocurrency or U.S. Treasury bonds, foreign-owned corporate securities, bank loans, government loans and trade credits, and so forth.[10]

Nevertheless, the contribution of multinational corporations to the internationalization of capital will be the primary empirical focus here. This emphasis is based on several considerations including limitations on the available evidence of international capital flows, our particular interest in their effect on class structure, and to reduce some very complex issues to manageable proportions in this space. The activities of multinational corporations are but one aspect of the internationalization and cross-penetration of capital.[11] Wherever possible other indicators will be provided.

Obviously, the growing interdependence of the global economy has many implications for national societies of the advanced and underdeveloped worlds including the unequal transfer of surplus, compromised political autonomy, and the ascendence of "semisovereign" global corporations. These critical issues have been dealt with in voluminous literature. Conversely, the question of how this process concretely affects social organization and class structure (particularly of the advanced countries) has been seriously neglected. Vital as it is to understand the workings of the global economic system, it is only when we can trace this process through to its effects on social groups, classes, and people—in a word, to see how it "comes home"—that we are able to apprehend the human impact of social change.

With that ambition in mind, the analysis centers on changes in class structure. This theoretical preference is informed by a belief that social class, particularly in the advanced industrial societies, is the most consequential (though never the only) basis for the organization of human groups and the determination of individual life chances. This does not deny that other bases of social organization such as community, status group, ethnicity, or nationality are important and

9. Stephen Hymer, "The Internationalization of Capital," *Journal of Economic Issues*, 6, No. 1 (1972): 91–111.

10. *Ibid.*, p. 91; Daniel J. B. Mitchell, *Labor Issues of American International Trade and Investment* (Baltimore: Johns Hopkins Press, 1976), p. 76.

11. Compare with James Hawley, "International Banking and the Internationalization of Capital," *U. S. Capitalism in Crisis, Review of Radical Political Economics*, 11, No. 4 (Winter 1980).

sometimes overriding.[12] It does, however, hold that class more typically determines the nature of group organization and life chances—a claim that always requires support[13] and one this discussion will endeavor to support in a particular context.

Classes are defined here in the Marxian tradition as common positions in the social relations of production. Following after recent developments in class theory,[14] the criteria underlying the social relations of production extend beyond ownership of the means of production and the sale of labor power. They include certain interstitial (or "ambiguous," as in Wright) positions with respect to ownership and control (e.g., managers and petty entrepreneurs) and with respect to authority relations in the division of labor (e.g., professional–technical, skilled–manual). These divisions correspond generally to what Poulantzas terms the "political" and "ideological" criteria of class determination and Giddens calls the "proximate bases of class structuration." Since the aim of this chapter is to suggest how class structures are changing in response to the global economy, we shall reserve further discussions of them for the conclusion where they may be fitted to the evidence presented.

The fundamental argument here is that the process of class formation is taking place increasingly at the international level—that the exigencies of the world economy are coming to have a greater bearing on the *intra*national organization of social classes than uniquely indigenous conditions. From a broad historical perspective Wallerstein[15] has discussed this process in terms of a worldwide division of labor, and others[16] have suggested the contours of an international ruling class. Yet, there are few available studies to substantiate the general argument and to detail its features in a concrete case.

Aspects of the Internationalization of Capital

A useful dictum in social science states that it is impossible to know what kind of a phenomenon one is presented with until you know how much of a phenomenon it is. What are the trends in the growth of internationalized capital, in its

12. Compare with Reinhard Bendix, "Inequality and Social Structure in the Theories of Marx and Weber," *American Sociological Review*, 39, No. 4 (April 1974): 149–161.

13. For example, Erik Olin Wright and Luca Perrone, "Marxist Class Categories and Income Inequality," *American Sociological Review*, 42 (February 1977): 32–55.

14. Giddens, *The Class Structure of the Advanced Societies*; Nicos Poulantzas, *Classes in Contemporary Capitalism* (London: New Left Books, 1975); Erik Olin Wright, "Class Boundaries in Advanced Capitalist Societies," *New Left Review* 98 (July–August 1976): 3–41.

15. Immanuel Wallerstein, "The Rise and Future Demise of the World Capitalist System: Concepts for Comparative Analysis," *Comparative Studies in Society and History*, 16 (September 1974): 387–415.

16. *E.g.* Walter R. Goldfrank, "Who Rules the World? Class Formation at the International Level," *Quarterly Journal of Ideology*, 1, No. 2 (Winter 1977): 32–37.

magnitude especially by contrast to the domestic economy, and in its nature with respect to areal and sectoral composition? The following descriptive material seeks to answer these questions and to show that the internationalization of capital plays a major role in the U.S. economy—one that has far-reaching implications both at home and abroad.

Perhaps the best place to begin is with trends in the distribution and volume of U.S. direct investment abroad in recent years. Table 5.1 indicates a number of benchmark observations. In 1976 U.S. direct investment abroad amounted to over $137 billion (book value) having increased more than fourfold since 1960 and nearly twofold in the most recent 6-year period. The great majority of this investment is in other developed countries, notably Western Europe and Canada. In fact, the *proportion* of total direct investment in the "developing" (poor) countries has been declining steadily since 1950 when it was 48.7% to 21.2% in 1976 (although these figures can be deceiving as we shall note next). Geographically the proportions are otherwise relatively stable with the additional exception of a sharp relative drop in the investment in Canada (63% of the total for the developed countries in 1950 versus 34% in 1976) by contrast to Western Europe (30% of the developed countries' total in 1950 versus 55% in 1976).

Several essential points concern the nature of this investment. First, in 1973 nearly 80% of the total direct investment involved U.S. ownership or control of

TABLE 5.1
U.S. Direct Investment Position Abroad at Year-end (millions of dollars)

Country	1950	1960	1970	1976
All countries	11,788	32,788	78,178	137,244
Developed countries	5,697	19,328	53,145	101,150
Canada	3,579	19,328	22,790	33,927
Europe	1,733	6,681	24,516	55,906
Japan	19	254	1,483	3,787
Australia, New Zealand, and South Africa	366	1,195	1,483	7,529
Developing countries	5,735	12,032	21,448	29,050
Latin America and other Western Hemisphere	4,576	9,271	14,760	23,536
Africa (excluding South Africa)	147	639	2,614	2,802
Middle East	692	1,139	1,617	−3,210
Asia and Pacific (excluding Japan, Australia, and New Zealand)	320	983	2,457	5,922
International and unallocated	356	1,418	3,586	7,044

Sources: 1950 and 1960 data: U.S. Department of Commerce, *Survey of Current Business*, August 1962, pp. 22–23; 1976 data: U.S. Department of Commerce, *Survey of Current Business*, August 1977, p. 45.

TABLE 5.2
Distribution of Domestic and Foreign Operations by Size-of-Asset Class, 1969

Asset sizes of U.S. corporations	Number of corporations[b]	Total taxable domestic corporate income[a]		Foreign tax-credit	
		Amount[b]	Percentage of total	Amount[b]	Percentage of total
Under $1,000,000	1,549.4	$11,656,952	15.1	$7,774	.2
$1,000,000–$50,000,000	105.1	18,754,174	24.3	122,127	3.1
$50,000,000–$100,000,000	1.9	3,246,166	4.2	80,969	2.0
$100,000,000–$250,000,000	1.4	5,948,713	7.7	201,856	5.1
$250,000,000 and above	1.1	37,556,550	48.7	3,574,722	89.6
Total	1,658.8	77,162,555	100.0	3,987,448	100.0

Source: "Statistics of Income, Corporation Income Tax Returns, 1969," U.S. Department of the Treasury, Internal Revenue Service. From Musgrave (1975: 13).
[a] Includes foreign branch earnings but excludes dividends from foreign incorporated affiliates.
[b] In thousands.

foreign-based enterprise, with portfolio investment accounting for the remaining 20%. Since 1950 the ratio of portfolio investment to direct ownership and control has declined precipitously indicating that "the vast bulk of the investments are in the form of wholly—or largely—owned foreign affiliates of U.S. corporations."[17] Second, direct foreign investment is overwhelmingly the province of the giant, oligopolistic corporations. Table 5.2 shows that nearly 90% of the foreign tax credits (an indirect, if by no means perfect indicator of the level of international activity) are claimed by corporations with assets greater than $250 million. In number these giant corporations are less than 1% of the total, yet receive nearly 50% of domestic corporate income. These figures suggest that their oligopolistic control is vastly greater in international business providing them with a decisive advantage over purely domestic competitors.

Third, although these data indicate that direct foreign investment involves mainly the largest U.S. firms operating in the more developed countries, certain interpretive precautions should be added. Some observers have used this type of evidence—and the fact that the repatriated earnings of U.S. corporations in any given year deriving from Third-World countries tends to relatively small (e.g., in

17. Pegsy B. Musgrave, *Direct Investment Abroad and the Multinationals: Effects on the United States Economy,* Subcommittee on Multinational Corporations, Committee on Foreign Relations, U.S. Senate, 94th Congress, 1st Session (August) (Washington: U. S. Government Printing Office, 1975).

the several billions)—to argue that U.S. "imperialism" is of inconsequential proportions.[18]

Although it is true that the larger volume of U.S. foreign profits derives from the more developed countries, the available figures on direct investment and earnings seriously understate the importance of the Third World to U.S. prosperity. Two important considerations help explain this fact. First, direct U.S. investment in the developing countries is a small proportion of corporate *assets* due to the widespread practice of local borrowing to finance U.S. controlled enterprises.[19] Second, since U.S. taxation on foreign earnings is deferred until repatriation and, therefore, profits tend to be reinvested abroad, the amounts showing up as repatriated earnings represent a reduced proportion of actual income. Moreover, there is ample evidence to conclude that multinationals operating in the Third World employ a variety of mechanisms (such as transfer pricing, transhipping through duty-free ports, and over- or under-evaluation of imports and exports) to disguise actual profits.[20]

If the true figures on U.S. assets and earnings abroad were known, it seems evident that the contribution of the Third World would be considerably larger than the available data suggest. Consequently, imperialism cannot be dismissed as an important element in U.S. prosperity. Nevertheless, just as those who would deny the importance of Third World are in error, it is equally mistaken to regard this aspect of the internationalization of capital as the single most important source of U.S. profit abroad.[21]

The magnitude of U.S. economic activities abroad is illustrated in a number of comparisons to the domestic economy. At the most general level, in the past 25 years the United States has assumed a greatly expanded role in the international economy, becoming the world's leading capital exporter. Some $200 billion of long-term capital has been sent abroad "amounting to over 20% of annual domestic corporate capital formation in recent years."[22] Table 5.3 (Column 5) indicates that U.S.-*owned assets* abroad in 1970 amounted to 7% of all manufacturing, the figure running higher in selected key industries (e.g., petro-

18. For example, S. M. Miller, Roy Bennett, and Cyril Alapatt, "Does the U. S. Economy Require Imperialism?," *Social Policy*, 1, No. 3, (September–October 1970): 13–19; Al Szymanski, "Capital Accumulation on a World Scale and the Necessity of Imperialism," *The Insurgent Sociologist*, 7, No. 2, (Spring 1977).

19. Musgrave, *Direct Investment Abroad and the Multinationals*; Richard S. Newfarmer and Willard J. Mueller, *Multinational Corporations in Brazil and Mexico: Structural Sources of Economic and Non-Economic Power*. Subcommittee on Multinational Corporations, Committee on Foreign Relations, United States Senate, 94th Congress, 1st Session (August) (Washington: U. S. Government Printing Office, 1975).

20. Ronald Müller, "The Multinational Corporation and the Underdevelopment of the Third World," in *The Political Economy of Development and Underdevelopment*, ed. Charles K. Wilbur (New York: Random House, 1973).

21. For example, Magdoff, *The Age of Imperialism*; Steve Babson, "The Multinational Corporation and Labor," *The Review of Radical Political Economics*, 5, No. 1 (Spring 1973): 19–36.

22. Musgrave, *Direct Investment Abroad and the Multinationals*, p. vii.

TABLE 5.3

Production Abroad Compared with Production in the United States: Domestic and Foreign Capital Stocks, 1970 (millions of dollars)

Industry	U.S. domestic corporate capital		Direct investment abroad		Foreign capital as percentage of domestic capital	
	$(1)^a$	$(2)^b$	$(3)^c$	$(4)^d$	$(5) = (3)\,(1)$	$(6) = (4)\,(2)$
All industries	2,367,449	497,875	78,178	57,053	3.3	11.5
All manufacturing	454,219	118,411	32,261	30,915	7.1	26.1
Chemicals	44,108	12,059	5,936	6,868	13.5	57.0
Motor vehicles	44,118	5,407	5,154	5,131	11.7	94.9
Machinery	84,158	15,840	7,671	6,411	9.1	48.4
Metals	74,656	26,779	2,755	2,619	3.7	9.8
Paper	—	7,798	—	2,007	—	25.7
Food	46,431	13,999	3,028	1,853	6.5	13.2
Wood products	—	3,719	—	1,296	—	34.8
Rubber	—	2,910	—	974	—	33.5
Petroleum	74,828	23,911	21,714	18,855	29.0	78.9
Mining	5,711	3,662	6,168	1,962	108.0	53.6
Other	1,832,691	351,891	18,035	5,321	1.0	1.5

Source: Musgrave (1975: 13).

[a] Book value of total assets reported on all active tax returns for U.S. corporations, "Statistics of Income, Corporation Income Tax Returns, 1969," less Col. (3). Manufacturing excludes petroleum refining, which is included in petroleum.

[b] Net fixed assets; equals gross book value of depreciable and depletable assets, less accumulated depreciation and depletion, plus and less Col. (4). Source: as Col. (1).

[c] Book value of U.S. owned assets of foreign affiliates. Source: For all industries, all manufacturing, petroleum, mining, and other, SCB, Sept. 1973: for 2-digit manufacturing breakdown, figures estimated by author by interpolation from Commerce Department's 1966 and 1970 direct investment surveys.

[d] Net value of property, plant and equipment of foreign affiliates. Source: Estimated by author from 1970 sample survey by blowing up balance sheet items to universe totals by factor based on sample firms share in 1966 universe totals.

leum, mining). *Net fixed assets* abroad (Column 6) are much higher as a percentage of the domestic economy—and even these figures are serious underestimates because of borrowing within foreign countries to capitalize U.S. controlled firms. But, the estimates show net fixed assets of foreign affiliates are 26% of the total for all U.S. manufacturing firms with substantial variation by industry up to the case of motor vehicles where nearly one-half of the industry's fixed assets are located abroad (i.e., assets abroad are 94.9% of those at home). A growing trend is shown by the fact that "gross capital formulation abroad has roughly tripled over the past decade, whereas domestic capital formation has only doubled."[23]

In a related vein, the labor force employed by U.S. manufacturing sub-

23. *Ibid.*, p. xii.

TABLE 5.4
Foreign Direct Investment Position in the U.S. at Year-end (millions of dollars)

Country	1962	1970	1973	1976
All countries	7,612	13,270	20,556	30,182
Canada	2,064	3,117	4,203	5,859
Europe	5,247	9,554	13,937	19,916
United Kingdom	2,474	4,127	5,403	5,699
Europe excluding United Kingdom	2,773	5,427	8,535	14,217
Japan	112	229	152	890
Other	189	369	2,264	3,518

Source: U.S. Department of Commerce, Survey of Current Business; October, 1977: 27; and February 1973: 30.

sidiaries abroad was 17% of all manufacturing employment in the U.S., although only 8% of the corresponding payroll (reflecting both lower wages and capital intensiveness). By 1968 the sales of foreign manufacturing subsidiaries had grown to more than 10% of all manufacturing sales in the United States. But, more striking, manufacturing sales abroad amounted to *more than twice* the value of U.S. manufactured exports. As a result, the profits of foreign affiliates of U.S. firms (with all the provisos mentioned regarding their underestimation) amounted in 1972 to 22% of domestic profits of *all* U.S. corporations.[24] Clearly, the vitality of the U.S. economy has come to depend intimately on its foreign extension.

Apropos of the cross-penetration model of international capital, foreign investment within the confines of the U.S. has also been on the increase. Table 5.4 indicates trends and levels of foreign investment in the United States. Although (by contrast to Table 5.1) the magnitude of foreign involvement in the U.S. economy is substantially less than its counterpart, it is growing rapidly (e.g., an increase of 50% in the most recent figures for 1973–1976). Illustratively, by 1973 foreign *long-term* investment in the United States had reached a value of $62 billion or 43% of U.S. long-term investment abroad.[25]

In its composition this investment is distributed in roughly the same proportions as U.S. investment abroad (i.e., somewhat less than one-half in manufacturing, more than 20% in petroleum, and the balance in trade, insurance, and other areas). There are important differences, however, in the investment patterns. Because of the larger scale of the economy, foreign investment in the United States is less significant and more multilateral than the heavy presence

24. *Ibid.*
25. *Ibid.*, p. 25.

146

of the United States in other nations. More important, although nearly 80% of U.S. investment abroad involves direct ownership or control, only about 25% of foreign investment in the United States takes this form.[26] Foreign investment in the United States is overwhelmingly in portfolio form, whereas the reverse holds for U.S. investment abroad. This fact alone has far-reaching implications for the impact of foreign control on domestic economies and leverage in international negotiations.

In summary, the evidence indicates the growing importance of the internationalization of capital not only with respect to external constraints on developing countries, but also for the domestic economies of the advanced nations including the United States. By virtue of its magnitude, steady expansion, and cross-penetration, the global economy is increasingly consequential for the social and economic organization of the nation-state. In the following sections we turn to some of the concrete manifestations of this process taking the United States and its changing class structure as an illustrative case.

Consequences of the Internationalization of Capital for Domestic Labor, Capital, and National Income

The Issues

Commenting on the domestic costs and benefits of multinational business, Babson writes:

> Much has been written by bourgeois and Marxist economists alike about the impact of (foreign) investment on third world countries, the international balance of payments, world trade, and diplomatic relations. Little, however, has been written about the effects of the multinational corporation on class relations in the United States, both because bourgeois economists prefer to ignore such questions as a matter of course, and because American Marxists have, until recently, been preoccupied with the Vietnam War and problems related to U.S. foreign policy.[27]

Musgrave argues that in our preoccupation with the loss of national control by capital-receiving countries and the balance of payments problems of capital-exporting countries,

> relatively little thought has been given to the effects of capital outflow on the structure of the U.S. economy, the level of income which it generates and the way in which it is distributed. This is unfortunate because from the longer-run point of

26. *Ibid.*
27. Babson, "The Multinational Corporation and Labor," p. 19.

view these may well be the most important aspects, along with the foreign policy implications which result from the concentrated influence of U.S. investments in foreign economies.[28]

Yet, the paucity of scholarly research has not restrained a heated debate in public policy circles surrounding the domestic costs and benefits of multinational business.

Although the multinational firm dates as far back as the Dutch West India Company (established in 1621), the Hudson's Bay Company (established in 1670), and originating in the United States, the expansion of International Telephone and Telegraph to Cuba and Central America just prior to 1920, it was only in the late 1960s that these firms became a public issue. The spectacular increase in U.S. foreign investment following World War II was initially greeted with enthusiasm by labor and the business community alike as the best solution for the economic recovery of war-torn countries and the development of the emerging ex-colonial nations.

U.S. policy actively supported this position until the late 1950s when it began to appear that gold and monetary reserves were declining. Contrary to bullish expectation, the balance of payments surplus began to deteriorate as investment abroad failed to generate the expected return flow of income. In part this was due to a heavy retention rate overseas encouraged by U.S. tax arrangements. During the 1960s legislative measures were taken (e.g., the Revenue Act of 1962) to improve the balance of payments through stricter (i.e., less preferential) taxation and control of foreign direct investment.

Successful in the short-run, these measures lead to a large increase in foreign borrowing that allowed for the expansion of international business without a concomitant increase in U.S. taxation under the revised system of tax deferral on foreign income. Moreover, the problem of export displacement was becoming a matter of concern: "Such factual evidence as was available in the early sixties suggested that foreign direct investment contributed relatively little to the U.S. export of capital goods and only modestly to that of intermediate goods, both gains which were offset by the affiliates' sales to the U.S."[29] Although these matters preoccupied economists and certain policy makers during the 1960s, public debate came only with the recession of 1973, which coincided with well-publicized plant closing in the electronic, apparel, and footwear industries as a great many U.S. firms sought lower production costs abroad.

Publicly the issue was joined by labor organizations arrayed against a multinational interest group coalition (including the multinational companies themselves, various lobby and "research" organizations, investors, and free trade

28. Musgrave, *Direct Investment Abroad and the Multinationals*, p. viii.
29. *Ibid.*, p. 4.

advocates). The intensity of the debate derives from more than self-interest. The issues are extremely complex and far outrun the available evidence.

Labor's position is based on a set of interrelated points. Investment abroad has led to deficits in balances of trade and payments to the disadvantage of the U.S. economy. Multinationals have exported U.S. jobs and advanced technologies that improve the position of foreign competitors. This has resulted in a decline of U.S. exports as well as a competitive disadvantage for U.S. manufactured goods from imports produced by extremely low wage, foreign labor. The result is a precipitous loss of U.S. jobs, undermining labor's negotiating power with potential "runaway" industries, and general decline in national economic vitality. More trenchantly, the "dimming of America" has been brought on by "soulless, anonymous multinational corporations" whose public statements and actions "make it continuously more difficult to determine whether they are simply non-American or un-American. The multinational has not only declared war on the jobs of American workers, but on the traditional concept of Americanism."[30]

In more measured language (and with the aid of academic research by economists at major universities), the multinational position disputes these claims of labor. Generally it argues that the *net* results of international business for the domestic economy are all on the positive side. Foreign earnings of U.S. multinationals exceed investments abroad making a positive contribution to the balance of payments. Indeed, deficits stem from government aid and lending. The largest U.S. corporations (which are also the multinationals) have expanded abroad and are outpacing the national average of profits and expanded employment at home. Most manufacturing abroad is sold in the country of production or exported to Third World countries. Only about 8% is reimported for sale in the United States and even then it benefits consumers through prices lower than domestically produced goods.

However, the fundamental argument emphasizes foreign investment as a *defensive* strategy. To survive and grow, the multinationals must compete and expand in markets abroad on an equal footing with foreign industry (which would otherwise displace imported goods emanating from the U.S.), as well as compete with foreign manufacturers in the U.S. market. Had the multinationals failed to take this course, sticking to investment and more costly production within the country, export markets would have been lost and domestic sales undercut by cheaper foreign imports. Nevertheless, although some noncompetitive U.S. industry may experience "adverse employment effects on a spot basis," foreign investment provides a net stimulus to U.S. employment. What begins as

---

30. AFL–CIO, "U. S. Multinationals—the Dimming of America," A report prepared by the AFL–CIO Maritime Trades Department Executive Board Meeting, February 15–16, 1973. Hearings before the Subcommittee on International Trade, Committee on Finance, United States Senate, 93rd Congress, 1st Session (February and March) (Washington: U. S. Government Printing Office, 1973), p. 450.

a defensive strategy leads to the production of components for further processing or assembly abroad, associated exports and capital equipment needed in foreign plants, white-collar and administrative jobs in home offices, and engineering jobs required to maintain technological advantage.

Boiling these arguments down to their bare essentials:

> The key questions centered on the possible displacement effect of production abroad on export sales from production at home. As it became clear that most direct investment abroad was (and is) carried out by the U.S. corporations which were also the major exporters and that sales abroad by their foreign affiliates were expanding much faster than were U.S. exports of the same industrial classification, the problem centered itself on the difficult but crucial question of whether investment abroad by the MNC's [multinational companies] was a substitute for investment and expanding production at home (thus displacing exports which could otherwise have taken place) or whether it served to supplement domestic investment, either by filling foreign markets which would otherwise have been lost to foreign competitors or by actually displacing such competitors abroad. These questions have not as yet been definitively answered.[31]

Nevertheless, if we disaggregate issues and consider them systematically it is possible to cut through many competing claims. Some conclusions about the domestic consequences of foreign investment can be drawn whatever the exigencies that prompt it. For example, on many issues labor and the multinationals simply talk past each other. Labor cites plant closings and distressed industries without considering off-setting employment gains in new activites (e.g., in multinational headquarters). The multinationals cite expanded production and employment among oligopolistic firms without considering the number of smaller firms and jobs these eliminate. By setting aside such transparent arguments and other hypothetical speculation attention can be focused on the available evidence concerning three key problems: employment (loss–gain), job displacement, and national income shares.

Employment

The most controversial issue surrounding foreign investment is whether or not it results in the "export of jobs." The evidence on this question is highly varied and fraught with ambiguity. The most frequently cited study concluding that foreign investment produces a net *loss* of U.S. jobs was conducted by a consulting firm under the auspices of the AFL–CIO.[32] Using Bureau of Labor Statistics it estimated that in 1969 there were 2.7 million jobs connected with export production—up from 2.5 million in 1966 or a gain of 200,000 jobs. However, it was also determined that 2.5 million jobs *would have been* required in 1969 to

31. Musgrave, *Direct Investment Abroad and the Multinationals*, p. 4.
32. AFL–CIO, *Needed: A Constructive Foreign Trade Policy. A Special Study Commissioned and Published by the Industrial Union Department*. Washington, 1971.

TABLE 5.5

Estimated Gains and Losses of U.S. Production vis-à-vis Foreign Affiliates of U.S. Firms by Manufacturing Industry, 1966 to 1970

	Estimated gain or loss (−) in U.S. exports relative to foreign affiliate sales	Estimated gain or loss (−) in U.S. production relative to imports foreign affiliates	Estimated net gain or loss (−) in U.S. sales relative to foreign affiliate sales in U.S. and host country markets	Total jobs represented in Column (3) (thousands)
	(1)	(2)	(3)	(4)
1. Food products	80.9	119.2	201.1	16.78
2. Paper and allied products	22.1	−38.6	−16.5	−1.18
3. Drugs, cosmetics, cleaning preparations	1,609.9		1,609.9	119.05
4. Plastic materials	86.9	29.6	116.5	−6.90
5. Industrial and other chemicals	−381.5		−381.5	−19.80
6. Rubber products	111.9	−27.2	84.7	4.50
7. Primary and fabricated metals	61.4	−13.3	60.1	3.90
8. Farm machinery and equipment	−17.4	−44.5	−61.9	−4.95
9. Office and computing machinery	125.5	−49.7	75.8	5.51
10. Other nonelectrical machinery	520.6		520.6	43.15
11. Household appliances	−4.2	−10.7	−14.9	−1.30
12. Other electrical machinery and equipment	856.3		856.3	65.94
13. Transportation equipment[a]	−3.8		−7.1	−.58
14. Textiles and apparel	−9.0	−67.3	−76.3	−8.49
15. Lumber, wood, furniture	2.3	−171.1	−168.8	−16.42
16. Printing and publishing	−1.6	−7.3	−8.9	−.82
17. Stone, clay, glass products	−1.1	13.8	12.7	1.02
18. Instruments	23.2	43.8	67.0	4.83
19. Other manufacturing	815.9		815.9	49.95
All manufacturing	3,899.3	−226.6	3,672.7	260.61

Source: Hawkins, 1976.

[a] Excludes auto trade between United States and Canada.

produce at home and volume of *imports competing with domestic products alone.* In 1966 the total number of export-related jobs so defined (i.e., those competing with imports) amounted to 1.8 million. Thus, presumably, in the absence of imports this segment would have grown from 1.8 to 2.5 million, or a gain of 700,000 jobs. Since the overall gain was only 200,000, it was concluded that roughly 500,000 jobs were lost during the 3-year period. Obviously, the study leaves much to be desired given its hypothetical basis and inattention to off-setting changes.

Yet, the evidence offered for the job-gain position is equally conjectural. Stobaugh and associates conducted a case study of the foreign investment decisions of firms in nine industrial groups based on company records and interviews with management.[33] Estimating the volume of "associated exports" connected with foreign investment it was concluded that 600,000 jobs were created dependent on exports. Similarly, the Emergency Committee for American Trade polled 117 U.S. multinational firms discovering that their domestic employment had increased by 900,000 jobs in the 1960s. This represented a proportionately larger increase than purely national firms (although it is not clear how many of those jobs could be directly connected to foreign investment). In a much more sophisticated analysis Hawkins estimated the gains and losses in U.S. exports, production, and sales relative to foreign affiliates of U.S. firms in 19 industrial groups (Table 5.5).[34] When production gains and losses are translated into the number of jobs needed to produce that output, both within the industries in question and from inputs purchased from other industries, it was found that 260,000 jobs were created through the activity of foreign affiliates between 1966–1970.

In a review of six related studies, Jadel and Stamm argue that very little can be concluded from all this evidence since

> labor assumes that if foreign investment were not made, the U.S. exports would be able to compete directly... [while] the other studies assume that underlying causal factors produced an environment in which American companies acted defensively to combat the potential erosion of competitive positions. They argue that if the final product is considered, more jobs would have been lost in the manufacturing sector if the foreign investments had not been made.[35]

Obviously, under such circumstances a simulation is required in which assumptions are allowed to vary in different cases. At the behest of the Senate

33. Robert Stobaugh, "How Investment Abroad Creates Jobs at Home," *Harvard Business Review,* 50, No. 5 (September–October 1972): 118–126.

34. Robert G. Hawkins, "The Multinational Corporation: A New Trade Policy Issue in the United States," in *The United States and International Markets,* eds. Robert G. Hawkins and Ingo Walters (Lexington, Mass.: Lexington Books, 1972).

35. Michael Jay Jadel and John H. Stamm, "The Battle Over Jobs: An Appraisal of Recent Publications on the Employment Effects of U. S. Multinational Corporations," in *American Labor and the Multinational Corporation,* ed. Duane Kujawa (New York: Preager, 1973), pp. 187–188.

Finance Committeee, the Tariff Commission conducted such an exercise for three hypothetical cases:

1. *Case 1* adopts the assumptions of multinational critics stating that "when a direct foreign investment takes place, investment at home drops absolutely and host-country investment increases absolutely . . . if the MNC had not made the investment, nobody else would have. The foreign investment substitutes directly for a domestic one that was not made."

2. *Case 2* reverses this assumption along lines compatible with the multinational position: "Foreign investment causes no fall in domestic investment at home, while it does substitute for domestic investment in the host country."

3. *Case 3*, though a compromise, "is closer to option one in the sense that it presumes no substitution in the host country. Host country investment rises absolutely and it would not have done so had the MNC not come along . . . no foreigner would have made the investment abroad; therefore, none of the potential bad effects of the MNC are assumed away by putting the onus on the foreigner. On the other hand, option three does *not* assume an absolute drop in domestic investment in the home country of the MNC."[36]

Next, the potential "gross job loss" under each of these conditions is estimated and then corrected for three off-setting conditions: (*a*) employment in the multinational headquarters attributed to foreign operations; (*b*) the effect of U.S. exports on affiliates abroad; and (*c*) employment in the U.S. by foreign-based multinationals. The results show a *net* U.S. *job loss* of 1.3 million in Case 1, 418,000 in Case 2, and a *net gain* of 488,000 in Case 3 for the single year of 1970. Since Case 3, though hypothetical, is regarded as more realistic than 1 or 2, the study's conclusion is that net gains are the more likely outcome.

Nevertheless, like any exercise this one is limited by its own assumptions. It is noteworthy that even in the more critical Case 1 it was not assumed, as critics claim, that U.S. domestic investment may *fall* as a result of foreign investment leading to a net job loss. Given that observation, and the fact that two of the three estimates suggest "negative" consequences, we can conjecture, at a minimum, that the optimistic claims of the multinationals are not supported.

A stronger position on the adverse effects of foreign investment on net employment in the United States is supported in more recent research by Frank and Freeman.[37] Their calculations include consideration of the market power of large corporations that can move abroad vis-à-vis their national competitors. Thus, indirect manufacturing job losses were estimated at 105,000 for the single

---

36. United States Senate, *Implications of Multinational Firms for World Trade and Investment and for U. S. Trade and Labor,* 93rd Congress, 1st Session (February) (Washington: U. S. Government Printing Office, 1973), pp. 647–648.

37. Robert H. Frank and Richard T. Freeman, "The Distributional Consequences of Direct Foreign Investment," in *The Impact of International Trade and Investment on Employment.* ed. William G. Dewald (Washington, D. C.: U. S. Government Printing Office, 1978).

year of 1970. The authors conclude that "even allowing for considerable deficiencies in the data, the net impact of foreign investment by U.S. multinationals is a substantial domestic employment demand reduction."[38] In a recent summary of these studies, Bluestone and Harrison[39] conclude that a summation of the net job loss owing to aspects of this process (direct plant shutdowns, effects on competitors, forward and backward linkages) amounts to 15 million between 1969 and 1976 or an average of 2.5 million jobs each year.

Our own summary is more cautious: At a minimum the job-gain position becomes less tenable as the evidence accumulates. In the past (i.e. until 1970) the actual numbers of jobs lost may have been small. Over the last decade the situation has changed as the pace of foreign investment has increased dramatically and the capacity of domestic and multinational firms to create new sources of employment has fallen. We believe that foreign investment is now producing a net reduction in jobs at an increasing rate.

Job Displacement

In light of the foregoing discussion it may come as a relief that reasonable agreement exists on the dislocations of industrial and occupational structure stemming from foreign investment. Although the multinationals regard export of certain lines of production as defensively necessary and ultimately generative of U.S. jobs and income, on the question of displacement their differences with labor are mainly rehetorical. Thus, the multinationals speak of "offshore production" and the need for "adjustment to temporary displacement" by government and workers, whereas labor talks of the "runaway shop" and "structural unemployment." No one disputes the fact that job displacement can be traced directly to the export of production facilities abroad in search of lower costs—including vastly reduced labor costs (although multinational spokespersons rank this factor low by contrast to other considerations).

Consider first the specific industries most affected by the export of production and job displacement. Table 5.5, which was presented with reference to net employment effects, is also useful here. The data indicate that in the aggregate more jobs are created than lost. But, on a sectoral basis, 9 of the 19 industries experienced varying degrees of job displacement with the categories hardest hit including: industrial and other chemicals; lumber, wood, and furniture; and textiles and apparel. From another vantage Table 5.6 shows the increase in expenditures on plant and equipment abroad versus at home. Here again, the growth abroad of the chemical industry is noted—although it is exceeded by motor vehicles and, particularly, petroleum.

38. *Ibid.*, p. 156.
39. Barry Bluestone and Bennet Harrison, *Capital and Communities: The Causes and Consequences of Private Disinvestment* (Washington, D. C.: The Progressive Alliance, 1980), p. 59.

TABLE 5.6

Plant and Equipment Expenditures at Home and Abroad (billions of dollars)[a]

Industry	Plant and equipment								
	Expenditures in United States			Expenditures abroad			Expenditures abroad as percentage of plant and equipment expenditures in United States		
	1957–1961	1962–1966	1967–1970	1957–1961	1962–1966	1967–1970	1957–1961	1962–1966	1967–1970
All industries									
All manufacturing	35.21	48.81	72.13	4.11	5.95	11.47	11.7	12.2	15.9
Chemicals	11.46	16.73	24.39	1.39	3.12	5.18	12.0	18.6	21.2
Motor vehicles	1.50	2.14	3.06	.24	.62	1.18	16.0	29.0	38.6
Machinery	.78	1.46	1.84	.31	.72	.81	39.7	49.3	44.0
Metals	1.65	2.66	4.00	.27	.72	1.48	16.4	27.1	37.0
Paper	.69	1.00	1.55	.10	.20	.24	14.4	20.0	15.5
Food	.86	1.13	2.26	.09	.18	.33	10.5	15.9	14.6
Rubber	.19	.30	.88	.08	.15	.18	42.1	50.0	20.5
Petroleum	2.75	3.48	5.29	1.75	2.05	3.54	63.6	58.9	66.9

Sources: Plant and equipment expenditures in United States: various September issues of "Survey of Current Business"; plant and equipment expenditures of foreign affiliates: "Survey of Current Business, March 1973," March and September 1972 and revised series for early years provided by Department of Commerce. Reprinted from Musgrave (1975: 14).

[a] All figures are averages.

For purposes of triangulation it is instructive to take another indicator, the distribution of petitions for Worker Adjustment Assistance provided under the Trade Expansion Act of 1962, designed to assist workers who lost their jobs as a direct result of import competition.[40] The largest number of petitions came from displaced workers in the fields of footwear, electronics (especially components, radio, and television), textiles, nonelectrical machinery, rubber products, and miscellaneous manufacturing (e.g., toys).

The data document what the average American consumer knows from experience—that it is very difficult to "buy American" if one is in the market for a radio, television, cothing, shoes, and sundry products. Barnet and Müller paraphrase George Meany to the effect that "20% of all cars, 40% of all glassware, about 60% of all sewing machines and calculators, all cassettes and nearly all radios, and 'large proportions of U.S. production of shirts, work clothes, shoes, knit goods' had already (by 1970) been displaced by imports, a substantial portion of which were coming from American-owned factories abroad."[41]

U.S. industry goes abroad for a variety of profit-oriented reasons including entry into new markets, U.S. and foreign tax advantages, cheap and docile labor, freedom from constraints on labor relations and environmental pollution. However, it is not cost advantageous for all industries to move abroad. The profile of "runaways" has certain characteristic features. In the physical sense these industries are relatively mobile producing goods that can be easily and cheaply transported over long distances (e.g., apparel and electronic components). They tend to be highly labor intensive and have low economies of scale, meaning that reduced labor costs are doubly advantageous since they constitute a larger proportion of all production costs. Describing textiles as an illustration par excellence of the "type of activities which the United States first attempted to transfer abroad," Hawkins notes, "It is an industry without large economies of scale; it is an industry with relatively low R & D intensity; it is an industry with a relatively high proportion of semi-skilled and unskilled workers; and it is a low wage industry."[42] As we shall note subsequently, these characteristics of the industry and jobs exported abroad involve, in turn, distinctive consequences for the occupational and class structure of the United States.

A study of the electronics industry[43] reveals the destination and volume of overseas production, particularly in the Third World. Table 5.7 shows some of

40. Mitchell, *Labor Issues of American International Trade and Investment.*
41. Richard Barnet and Ronald Müller, "Global Reach," part II. *The New Yorker,* December 9, 1974, p. 131.
42. Robert G. Hawkins, "Additional Statement," *Foreign Investment and U. S. Jobs,* Hearings before the Subcommittee on International Policy, Committee on International Relations, House of Representatives, 94th Congress, 2nd Session, Part 1 (January–February 1976) (Washington: U. S. Government Printing Office), p. 69.
43. NACLA, "Electronics: The Global Industry," *Latin America and Empire Report,* XI, No. 4 (April 1977).

TABLE 5.7
U.S. Electronics Runaways by Region

Latin America		Asia		Europe[a]	
Mexico	193	Hong Kong	45	Spain	29
Puerto Rico	140	Taiwan	45	Ireland	22
Jamaica	9	India	32	Scotland	18
Barbados	5	Singapore	30	Portugal	14
El Salvador	5	Malaysia	23	Malta	1
Dominican Republic	4	South Korea	19		
Trinidad and Tobago	4	Philippines	17		
Curaçao	3	Thailand	8		
Haiti	3	Indonesia	6		
Bermuda	2	Okinawa	1		
Virgin Island	2				

Source: Compiled by NACLA (1977). Reprinted by permission.
[a]Only includes lower wage, "gateway" areas.

the favorite sites for new plants: Mexico and Puerto Rico dominating in Latin America; Hong Kong and Taiwan in Asia; and, for low-wage countries in Europe (a curious limitation), Spain and Ireland.

In electronics and textiles a great deal of offshore production is for the purpose of reexport or shipment back to the United States. Under provisions 806.30 and 807.00 of the Tariff Schedules of the United States, tariffs on reimports are waived and duties paid only on the value added in assembly. For the electronics industry alone, Table 5.8 indicates the spectacular rise in value of this production between 1966 and 1977. A significant amount of job displacement in these industries results from special trade arrangements.

TABLE 5.8
Value of Electronics Products Imported into the United States under Items 806.30 and 807.00

Product description	1966	1975
Television receivers	$ 9,515	$ 103,379
Television apparatus and parts	26,041	287,736
Radio apparatus and parts	11,904	133,690
Phonographs and parts	11,083	31,051
Semiconductors and parts	51,584	617,499
Electronic memories	12,373	927,415
Consumer electronic products and parts	122,500	1,241,233

Sources: The data in this table is from NACLA (1977). NACLA compiled the data from the following sources: 1970: Economic Factors Affecting the Use of Items 807.00 and 806.30 of the Tariff Schedules of the United States. Tariff Commission Publication 339 (September 1970), Tables 1 and 22; 1975: House of Representatives, Committee on Ways and Means Subcommittee on Trade, Background Information and Compilation of Materials on Items 807.00 and 806.30, Tables 2 and 5. Reprinted by permission.

To specify even further the source of these job-displacing imports, the U.S.-Mexico Border Industrialization Program (which benefits from both provisions 806.03 and 807.00 as well as additional tax and tariff concessions) by 1973 attracted 448 U.S. assembly firms with an investment of over $63 million. More than one-half of this was in electronics followed at some distance by textiles, shoes, sporting goods, toys, and so forth. The vast majority of employees in these assembly plants were women earning $3.50–$5.50 a day by contrast to the U.S. factory worker average wage of $25.00 per day.[44]

Turning from job displacement by industry or sector to the effects *within* industry, the evidence again is unequivocal. The loss of jobs resulting from production abroad tends to be concentrated in the ranks of blue collar, lower wage, skilled, and semiskilled workers. Conversely, the alleged job creation stemming from exported production is among technical and managerial personnel.[45] "The industry structures of the gainers and losers indicate that higher wage, more skilled jobs tend to be created while lower paid, lower skilled jobs are lost to foreign affiliates."[46] And the same point in a more critical vein, "No doubt foreign investment does benefit white collar workers, management, and certain highly skilled sectors of labor. But it is to the disadvantage of other workers, particularly the lower ranks of white and black blue-colar workers."[47]

Exported jobs tend to be in the more labor intensive, traditional manufacturing fields that formerly absorbed the labor of less affluent workers and ethnic minorities. The garment and footwear industries are prototypical. Although *some* new clerical and managerial positions replace these losses, it is doubtful on an individual basis that redundant workers can be retrained to qualify for those jobs involving completely different skills. Moreover, with the exception of several poorly funded and narrow programs of "worker adjustment assistance,"[48] the burden of displacement falls entirely on the individual worker.

Income Shares

Optimistic students of foreign investment who regard job-displacing effects as a temporary aberration find it difficult to explain away its regressive consequences for the distribution of national income (or the "factor shares" accruing to labor

44. NACLA, "Hit and Run: U. S. Runaway Shops on the Mexican Border." *Latin America and Empire Report*, IX, No. 5 (July–August 1975); Raul A. Fernandez, "The Border Industrial Program of the United States–Mexican Border," *The Review of Radical Political Economics*, 5, No. 1 (Spring 1973): 37–52.

45. Jose de la Torre, Robert B. Stobaugh, and Piero Telesio, "U. S. Multinational Enterprise and Changes in the Skill Composition of U. S. Employment," in *American Labor and the Multinational Corporation*, ed. Duane Kujawa (New York: Preager, 1973).

46. Hawkins, 1976, "Additional Statement," p. 68.

47. Robert Gilpin, *The Multinational Corporation and the National Interest*. Committee on Labor and Public Welfare, United States Senate, 93rd Congress, 1st Session (October, 1973) (Washington: U. S. Government Printing Office).

48. Mitchell, *Labor Issues of American International Trade and Investment*.

and capital). Indeed, the proponents of multinational business tend to be silent on this issue, judging perhaps that, in the absence of any effective rebuttal, words are best left unsaid.

The major thrust of Musgrave's[49] important study deals with the consequences of multinational direct investment abroad for aggregate national income and its distribution. These effects are considered more important than short-run consequences for employment, prices, and the balance of payments. Although the procedures for arriving at the conclusions of the study are complex, the results are clear;

> In the long run, perhaps the major effect of foreign investment is through its impact on domestic capital formation in the U.S. To the extent that domestic capital formation is displaced, foreign investment will *reduce the level of income originating within the U.S. as well as the labor share* in national income. While the effects on total income are fairly small, our estimates suggest a *substantial distributional effect adverse to the labor* share.[50]

In principle the method for arriving at these conclusions is fairly straightforward. Those industries in which foreign investment is particularly prominent are analyzed in terms of the relationships between labor input, capital stock, and income generated. Next, incomes are simulated for the foreign capital stock of U.S. direct investors and "transferred" back to the U.S. economy as of 1968. "The difference between the simulated levels of U.S. national income and factor shares and the actual observed levels are then held to be the consequence of having invested that capital abroad."[51] The simulation is performed under two assumptions—"full displacement," which assumes that investment abroad substitutes fully for investment that would have been made in the United States, and "partial displacement," which assumes that a portion of foreign investment responds to new opportunities abroad that would not have existed domestically and thus is not lost to productive use within the country. Table 5.9 indicates the results of this exercise.

Whether one assumes full or partial displacement of domestic investment, the *level of income* originating in the United States would have been between $5–10 billion higher—amounts that are relatively negligible proportionately (i.e., two- to three-tenths of 1% of the actual 1968 level).

However, substantial differences appear in connection with income *distribution* under the two conditions. In the absence of foreign investment labor income would have been $10 billion higher and income to capital $8 billion less—a 4% increase for labor and a 17% reduction for capital. These conclusions derive from the first (full displacement) model, but estimates from the second (partial

---

49. Musgrave, *Direct Investment Abroad and the Multinationals.*
50. *Ibid.*, p. xix, emphasis added.
51. *Ibid.*, p. 91.

TABLE 5.9

Estimated Effect on 1968 Income of Replacing Foreign with Additional Domestic Capital Stock[a]

	Actual value (billions)	Hypothetical values					
		Absolute (billions)		Percentage change			
		Full displacement	Partial displacement[c]	Full displacement	Partial displacement[c]		
Income[b]							
Domestic income originating in United States	$381.8	$392.8	$387.6	+0.3	+0.2		
U.S. national income	390.5	392.8	387.6	+.1	-.1		
U.S. labor income after tax	259.9	269.8	265.1	+3.8	+2.0		
U.S. capital income after tax	47.7	39.6	39.7	+16.8	-16.9		
U.S. tax revenue	82.9	83.4	82.8	+.6	-.1		
Factor shares[d]							
Labor income share (percentage)	77.2	79.7	79.3	+3.2	+2.7		
Capital income share (percentage)	22.8	20.3	20.7	-11.0	-9.2		

Source: Musgrave, 1975.

[a] Elasticity of substitution equal of 0.75.

[b] Income measurements refer to the nonfinancial corporate sector only.

[c] Estimated displacement of 48%. If no displacement is assumed, Lines 1, 3, and 5 remain unchanged at actual 1968 levels, whereas Lines 2 and 4 are raised by the foreign-investment income of $8.7 billion.

[d] Shares refer to labor and capital income before tax as percent of national income (Line 2).

displacement) one differ only in a somewhat lesser gain to labor. Stated conversely, under reasonable assumptions foreign investment may result in a net loss to labor of 3% of national income and a net gain of 10% to capital in a *single year*. When this result is coupled with previous evidence of the rapidly growing volume of foreign investment, the cumulative effect is a markedly more regressive distribution of income in the United States.

Additional evidence is available to support this conclusion. The previously mentioned work of Frank and Freeman shows that foreign investment reduces labor's share of national income between 2–6% yearly.[52] Gilpin argues that "the effect of foreign investment is to decrease the capital stock with which Americans work; this decreases the productivity of American labor and real wages below what would have been if foreign investment had not taken place."[53] Similarly, Barnet and Müller reason that

> the deterioration of income distribution appears to have gathered momentum in the same years during which the process of concentration and globalization in the United States economy also became evident. Mere coincidence in time is not the same as a causal connection, but there is strong evidence for suspecting that the behavior of global corporations has materially contributed to the worsening pattern of income distribution.[54]

Moreover, declining shares of national income can be traced directly to the stratum of skilled and semiskilled blue-collar workers.

Conclusion

On balance we may conclude that the internationalization of capital in the form of foreign investment is producing a new species of class inequality in the United States. Particularly affected are traditional segments of the working class, losing in sources of employment and their former share of national income. Although these effects are clearly demonstrable, advocates of multinational business hasten to add that there are many positive features of this process. The nation as a whole is said to benefit from the capture of new markets, particularly in light of what "would have happened" to corporate profits, jobs, domestic competition from imports, and traditional export markets had capital not gone abroad.

There is no doubt that foreign investment has been both defensive to some extent[55] and enormously profitable to certain segments of the economy, notably

---

52. Frank and Freeman, "The Distributional Consequences of Direct Foreign Investment," p. 165.

53. Gilpin, *The Multinational Corporation and the National Interest*, p. 8.

54. Barnet and Müller, "Global Reach," pp. 121–122.

55. Bob Rowthorn, "Imperialism in the Seventies—Unity or Rivalry," *New Left Review*, 69 (September–October 1971): 31–59.

to the oligopolistic corporations. However, the evidence warrants a good deal of skepticism about alleged positive side effects. There is no conclusive proof of net gains in employment, for example. Moreover, whereas there are certainly some jobs created to absorb structurally (rather than individually) the displaced labor force, recent evidence suggests that this capacity is dwindling.

The early period of multinational expansion may have produced net gains in employment, but "if one looks at the period from 1960 to 1965 and the period from 1965 to 1970 separately, a different picture emerges. (The justification for separating these two periods is that the pace of globalization greatly increased in the second half of the decade and the character of foreign investment changed in significant ways.) It appears, in fact, that the ability of corporations to create new jobs is drastically declining." A study of 74 large corporations sponsored by the Tariff Commission reports that

> in the first half of the decade, the sample companies were creating new jobs at a rate sixty-seven percent higher than the national average, but by the second half their job creation rate was just under five per cent higher. . . . In the latter half of the sixties, the rate of job creation in the entire manufacturing sector registered a decline of more than eight per cent, but the decline for the sample companies was forty per cent.[56]

Without positing the imminent collapse of the U.S. economy, it is clear that a number of far-reaching structural changes are afoot. Suggestively, Barnet and Müller offer the analogy of "Latin Americanization" of the United States—the country becoming increasingly dependent on the export of raw materials rather than manufactures (for example, in 1978 only the heavy export of corn and soybeans averted a disasterous balance of payments deficit aggrieved by increasing petroleum imports), whereas the standard of living declines for the majority of the population: "Our large, prosperous middle class, long considered the foundation of American stability, is increasingly squeezed by shrinking employment opportunities, high taxes, and inflationary prices."[57] In a similar vein, Gilpin asks "is the United States as a nation repeating the error committed by other once great economic powers such as the Netherlands in the seventeenth century and Great Britain in the nineteenth century of overinvesting abroad to the detriment of the home economy?"[58] He concludes that this has been the case in recent years as the United States increasingly became a rentier economy of exported production.

Those who hold that the United States is overinvested abroad to the detriment of the domestic economy (both in the short run for labor, but also in the long run

56. Barnet and Müller, "Global Reach," pp. 127–128.
57. *Ibid.*, p. 100.
58. Gilpin, *The Multinational Corporation and the National Interest*, p. xiv.

for capital) point to a number of distressing indicators. In the quest for quicker and easier profits abroad U.S. corporations have failed to develop technological innovations that would maintain their superiority in foreign markets. No major technological revolutions have come along in the last 20 years (although some now see that possibility in genetic engineering) and during that period exported production has steadily reached into the more technically sophisticated ranks of domestic production. Perhaps partly as a result, the overall performance of U.S. multinationals has been inferior to that of German and Japanese firms. Citing research on this point Hymer and Rowthorn conclude that "the bad performance of the United Kingdom and the United States *could* be explained by the fact that their firms have tended to expand by investing rather than exporting."[59]

Defensive arguments of the multinational firms not withstanding, critics claim that there *are* many areas of vitally needed domestic investment in fields such as energy, transportation, urban redevelopment, and environmental protection. Although profits may not be as quickly or easily realized in these areas, their long-term advantages for the national interest include potential job creation, a more egalitarian distribution of income, reclaimed technological superiority, and a general enhancement of the quality of life.[60] Whether recent challenges to U.S. hegemony in the global economy will lead to a revitalization of the domestic economy remains an open question. Assuming this task were undertaken, it would require many years to reverse the social and economic consequences of the internationalization of capital.

In most of the arguments reviewed here and in the research evidence cited for their evaluation, the effects of the internationalization of capital are treated from the standpoint of structural changes among aggregates. Although this is necessary at one level, it tends to obscure the fact that the problem is ultimately experienced by individual workers and their families. Even though the effects on individuals are difficult to measure, we must not be lured into any technocratic myopia that sees the problem only in the analysis rather than among the people whose experience provides the statistics. If it is beguiling to think about the reallocation of "human capital," this does not diminish the facts of human suffering.

When workers lose their jobs they also lose the intangibles of self-esteem and respect in the eyes of their families and communities. They lose, obviously, income and what is sometimes more disastrous, their health insurance benefits (the cost of continuing coverage often exceeding unemployment payments). Sometimes pension rights are lost, mortgages foreclosed, and family savings depleted to the point of bankruptcy in the effort to keep afloat. Research has

59. Stephen Hymer and Robert Rowthorn, "Multinational Corporations and International Oligopoly: The Non-American Challenge," in *The International Corporation: A Symposium*, ed. Charles P. Kindleberger (Cambridge: MIT Press, 1970), p. 84.
60. Gilpin, *The Multinational Corporation and the National Interest.*

shown that displaced workers experience inordinately long periods of unemployment and, if they are fortunate enough to find subsequent employment, their occupational status and income is typically lower.[61] One study indicates that where nearly all workers whose jobs were eliminated by plant closure suffered long-term income loss (i.e., in those jobs they found afterwards), those who accepted retraining subsequently did worse than those who elected not to.[62] With the exception of such dubious retraining efforts, it should be stressed that the costs of displacement are borne entirely by the individual worker with no real responsibility attaching to government or the firm. Contrary to structural analyses of temporary displacement and readjustment, the effects on individual workers tend to be degrading and permanent.

Institutional Consequences of the Internationalization of Capital

For those not given to abstract speculation, the concrete evidence presented so far indicates that the effects on the level of employment, occupational structure, and national income portend qualitative changes in social class structure. These tangible consequences of the internationalization of capital are closely associated with a set of changing institutional relationships that are germane to theoretical ideas on class structure. We shall briefly characterize these institutional changes under several headings and subsequently integrate them into the analysis of social class.

Corporate Oligopoly

It has been shown in Tables 5.2 and 5.3 that investment abroad is dominated by the very largest U.S. firms whose share of internationally derived profits is greater than their domestic share. Moreover, the investment and profits of these companies abroad are growing faster than the domestic economy. When these facts are coupled with the growing concentration of corporate assets within the United States stemming from mergers and acquisitions, the familiar trend toward corporate oligopoly is more fully documented. What this analysis adds to a domestic appraisal is that the more vital contribution to concentration of corporate assets comes from the advantages accruing to the giant firms in their control of foreign markets.

Size is a major determinant of overseas expansion and, in turn, provides the multinational with a distinct advantage in the home market because of its better

---

61. Bluestone and Harrison, *Capital and Communities*, chap. 3.
62. James L. Stern, "Consequences of Plant Closure," *Journal of Human Resources*, 7, No. 1 (Winter 1972): 3–25.

profit position and ability to reimport for domestic consumption goods assembled in its offshore production sites. Two trends are closely related. On one hand, "almost 60 percent of U.S. overseas assets are monopolized by the nation's 45 largest corporations"[63] or 1% of all the U.S. firms with operations abroad earn 90% of foreign profits (Table 5.2). On the other hand, in 1974 "the 500 largest industrials (accounted for) 65 percent of the sales of all U. S. industrial corporations, 76 percent of the employees, and 79 percent of the profits,"[64] proportions that have been rising steadily in recent decades.[65]

Organized Labor

Although difficult to quantify, a corollary to the growth of corporate oligopoly is the relative decline in the power of organized labor. The ease with which capital has moved abroad in recent years makes the threat and reality of plant closing or production cutbacks powerful tools for promoting labor acquiesence. Babson regards this new corporate advantage over organized labor as far more important than any net gain or loss in jobs,

> for the underlying question is not how many people actually are laid off, but what effect the threat of being laid off has on the balance of power between workers and owners. In this case, the option to move abroad does not have to be exercised by management to achieve its desired effects. Wages can be driven down, organizing efforts diffused and the speed of the line increased simply because the option exists. All the company has to do is periodically threaten (or legally "suggest") that it might have to move overseas if workers make "unreasonable" demands. Older and married workers afraid of losing their jobs, and not being able to find another, would become cautious about the sort of demands they make on employers, while the pressures would increase on conservative union bureaucracies to suppress rank and file militants.[66]

Illustratively, Babson cites the following case:

> In 1971, Frigidaire started laying off workers in its Dayton, Ohio plant and threatened to close down production altogether if it could not reduce labor costs. Harold Campbell, the general manager, announced that the company was considering three alternative strategies for getting the company out of the red: having another domestic manufacturer build Frigidaire appliances; relocating its plant outside the Dayton labor market; or having Frigidaire appliances manufactured in Japan. Faced with this threat, the IUE local renegotiated its contract, accepting wage reductions of up to $20 a week and a two-year wage freeze in return for the

63. Babson, "The Multinational Corporation and Labor," p. 19.
64. Fortune Double 500 Directory (New York: Time Inc., 1974), p. 3.
65. Willard F. Mueller, "Recent Changes in Industrial Concentration and the Current Merger Movement," in American Society, Inc.: Studies in the Social Structure and Political Economy of the United States, 2nd edition, ed. Maurice Zeitlin (Chicago: Rand McNally, 1977).
66. Babson, "The Multinational Corporation and Labor," p. 26.

rehiring of 850 workers and a promise from Frigidaire to keep production in Dayton.[67]

Another source of weakness within the ranks of labor stems from the fact that the major federations are divided on the issue. Both the AFL–CIO and the UAW have taken strong stands against the runaway shop, items 806.30 and 807.00 of the Tariff Schedules, and in support of the ill-fated Hartke–Burke (trade and tax deferral reform) bill. However, the Teamsters, whose members are drawn mainly from the service sector rather than manufacturing, have remained indifferent. Moreover, the UAW and AFL–CIO are split with respect to the policies they advocate for preventing the runaway shop—the UAW stressing greater efforts at full employment while avoiding protectionist measures, and the AFL–CIO advocating protectionism and closer regulation of the multinationals.[68]

Reform measures supported by organized labor have fallen on deaf ears in Congress and it appears labor's power in the legislative arena is as severely weakened as in negotiation with management. Theoretically the appropriate labor response would be cross-national organization covering key industries and affiliates. Although there are several recent examples of binational union cooperation within particular industries (e.g., the automotive industry in Europe), any labor international involving U.S. unions appears as the remotest of possibilities.

The Competitive Sector and Migrant Labor

So far attention has focused on the institutional consequences of the internationalization of capital for the dominant partners of the U.S. economy, the oliogopolistic corporations and organized labor. This excludes small enterprise and the unorganized and migratory sections of the labor force—those junior partners whose livelihood is indirectly affected by changes in the more dominant sectors of the economy.

Movements in the internationalization of capital have combined with domestic trends toward monopoly severely limiting the operation of smaller, less unionized, lower wage, more labor intensive firms that make up the competitive sector of the U.S. economy.[69] The competitive sector is subject to dual pressures. On one hand, it is highly vulnerable to cheaper imports and the incursions of big capital into its traditional provinces such as light manufacturing, construction, and retail sales, all of which are becoming vertically integrated. On the other hand, the competitive sector is increasingly the locus for job seeking by new and displaced workers.[70] As a result, the competitive sector is more "over-

67. *Ibid.*, p. 27.
68. Alberto Martinelli, "Multinational Corporations, National Economic Policies, and Labor Unions," in *Stress and Contradiction in Modern Capitalism,* eds. Leon N. Lindberg, Robert Alford, Colin Crough, and Claus Offe (Lexington, Mass.: D. C. Heath, 1975).
69. James O'Connor, *The Fiscal Crisis of the State* (New York: St. Martin's Press, 1973).
70. Bluestone and Harrison, *Capital and Communities,* p. 74.

crowded" in terms of both the number of enterprises competing for dwindling market shares and the number of available workers. The state attempts, without great success, to manage this dilemma through public employment, "manpower" programs, and unemployment or welfare benefits. Nevertheless, because the forces producing the situation continue, public aid recipients, hard-core unemployment, and welfare dependency continue to grow.

Competitive sector firms now faced with keener competition naturally seek ways to reduce production costs generally and labor costs specifically. Lacking the resources of multinationals to export production to areas of cheap labor, they frequently resort to the converse—the employment of "imported" labor in the presence of immigrant workers. As we noted in Chapter 2: "Not all enterprises can take advantage, however, of technology and labor reserves in the periphery. Competitive firms may lack the capital for large scale technological innovation. Even middle-sized enterprises lack the experience, 'know how,' and resources to venture themselves into a foreign country. Thus, important layers of American capitalism continue to be dependent on finding cheap sources of labor in the local market."

Chapter 2 examines international migration in detail. Here we need only add to that analysis the observation that it ties directly into the international movement of capital as both affect the organization of social class. As a result of the internationalization of capital, the U.S. is witnessing an internationalization of labor similar to the Western European countries.[71]

The result of this process is the creation of a new "underclass" of disenfranchised workers that may be used to discipline domestic workers, chasten their demands, and to absorb many of their jobs if need be. The net result is to shore-up the ailing competitive sector to the disadvantage of the less privileged, minority, and female elements of the domestic labor force.

Authority Relations in Industry

The distribution of authority within enterprise is another determinant of class position since it affects the organization of production, occupational benefits, and mobility on a localized basis. The evidence reviewed suggests that the internationalization of capital has resulted in a shift of the industrial work force from line to staff positions—the creation of a proportionately larger segment of professional, technical, and managerial personnel. This shift is fed by two streams—elimination or displacement of skilled blue-collar workers and increasing managerial functions that coordinate global production. This, along with other technical advances in industry, has resulted in "the extension of manage-

71. Stephen Castles and Godula Kosack, *Immigrant Workers and Class Struggle in Western Europe* (London: Oxford University Press, 1973); Manuel Castells, "Immigrant Workers and Class Struggles in Advanced Capitalism: The Western European Experience," *Politics and Society*, 5 (1975): 33–66.

rial control, in the sense of the effective power of managers to determine the policies which govern the fate of the large-scale corporation."[72]

The same trend has expanded the ranks of white-collar clerical workers who, however, view themselves as belonging to management and participate in the delegation of authority.[73] This circumstance provides additional disadvantages for skilled and semiskilled blue-collar workers. Beyond the weakness engendered by the threat and reality of runaway industry, labor that remains in domestic employment is both less numerous and less in possession of authority over its own ranks. This relative powerlessness is conducive to economistic settlements with management where job security and a semblance of labor control outweigh more aggressive demands for benefits and better working conditions, and where wage increases are pegged to productivity gains. Generally industrial class conflict is dampened and encapsulated from spreading into broader political questions.[74]

Urban and Regional Effects

Fears over the consequences of foreign investment expressed by organized labor are matched only by those of local and regional officials who have seen their economies devastated by the flight of jobs and tax revenues. Granted, many of these losses have been at the hands of U.S. suburbs and the "sunbelt,"[75] but movement abroad has contributed significantly to the general trend and in some regions has been the major setback. As Barnet and Müller frame the general problem:

> The immediate and noticeable impacts of the multinationals are felt in cities and towns where factories are situated or goods are sold. The essential strategy of the international company makes it an antagonist of local interests everywhere. The local community in the United States has the same ambivalent relationship to global corporations as do underdeveloped countries. There is always a price to absentee ownership. The company president in New York cannot be expected to concern himself with the traffic, housing, pollution, or fiscal problems of Schenectady or any other city where his plants may be situated. This is no less true, as is now becoming more common, when the president of the parent company lives in Tokyo. Local communities in the United States face the same fundamental issues of public policy, as do Latin American republics. How much foreign—i.e., non-local-investment do they wish to accept? On what terms? What does it mean to have the local economy controlled from outside?[76]

72. Giddens, *The Class Structures of the Advanced Societies*, p. 172.
73. David Lockwood, *The Blackcoated Worker* (London: Allen and Unwin, 1958).
74. Ralf Dahrendorf, *Class and Class Conflict in Industrial Society* (Stanford: Stanford University Press, 1959); Giddins, *The Class Structures of the Advanced Societies.*
75. Alfred Watkins and David Perry, *Sun-Belt Cities* (Beverly Hills: Sage, 1978).
76. Barnet and Müller, "Global Reach," p. 152.

The northeastern United States, and New England in particular, have suffered most from runaway industry. Not only is the region's industrial plant old, it specialized heavily in such candidates for exported production as textiles, shoes, electronics, and home appliances.

New England serves in this respect as a possible model of the entire country's future, for it was both the first area to develop industrially and one of the first to stagnate and decline. In the 1880's companies had already begun to move textile production, the region's major industry, south. Now, in the last decade, after 90 years of disinvestment in textiles and a wide range of other industries New England's average weekly wage is $8-$10 below the national average, while unemployment has been appreciably higher than national figures in four of the last five recessions. In October of 1971, for example, when national unemployment stood at 5.8 percent, New England's was at 7.8 percent, with a half dozen of its manufacturing cities over 10 percent. The export of production clearly has not aided New England's workers; there is no reason to assume it will serve the long-run interests of workers nationally.[77]

Although older manufacturing cities have been hardest hit in this process, textile centers in the South and electronics throughout the country have also lost jobs. This contributes to the decline in employment and population occurring in most of the nation's large central cities since 1960.[78] As a consequence, the cities find themselves in a familiar double-bind. On one hand, local tax revenue falls in the absence of former contributing workers and businesses as well as the sales they generated. On the other hand, local expenditures rise in public assistance for those left behind. Analysts of the New York fiscal crisis see this situation spreading to other cities, tracing its origins to the loss of jobs (over one-half million in New York between 1969 and 1976) and, ultimately, to broader movements of capital.[79]

Similar shocks to the local economy have been repeated in urban areas throughout the country. A typical example was reported by the *Wall Street Journal* (April 5, 1979) under the headline "Sioux City Still Suffers after Its Top Employer Moves Business Abroad—Zenith's Pullout a Year Ago in Face of Import Rivalry Sends Continuing Ripples."

Zenith was the biggest employer in this manufacturing and meatpacking city of 80,000 population. When business was going strong, nearly 2,000 workers made parts for stereo and television sets in a huge plant on the edge of town. But Zenith closed the plant a year ago. It moved its business to Mexico and Taiwan to compete better with the Japanese and other imports to the U.S., and the 1,400 remaining

77. Babson, "The Multinational Corporation and Labor," pp. 27–28.
78. William B. Neenan, *The Political Economy of Urban Areas* (Chicago: Markham, 1972).
79. E.g., William K. Tabb, "The New York City Fiscal Crisis," in *Marxism and the Metropolis: New Perspectives in Urban Political Economy*, eds. William K. Tabb and Larry Sawers (New York: Oxford University Press, 1978).

workers were out on the street. . . . Besides affecting laid-off workers, the closing dealt a blow to small-business men who supplied the plant with parts. . . . Some prominent people have been caught in the rubble. Three of the biggest home builders in town have gone out of business. Longstanding real-estate firms have been financially shaken.

The Sioux City experience may be atypical in the sense that few cities have lost their major employer at one stroke. But major cities like Chicago have seen similar closings (especially in the electronics industry) so often that their cumulative effect is likely the same.

No doubt the "urban crisis" stems primarily from the redistribution of domestic investment and profit. The export of production abroad contributes directly, if incrementally, to the loss of manufacturing jobs. It also contributes to the exodus of corporate headquarters of firms with overseas production from the cities and, occasionally, from the country.[80] The important question for the future of the urban crisis is whether the travels of these firms and factories to the suburbs and Sunbelt areas are simply a way station en route abroad.

Patterns of Foreign Investment in the United States

As we have shown, although foreign investment in the U.S. is substantial ($62 billion in 1973 or about 43% of U.S. long term investment abroad) and increasing, its consequences for the domestic economy are less disruptive (than U.S. investment in other countries) since most of it is in the form of portfolio investment rather than direct ownership and control. Despite the fact that foreign companies acquired 340 U.S. firms valued at $5.5 billion between 1976–1978, the larger investors still prefer equity. For example, Rhone-Poulenc "the ninth-largest chemical company in the world and the third-largest of all firms in France" recently purchased 20% of Chicago based Morton–Norwich explaining, "we'd rather have a smaller piece of a bigger pie."[81] Xenophobic worries about Arab investments in real estate and Japanese in tourism notwithstanding, the United States is in no danger of losing control over its domestic economy.

But, the evidence of true cross-penetration of capital is remarkable and the object of concern in leading financial circles as indicated by the following lead articles in the *Wall Street Journal*. On November 24, 1978 they reported a "Bank Invasion—Many Foreign Lenders Set Up Branches Here, Offer Stiff Competition." The article goes on to say that the number of foreign banks in the United States increased from 152 in late 1974 to 290, while improving their share of big business loans from 12% to 17%. In addition to serving their own multinationals, foreign banks were moving into all of the conventional investment fields.

80. Leland S. Burns and Wing Ning Pang, "Big Business in the Big City: Corporate Headquarters in the C.B.D.," *Urban Affairs Quarterly*, 12, No. 4 (June 1977): 533–544.
81. *Chicago Sun-Times*, "French firm goes international because 'nobody knew about us,'" July 2, 1978, p. 12.

On April 20, 1979 the *Journal* announced "Foreign Firms Step Up Takeovers in the U.S. and Worry is Rising." In the first quarter of the year, 63 acquisitions of domestic corporations by foreign buyers had taken place, up from 37 in the previous year. Especially bothersome was the fact that several symbols of Americana were passing into foreign control. A French group had taken over the Korvette's retail chain. Another group from Germany purchased 42% of the Great Atlantic and Pacific Tea Company (A & P). And Woolworth's, the most familiar Main Street landmark, was being eyed by Canadian interests.

Most celebrated is the foreign acquisition of real estate and farm land. Under the lead "Pieces of America," the *Journal* of September 26, 1979 reported "Real-Estate Purchases by Foreigners Climb, Stirring Wide Debate." Counted in the billions for a single year, much of this investment is in commercial buildings and private homes. But it was the purchase of farm land that aroused greatest concern resulting in legislation signed by President Carter in October of 1979 requiring the registration of new foreign ownership with the Department of Agriculture.

This trend toward cross-penetration is recent and may prove highly cyclical. Its dramatic rise is closely related to the declining value of the dollar among international currencies. In consequence, purchases in the United States are relatively cheap and provide the foreign bargain hunter with the additional advantages of political stability and favorable tax laws.

Problems of unemployment and regional decline have led to some unusual concessions to attract foreign industry. Perhaps the best known case is the Volkswagen plant in East Huntingdon, Pennsylvania. In an account appropriately entitled "The Rabbit that Ate Pennsylvania," Chernow claims

> Governor Milton Shapp pledged more than $70 million to the German automaker if it would set up shop in the state. He turned Pennsylvanians, willy-nilly, into Volkswagen stockholders, hitching their fortunes to a single, shaky corporation. In the annals of American corporate rip-offs, the Great Volkswagen Giveaway looks as if it will easily surpass the 1971 Congressional loan to Lockheed. As we shall see, it also sheds a chilling light on the plight of New York City and other localities that must pay ransom to corporations in order to weather the present recession.[82]

Promising some 5000 jobs for the production of 200,000 VW Rabbits each year, the plant was sought after by officials in Maryland and Ohio allowing the firm to play these against Pennsylvania for the best arrangement. Evidently the strategy was successful as Chernow lists the following concessions VW received:

> (1) Pennsylvania will spend $40 million to buy and refurbish the Chrysler plant, then lease it back to Volkswagen over a 30-year term. For the first 20 years, Volkswagen will pay interest at the microscopic rate of one and three-quarter percent.

82. Ron Chernow, "The Rabbit that Ate Pennsylvania: Governor Shapp Builds Volkswagen at $70-million Hutch." *Mother Jones*, 3, No. 1 (January 1978): p. 19.

(2) The two big Pennsylvania pension funds—for state employees and for teachers—will pitch in a $6 million loan to Volkswagen at 8.5 percent interest over 15 years.

(3) The state will float $10 million in bonds for a special rail spur to whisk the Rabbits to Chessies B & O Railroad. Also, it will issue another $15 million in highway construction bonds so that Rabbit-laden trucks can speed down to the Pennsylvania Turnpike and other local arteries.

(4) The local authorities, with noble self-effacement, will forego 95 percent of VW's taxes for the first two years, 50 percent for the next three. Homeowners take note: the giant German automaker will pay $3,550 to East Huntingdon township in property taxes this year.[83]

The risks involved in this venture are assumed largely by Pennsylvania taxpayers. If it fails, if the cars do not sell or if the dollar advances on the German mark making German-built Rabbits cheaper, the state has incurred heavy financial losses. If it succeeds the investment may be recovered in jobs and taxes, with the profits going to German owners. Losses will be socialized and profits privitized.

An ironic footnote to this story is that once the plant began production it was hit by a wildcat strike of United Auto Workers (UAW) union locals. As a strong advocate of manufacture within the country the UAW had also enticed VW with contracts well below "Detroit scale." This, in turn, was designed to attract assembly plants of Toyota, Datsun, and Honda, all adding substantially to the UAW job roles. But, the Pennsylvania locals had little sympathy with these international manuevers and led a successful walk-out under the banner "No Money, No Bunny."

At the moment it is impossible to judge whether these developments that are so closely linked to the value of international currencies are typical. Nevertheless, when the elimination of artificial supports of the U.S. dollar abroad is coupled with the new strength of other national economies and rising energy costs, it is safe to assume that the domestic economy will continue to intertwine with the international.

Conclusion

In this section concern has shifted from a quantitative assessment of the major occupational and income effects of the internationalization of capital to a more qualitative evaluation of changing institutional arrangements. These changes are difficult to demonstrate conclusively owing to their complex and subtle nature. Moreover, constant recognition must be given the facts that (a) the changes described are not singularly caused by the internationalization of capital (in contrast to contributory domestic events); and (b), these tendencies may be offset by forces at the national level. When all is said, however, some consequences can be specified precisely whereas others are plausible and merit closer attention.

83. *Ibid.*, p. 22.

From an institutional standpoint the United States is undergoing fundamental realignments in the position and power of labor, the corporate oligopoly, and the multinationals themselves. In broad strokes, the former is losing some of the bargaining power it once held whereas the latter are becoming stronger with respect to both labor and government. Indirectly, these changes are adversely felt in the competitive sector and among the least privileged and immigrant workers. The same forces have focused effects in regional decline and urban crises. Any one of these themes could be pursued in its more fine-grained distributional consequences. For present purposes these themes will be integrated around the concept of class structure, which is a basic feature of social organization in its own right and also mediates other forms of social change.

The Changing Structure of Social Class

Obviously, the internationalization of capital is a complex process operating at many levels from the life chances of individuals in the advanced and developing societies to the fate of nations within the world system. For our purposes, attention focuses on those consequences that can be traced directly to the class structures of the advanced countries. This focus is guided partly by considerations of substantive interest and previous neglect, and partly by the theoretical assumption that social class is one prominent determinant of social organization and individual lifestyle in developed societies. The concept social class—or more vaguely "stratification"—has been clouded with ambiguity. Usages range from popular bromides about the "great middle class" to psychologistic self-perceptions of social standing and very abstract notions of social formations. Recently, a number of contributions have helped reclaim the concept of class for sociological analysis by returning to the essentials of Marx and Weber. Following in the endeavor, we accept the view that "classes constitute common positions within social *relations* of production, and this means that classes must always be understood in terms of their relationship to other classes. Thus, the theoretical starting point of a class analysis is to decode the social relations of production within a particular society in order to uncover the class positions which they determine."[84]

The *social relations of production* are understood to consist of patterns of human interaction that arise out of, and in turn reshape, particular forms of material production.[85] The latter, constituting the *means of production* (i.e. technique), combine with the social relations in the overall organization or *mode*

---

84. Wright and Perrone, "Marxist Class Categories and Income Inequality," p. 33.

85. Cf., Harry Braverman, *Labor and Monopoly Capitalism: The Degradation of Work in the Twentieth Century* (New York: Monthly Review, 1974).

of production.[86] Class analysis based on "decoding" the social relations of production endeavors, first, to determine how these relations are affected by the internationalization of capital, and second, how the new social relations qualitatively change the nature and distribution of inequality. Even within this delimited arena the effects of the internationalization of capital are diverse. For the sake of clarity we shall consider the main effects under four headings.

Internationalization of a Capitalist Class

Although in its early stages of formation, and still encumbered by rival national interests, the contours of an international capitalist class are emerging. In its implications for class structure this development will prove as monumental as its historical antecedent—the shift from local entrepreneurial to national conglomerate capital.[87] One indicator of this trend is the cross-penetration of investment by country and firm in the practice of joint ventures. While competing on one level, many U.S. firms have invested heavily in Japanese electronics[88] and European manufacturing and bond markets.[89] Conversely, as we have seen, foreign portfolio investment in the United States is even more common.

> The large firms of the world are all competing for these various sources of future growth, but in an oligopolistic rather than a cut throat way. They recognize their mutual interdependence and strive to share in the pie without destroying it. As they do so, they come to be less and less dependent on their home country's economy for their profits, and more and more dependent on the world economy. Conflicts between firms on the basis of nationality are thereby transformed into international oligopolistic market sharing and collusion.[90]

Joint ventures are only one leg of this international cooperation. Regional markets such as the EEC bring together European firms with those of the United States and other countries to coordinate investment plans. The world's oil companies, by virtue of their ability to pass on price increases to consumers, collaborate more closely with OPEC countries than with any national interest. This collaboration is facilitated by foreign assignments of managerial personnel and the employment of foreign nationals. "The ability of the international capitalist system to extend its domain by broadening and 'internationalizing' the ranks of its managers and even ruling class must be taken seriously and its limitations realistically evaluated. This represents the 'Merrill, Lynch, and Yamini' solution to the energy crisis."[91]

86. Giddens, *The Class Structure of the Advanced Societies*, p. 86.
87. C. Wright Mills, *The Power Elite* (New York: Oxford University Press, 1956).
88. NACLA, 1977, "Hit and Run."
89. Hymer, "The Internationalization of Capital."
90. *Ibid.*, p. 98.
91. Joe Stork, *Middle East Oil and the Energy Crisis* (New York: Monthly Review, 1975), pp. 283–284.

have become the dominant criteria of upward mobility and a reasonable livelihood. Obviously, education has long been an important determinant of social standing. But, something new has been added. Namely, skilled labor and nonprofessional or nontechnical education are attributes of declining occupational currency. On a broad set of dimensions (e.g., income, authority in industry, power in labor disputes) the class position of blue-collar workers is deteriorating with respect to mobility and life chances.

The explanation for this lies in a structural shift in the composition of the labor force that has displaced large numbers of blue-collar jobs due in large part to the export of jobs. Redundant workers are not easily retrained and reabsorbed at higher skill levels. Moreover, it is questionable whether at present and in the immediate future the U.S. economy will be capable of creating new technical and professional positions at anywhere near the continuing (perhaps escalating) rate of job displacement. A reasonable prediction is that more new and displaced workers will be pushed downward into the ranks of the competitive sector—a question we shall consider shortly.

Several consequences follow from the increasing professionalization of modal locations in the class structure. First, these newly professionalized groups see their positions and interests as coincident with top management and capital, at least in the short run. This suggests a decline in conventional labor–management conflict and the aggrandizement of the power of capital. Second, and somewhat related, the new groups of professional, technical, and clerical workers are not necessarily better off. The appearance of mobility derives only from an anachronistic comparison with the class structure of earlier times when blue-collar jobs predominated. In *structural* terms the new class of professional workers may occupy a position equivalent to the old working class and, indeed, certain elements of it such as clerical workers may actually be worse off and downwardly mobile.[96] This interpretation is suggested indirectly by the evidence on national income shares. Third, the positions of this new professional class are characteristically volatile. They are challenged by the aspirations of displaced workers, subject to escalating educational standards, and vulnerable to major shifts in product lines (as in the case of the depressed aerospace industry).

Popular belief in upward mobility through "professional advancement" is now questionable. Professionalization is now less a matter of social mobility than a symptom of class realignment occasioned, in part, by the export of working class positions and the rise of international capital.

The Immiseration of the Competitive Sector

We have examined the dual pressures on the competitive sector resulting from the invasion of its traditional preserves by oligopolistic capital and its exported

96. Giddens, *The Class Structure of the Advanced Societies*; S. M. Miller, "Comparative Social Mobility," *Current Sociology*, 1, 1960.

production on one hand, and from the swelling of its labor pool by displaced and immigrant workers on the other. The resultant "overcrowding" produces keener competition among small firms in a dwindling market and among overabundant workers. Petty entrepreneurs are "proletarianized," but the more substantial consequence of this process is to introduce competitive rivalries among workers divided along occupational, racial, and nationality lines.

The declining, blue-collar, unionized labor force endeavors to maintain its status by restricting its ranks to new entrants in exchange for job security and productivity-linked benefits. New and displaced workers in the competitive sector find it difficult to move up to positions that are either evaporating or closely guarded by union patronage. On the other side, hard-pressed employers in the competitive sector increasingly turn to a more docile and exploitable labor force in the presence of illegal immigrants. If we can trust the estimates, the number of undocumented workers in the United States constitutes about 15% of the 100 million available workers (at least 7% of whom are presently unemployed), which is far from a marginal phenomenon, particularly for the competitive sector where they are disproportionately concentrated (cf. Chapter 2).

These circumstances lead to the immiseration of increasing numbers of petty entrepreneurs and workers in the competitive sector. Profits are held low in the absence of room to expand and wages are kept down by labor reserves. Although the welfare roles reflect some of the consequences of this situation, they are the tip of an iceberg made up of unemployment, underemployment, unreported (i.e., long-term) unemployment, "voluntary" and early retirement, attenuated potential employment (e.g., spouses), and so forth. The competitive sector has become the dumping ground of oligopolistic and international capital.

An intriguing recent development that relates to our general theme of global interdependence and the previous discussion of the urban economy in peripheral societies (Chapter 3) is the appearance of an informal economy in the *advanced* countries. As a dumping ground the competitive sector has definite limits that shade into (informal) underemployment and unremunerated work. Structural changes in the manufacturing and saturation of the service sector imply a labor surplus outside formal boundaries. Employment in manufacturing is certain to decline in the 1980s and since the early 1970s the service sector has abated in its compensatory expansion.

> In the short term employment in manufacturing industry is likely to decline, partly due to the need to be competitive and to maintain high productivity by increasing output per man, and partly due to the restructuring of capital and the shift of certain kinds of industrial production to the newly industrializing countries. Unemployment in more advanced countries may be a form of hidden aid subsidy to the less industrially advanced. At the same time the cost of providing services is increasing so that we are obliged to serve ourselves in banks, shops and filling stations or provide services for ourselves with our own tools and capital equipment.

178

A new point may be introduced here: It may be more satisfying and rewarding to produce our own service or to engage in reciprocal exchanges with others.[97]

Pahl distinguishes between the household economy, the communal economy (the exchange of services among neighbors), and the informal economy proper (involving cash payment) arguing from his own exploratory research and other work that these are expanding to the point of constituting a key feature of advanced capitalist economies. Through do-it-yourself services *and* production (e.g., of food), new "work exchanges" that we see in the United States (causing real concern to the Internal Revenue Service), and informal transitory employment, a new phenomenon is emerging with apt parallels in the Third World.

Indeed, another analysis suggests that the new informal economy in the advanced societies may serve the formal sector in ways that are analogous to our discussion of the urban economy in the periphery. Proceeding from the global crisis of accumulation and surplus labor in the advanced countries, now hemmed-in by the overexploitation of the Third World, an "internal solution" may be sought: "One option is for capitalism to expand these marginal sectors whose features are low wages, irregular employment and super-exploitation of labour, by diverting some of the economic activities which were previously carried out in the great industrial concerns."[98] Although the informal economy of the advanced societies pales in its significance when compared to the role these activities play in the periphery, the important point (in addition to its probable expansion) is its theoretical significance underlining the absolute necessity of understanding these developments from the standpoint of the international determination of the labor process and class structure.

The Contribution of the Public Sector to a Class State

Far from being a passive observer or regulator of this process, the state participates directly in the forces of class determination. As numerous analysts have argued[99] the state performs the dual functions of providing the conditions for the accumulation of capital and of legitimation of its consequences. In connection with the first of these functions, the state provides the *social capital* necessary for profitable private accumulation in the form of "social consumption" or the

97. R. E. Pahl, "Employment, Work and the Domestic Division of Labor," *International Journal of Urban and Regional Research*, 4:1 (March 1980): 5.

98. Enzo Mingione, "Capitalist Crisis, Neo-Dualism, and Marginalization," *International Journal of Urban and Regional Research*, 2:2 (June 1978): 215.

99. For example, O'Connor, *The Corporations and the State*; Alan Wolfe, "New Directions in the Marxist Theory of Politics," *Politics and Society*, IX, No. 2 (1974): 131–159; David Gold, Clarence Y. H. Lo, and Erik Olin Wright, "Recent Developments in Marxist Theories of the Capitalist State," parts I and II, *Monthly Review*, 27, No. 5 (October 1975): 29–43; and No. 6 (November, 1975): 36–51.

projects and services that lower the costs of the reproduction of labor (e.g., transportation, health services, unemployment insurance, and social security), and "social investment" or projects and services to increase the productivity of labor (e.g., infrastructure, education). With regard to the second function of legitimation the state provides *social expenses* in the form of welfare and social control.[100]

In the area of foreign investment and the export of production, the state subsidizes multinational corporations through tax deferral and special tariff provisions on one hand, while attempting to legitimate the contradictions of this process with manpower programs and worker adjustment assistance on the other. At the same time, state policy on immigrant labor vacillates between benign and aggressive enforcement within a policy that ultimately ensures a cheap and disposable labor reserve. The state is involved in a basic contradiction since its efforts to curb domestic inflation, unemployment, and income inequality are frustrated by the foreign investment that it encourages and that contributes directly to these problems. O'Connor's[101] description of the fiscal crisis of the state, although cast strictly on the domestic level, can be fruitfully extended to the global economy, which contributes significantly to fiscal woes at home.

The state deals with these contradictions in contradictory ways that reflect the great political power of the oligopolistic corporations. Although tax-payer rebellions lash out at the most visible targets of public services to the local community, organized labor has been unsuccessful at mobilizing public support for the regulation of the multinationals. The connection between domestic ills and international business has been successfully mystified by the "research" organizations of the multinational corporations and their academic collaborators. With few exceptions, Congress has sided with the multinational lobby. Although the situation is rife with organized political action, the more characteristic response has been fratricidal conflict among variously affected occupational, racial, and nationality groups within the working class. For example, the conflict shows up as union resistance to new programs for equal opportunity and xenophobic agitation to do something about the presumed threat to U.S. jobs from migrant workers (cf. Chapter 2).

Of course, historically the classical response of the state of the occupational dislocations in manufacturing and agriculture has been the expansion of welfare services and, particularly, public employment. As the various analyses of economic and fiscal crisis suggest,[102] and as contemporary austerity policies demonstrate, this recourse is increasingly unavailable. In the short run the fundamental contradiction of increasingly internationalized capital *and* of the immiseration of broad segments of labor that our analysis points to can only grow in severity.

100. O'Connor, *The Corporations and the State.*
101. *Ibid.*
102. *Ibid.* Manuel Castells, *The Economic Crisis and the American Society* (Princeton: Princeton University Press, 1980).

Conclusion

This chapter has pursued several closely related purposes. We began with the premise that recent advances in the study of development emphasizing dependency or (better) an interdependent global political economy, ironically fail to carry the position to its logical conclusion—to analyze the manner in which the dominant core countries are affected by the expansion of the world-capitalist system. The implications of *inter*dependence have not been seriously entertained as research on underdevelopment continues to stress the exploitation of peripheral societies to the presumably unalloyed advantage of the advanced ones.

Once this bias is redressed it is clear that the internationalization of capital and labor has a pervasive influence on advanced countrires such as the United States. In the daily social and economic life of the country a panorama of events become more salient and interpretable from this vantage. Plant closings, the decline of conventional sources of industrial employment, growing numbers of migrant workers, small business failures, the squeeze on competitive enterprise, urban and regional crises, large numbers of once productive workers whose skills are suddenly not needed, the declining fortunes of workers and families caught in this process—all can be traced in important part to international movements of capital. At this juncture the sociological imagination serves us well by making the connection between "the personal troubles of milieu" and "the public issues of social structure." It enables people "to use information and to develop reason in order to achieve lucid summations of what is going on in the world and what may be happening to themselves."[103]

As the problem itself, its full comprehension traverses several levels of explanation. At the national level the trends and forces of international capital can be translated into the classical mode of class analysis. Accordingly, new forms of class polarization and inequality are taking shape. On one side, the traditional petty bourgeoisie and industrial working classes are increasingly encroached on or threatened with redundancy. On the other side, oligopolistic firms and their managerial and technical employ expand capitalizing on their international franchise and inflated position of power relative to the domestic economy alone. Precariously situated between are skilled workers and service personnel whose professionalization may keep them nominally in the camp of management, but whose life chances are scarcely improved even if they manage to keep pace. Meanwhile, the marginalized and underemployed working class continues growing, adding redundant workers to its overcrowded ranks of minorities and the least skilled.

Most of our general social theory fails to reckon with these changes. The notion of postindustrial society, for example, can now be understood as a highly

103. C. Wright Mills, *The Sociological Imagination* (New York: Oxford University Press, 1959), p. 5.

selective analysis that extracts from context certain changes in the professionalization of the labor force and the relative expansion of the service sector, interpreting these as universal. Not only does the theory ignore the existence of the working class losers in the process, it assumes unrealistically an easy conversion to and unlimited expansion of technical and service occupations. The limited circumstance of winners in the process is taken as the model of a new society. Theories of late capitalism come much closer to the mark by virtue of their focus on the international concentration and centralization of capital, which implies new forms of class polarization. Nevertheless, with its heavy emphasis on the economic causes and consequences of this fact, the social structural implications of the theory need to be developed and evaluated with evidence similar to what has been presented here.

Recent efforts to reclaim class analysis in the tradition of Marx and Weber, although themselves divergent, complement this discussion. Giddens characterizes the process of class "structuration" along a set of dimensions that include ownership and labor power, but add education, the division of labor in enterprise, authority relations, and consumption patterns.[104] With this scheme he is able to contrast both the importance of various bases of class formation and the degree of structuration (vs. fluidity or mobility) across societies. Wright hews more closely to the Marxist tradition developing a multidimensional framework of economic, political, and ideological bases of class whose intersection produces both consistent and contradictory (ambiguous) locations within class relations.[105] Contradictory locations occur between the proletariate and the bourgeoisie (among top and middle managers, technocrats, foremen, and line supervisors), between the proletariate and the petty bourgeoisie (semiautonomous employees), and between the petty bourgeoisie and the bourgeoisie (small employers). The scheme is used to portray differences in the consistency of class structures and changes over time. Illustratively,

> The development of capitalist enterprise has thus pushed foremen in two opposing directions: they have moved further from workers by becoming less involved in direct production, and they have moved closer to workers by gradually having their personal power bureaucratized. Superficially at least, it would seem that the first of these tendencies probably dominated during the first part of this century, while the second tendency probably dominates today. In any event, when the control of supervisors over labor power becomes so attenuated that the supervisor lacks even the capacity to invoke negative sanctions, then the position really merges with the working class proper and should no longer be thought of as a contradictory location.[106]

Generally, political and idealogical factors assume a more important role in the determination of class positions to the extent that these positions occupy

104. Giddens, *The Class Structure of the Advanced Societies.*
105. Wright, "Class Boundaries in Advanced Capitalist Societies."
106. *Ibid.,* p. 34.

contradictory locations. For example, although technicians are close to workers on the dimensions of class relations at the economic level, the status division between mental and manual labor (ideology) pushes them closer to management. Conversely, a strong union among white-collar workers (political) would push them closer to the working class.

The utility of the theories is illustrated in application to the consequences of the internationalization of capital. From the standpoint of Giddens's analysis, foreign investment leads to a greater concentration of ownership (oligopoly) and of income (factor shares). A greater premium attaches to the education necessary to command the higher skilled and technical jobs resulting from displacement, whereas the possession of sheer labor power is of declining value in a more competitive market. Within enterprise the division of labor between mental and manual work becomes sharper, and with the expansion of managerial control the possession of authority shifts more decisively against labor. In short, class structuration becomes more rigid and class position more decisive for the distribution of life and mobility chances.

A similar conclusion derives from Wright's analysis. The increasing concentration of ownership and control over the physical means of production fortifies the position of the bourgeoisie. Shifts in the skill levels and authority relations within the occupational structure "push" managers and technocrats closer to bourgeois interests and foremen closer to workers. Semiautonomous employees and small employers lose their independence, if not their livelihood, with the trend to the bureaucratization of management authority and corporate incursions on the competitive sector. In these terms, contradictory locations within class relations are increasingly absorbed into a more determinate and polarized structure. Here, as in the case of Giddens's framework, class structure is not only more rigid but also has been altered in a direction conducive to greater social and economic inequality.

Yet, class analyses at this level carry us only part of the distance since they are still embedded in an intranational perspective. They artifically truncate the full explanation by virtue of their neglect of international forces. These forces are increasingly decisive in determining those very patterns of ownership, the labor market, the division of labor, changing authority and power relations, and so forth—mistakenly seeing these as first causes of national origin. Increasingly the process of class formation takes place at a global level. For the last decade, at least, this fact has informed analysis of the underdeveloped societies. We may now appreciate its validity for the advanced countries and, therefore, in an integral world-system perspective.

Only on a narrowly descriptive basis can the United States be regarded as a postindustrial society. True, the economy of the continental United States contains less industrial production and employment as a proportion of its gross product than it did at an earlier time. But U.S. "society" has been exported along with a good deal of its wealth, technology, and production. Not only does the

U.S. economy and society exist all over the globe, but the implications of that fact are felt forcefully in the changing structure of the domestic economy and society. Once we have shed our national blinders postindustrial society dissolves into a nationally interpenetrated global economy with its own division of labor that concentrates production in the enclaves of cheap labor, secondary markets, and easy access, while concentrating its financial, managerial, and technical direction in the metropolitan core.

Class formation on a global level cuts across national boundaries placing geographically distant groups in similar strata despite their local furnishings. The working class of core countries, for example, does not benefit systematically from upgrading associated with the export of less skilled, dirty work. Cheap labor abroad enhances profit, although working under primitive labor relations. Obviously, in the particular setting these are apt to be desirable jobs. A small fraction of the Third-World labor force is upgraded and drawn closer to the material position of workers in the advanced countries, thus widening the gap between formal and informal sector workers in the periphery. At the same time this process differentially affects U.S. workers. Many are displaced and unemployed whereas a lesser number may be reabsorbed at a higher level. Nevertheless, the main effect in the long run is to degrade the labor process in general leading to an accentuation of worldwide class inequality. Polarization, stemming from the fact that core and periphery workers increasingly share a common situation, is engendered further in the periphery as a dependent bourgeoisie allies with multinational business. The fact that there are winners and losers at both ends of the core–periphery relationship reemphasizes the new global basis of stratification. The emerging pattern is one of internationally stratified classes rather than of countries.

Finally, it should be stressed that trends in the internationalization of capital have their own cycles. The period that informs many of the conclusions of this chapter (1950–1980) was a revolutionary era for the world economy. Recent developments, especially the omnipresent energy question, suggest that important changes in what we have described are already afoot. From the standpoint of the United States, the decline of the dollar and rising costs of production and wages in Europe have had salutory effects. Disinvestment in Europe is accelerating as U.S. and foreign capital is returning to the country. With the weakened dollar, U.S. exports are more competitive in world markets. Production that once went abroad may now find a competitive edge by staying at home. Yet, these monetary and locational shifts are of secondary importance to the global economic crisis of overproduction and overaccumulation, which is the legacy of the internationalization of capital.[107] The 1980s are bound to see realignments

107. Ernest Mandel, *The Second Slump: A Marxist Analysis of Recession in the Seventies* (London: NLB, 1978).

184

of the global economy and attendant changes in class structures. Some of the conclusions advanced here will doubtless require reevaluation and modification, just as they require assessment in other core countries. These provisos, of course, only reemphasize what has been taken as axiomatic all along—that the global political economy is the appropriate starting point for an understanding of the advanced and underdeveloped societies alike.

6

Conclusion

Whatever else may be asserted and argued about the world today, one fundamental fact remains. Never in history have the connections among societies been closer. Political and economic changes in virtually any corner of the globe reverberate through an increasingly resonant network of interdependence. This, of course, is dramatically illustrated in the geopolitics of petroleum. Revolution and its aftermath in Iran intrude on the daily life of Americans and Europeans. Nigeria and Mexico have become formidable continental powers whose policies the metropolitan countries must reckon among major diplomatic constraints. Guest workers and Bedouin soldiers in Saudi Arabia hold potential trump cards in the volatile game of international politics.

Yet the drama of world energy supplies is only a part of global interdependence. Through countless material objects citizens of the advanced and underdeveloped societies are in daily communion. A great deal of business in the developed societies succeeds or fails to the extent it is able to cultivate worldly connections. Societies on the periphery are dominated by the world-system presence and, particularly, by the drastic inflation it has brought recently. Production for export, the rising costs of imports, and multinational invasion of local markets not only shape the organization of the formal sector, they reach down to the street vendor and backyard mechanic structuring the behavior of the informal economy.

In the generation spanning World War II and 1980 the world-system has simultaneously become more interdependent and undergone a radical change in its scope, member states, and alignments. History may reflect on this generation as the brief reign of America Empire—an arrangement soon eclipsed by core competition and multinationalism. The period witnessed the resurgent economic power of Japan and Western Europe, China's deliberate move into world affairs, the progressive elimination of the "external arena" (of states unincorporated in the global economy), and the growing importance of certain

187

semiperipheral and peripheral states as crucial commodity producers, markets, and political allies.

Naturally, these changes played havoc with conventional theories of modernization and development. As we have suggested previously, notions of individual modernity and structural differentiation gave way to the *realpolitik* of dependency. But the latter soon became vulnerable to changing global conditions. Core-power rivalries, a new assertiveness in Third World countries with vital resources, the opportunities for struggle and renegotiated ties made possible by these and related circumstances—all led to a situation that had outgrown the economistic premises and simplistic "mechanisms of domination" so central to dependency theory.

Theories of accumulation and exchange in the capitalist world-system superseded these difficulties and promised, particularly in their *implications*, the scope and flexibility appropriate to a changing interdependent world. The core, semi-periphery and periphery represented both shifting entities and fundamental processes. The system was characterized by exchanges under changing economic and political circumstances. But most of the exceptional work within this approach is distantly historical and highly general. At the moment its appeal is mainly to intuition and promise—which is a good thing. It remains to be seen how well we can capture concrete contemporary developments at close range *and* explicitly relate them to the broader thrust of theory. That, in a word, is the issue we have pursued in these pages.

Focusing on a limited range of key issues, the chapters in this volume have two purposes. First, they endeavor to describe in empirical detail the actual operation of processes of exchange and domination as these affect sectors, classes, and people. The international movement of capital, labor, and ideas, and emergent social formations in the periphery (the informal urban economy) and core (the class structure of multinationalism), are central, perhaps even representative, manifestations of the contemporary global economy.

Of course, there are others that merit empirically grounded descriptions of the changing international political economy: practices of international banking and finance, military organizations and alignments, changes in agricultural organization and export, world demand for critical resources and producer cooperatives from OPEC on down, state policy and emergent political regimes, and many others. Our efforts, naturally, are only a beginning and may be more instructive about how to take the next steps in the advancement of development theory than for any definitive conclusions about the future of the world-system.

Second, these chapters attempt, beyond description, to establish links between the appropriately grand theory of the world-system and concrete processes—to work out a global systems analysis at the level of contemporary issues and settings. We have tried to show, for example, that the informal urban economy—the engaging activity of street life and entrepreneurial inventiveness that charms observers of the Third World as a vestige of local tradition—is actually a product of multinational capitalist development. Its very organization, activity, and subsidizing contribution (or "function") can only be understood from the broader theoretical vantage.

Similarly, changing patterns of employment and social class in core countries like the United States cannot be understood from a domestic perspective, most contemporary and parochial sociology not withstanding. It is not the mixed blessing of progress and postindustrialism that explains the plight of an unemployed electronics worker making ends meet by part-time work in a fast-food franchise. It is instead the long chain of circumstance that links this person to the Taiwanese or Mexican assembly-plant worker (who consumes the products and services of the local informal economy and migrates or not depending on the availability of this work) through the mechanisms of international capitalist development. For good or ill the life chances of these two individuals derive from their unavoidable participation in a single process of social class determination. Grandiose as it seems, the world-system is a matter of daily experience for most of us.

Assuming that these connections are sufficiently apparent or implied, the question arises whether or not we have discovered anything remarkable. That is, beyond the more and less original interpretations that animate the individual chapters, as a whole do they suggest new avenues of generalization? We believe they do.

Reflecting on the processes and emergent forms of international migration, peripheral informal economy, core class structure, and ideologies of inequality, all seem to demonstrate a fundamental *transformation of the labor process* extending from the center to the periphery of the world-system. Belaboring a general point, first, labor processes throughout the world are increasingly interdependent. They are linked by multinational and interpenetrating structures of capital. The costs of actual labor and its reproduction in distant parts of the globe increasingly enter into a single set of calculations informing strategies of investment, production, and employment.

Second, labor supply (both professional–technical and skilled–manual) is mobile, flexible, and elastic within broad international limits. A panoply of official and informal labor migration systems makes it more readily obtainable and disposable. This, in turn, allows shifting and tailored requirements of labor demand. Local qualities and aspirations of labor are less constraining on decisions about investment and how production is organized. Coupled with the fact that capital and certain forms of production are also more mobile, the opportunities for rationalization (of investment, production, and marketing) multiply.

Third, these considerations lead to greater unity in the system of internationally stratified labor. As world-systems theorists have stressed, the division of labor is world wide. But, this principle needs to be pursued further. Class formation on a global level, as we have seen, means that geographically dispersed labor is not only part of the same stratification system, but increasingly occupies common locations within that system apart from its residence in the core, semiperiphery, or periphery. Labor in the core is not located in a nested hierarchy in which it gains from peripheral exploitation what it loses to domestic upper classes. Rather, core and periphery hierarchies interpenetrate sharing some (increasingly) common positions and attendant fortunes.

Moreover, the same process that produces greater rationalization and unity of class structure also generates greater polarization and worldwide class inequality. The long-recognized "auxiliary bourgeoisie" of the Third World, an appendage to core capital, has its counterpart in labor—not an "aristocracy of labor" (both terms misleadingly imply anomalies) but a stratified and segmented labor market that increasingly resembles the (changing) core system by virtue of their common determination.

Finally, the most tangible and theoretically significant implications of this transformation concern the methods of labor control. In historical perspective, world-system analyses have depended upon the generalization that the core, semiperiphery, and periphery rely, respectively, on wage, "coerced cash-crop," and slave labor. Whatever the historical utility of this distribution, contemporary arrangements appear to have changed. Collectively, our results suggest a possible redefinition of the historical division of labor in the world-system based on emerging modes of labor control and utilization.

Central to our proposed reconceptualizations of the international division of labor are the following points. Highly differentiated systems of wage labor are more inclusive and nonwage labor is more typically organized in the informal economy (as distinct from subsistence and petty commodity production). Perhaps more important, the geographical division of labor (in that sense of core, etc.) is yielding to a cross-national intermixture of labor processes. The *core labor process* involves increasingly professional, technical, and managerial functions that are more polarized with respect to other forms of labor. The *semiperipheral labor process* is based on labor intensive production of the traditional (though increasingly deskilled) industrial form and the commercial and services activity of the competitive sector. The *peripheral labor process* involves the activities of the informal economy as a source of labor absorption and subsidization. Naturally, these transformed labor processes are variously distributed in the advanced and less developed societies. But they are, first, coexistent everywhere in different combinations (including a growing informal economy in the advanced countries), and, second, interrelated in terms of cause and functional reciprocity.

When we say that the labor process has been transformed under global capitalism, we mean something more than the fact that the distribution and mix of labor in different areas has changed. We also mean that new forms of labor activity and organization have emerged. Migrant labor, for example, is not only organized differently (e.g., as transitory, unprotected by citizenship rights, more exploited, and as a method to control local labor), it also performs tasks that would not exist without it. The informal economy creates jobs that did not exist as jobs before. And the technical and managerial tasks of core labor can exist in more pure isolation from the production process performing newly created functions of coordination. Of course, many of the same tasks are performed, but they are performed under conditions of organization and segmentation that constitute a different experience of labor.

Research on the continuing development of the global political economy can profitably focus on the contradictions and limits of the processes described here. For example, when do useful systems of labor migration turn into fetters on rational production as the dependency on that labor, as well as the aspirations of workers, make it less docile and expendable? At what point do labor importing economies become vulnerable to their own requirements, since cheap labor is apt, with time, to become less cheap? When do class inequalities of degraded core labor, immiserated competitive sector labor, and the saturation of the informal economy with surplus labor, advance to common class consciousness and political alliances on a national and international basis? At what point do ideologies of inequality become transparent reflections of international class interests? More generally, what are the restraints on the internationalization of capital and labor that the core countries will be willing to accept and what will they do when they are not?

At bottom these issues relate to the question of worker *responses* to the transformation of the labor process described so far. Are there parallel and emerging patterns of class struggle that we can explain from a perspective that complements the analysis of labor transformation? Although the chapters do not deal directly with this issue, they touch on it at various junctures and provide some bases for inference when related to other work.

In the advanced countries the response of labor to date has been mixed and mild. The runaway shop, loss of jobs, and labor displacement are vocal concerns in the American labor movement, although they have not led to aggressive action or a unified stance. As we noted in Chapter 5, the major unions are divided on the issue and labor force reductions have typically been softened by economistic concessions to unaffected workers or through publicly financed retraining programs. This, of course, comes in the context of a generally weakened labor movement according to the previous argument.

Nevertheless, there are clear signs of labor protest and innovative organizational responses. Unions continue to oppose the runaway shop and lobby for import restrictions. Albeit through ameliorative measures, the state has been persuaded of its responsibility for certain kinds of dislocation. More aggressively,

European unions have begun to develop strategies for confronting multinational corporations with coordinated actions in separate countries. This may be particularly effective within a single industry with dispersed sites for fabricating parts (e.g. the automotive) and, therefore, an object lesson to the American "international" brotherhoods with locals in the United States and Canada.

More intriguing developments loom, for example, in the efforts of some unions to deal directly with the problem of undocumented workers. The American Farm Workers have had some success (and much grief) with attracting migrant labor to their ranks and discouraging its use in strike breaking. The International Ladies Garment Workers Union is currently engaged in a campaign to organize the vast number of illegal aliens in the clothing industry. Obviously, the issue of whether and how one can organize noncitizens is troublesome, but at least this strategy appears more pragmatic than attempting to buck the powerful forces that profit from their entry into the economy.

Grassroots organization of migrant labor related to broader problems of the developed societies is also taking place. In the United States, committees for the defense of migrant workers have been established in the midwestern and western states. Typically these articulate with the growing political movement of Hispanic Americans. The potential electoral strength of this movement, in turn, has tempered proposals for the deportation or other repressive treatment of the millions of foreign nationals working within the country. Similarly in Paris, urban neighborhoods comprised largely of migrant workers have organized successful political movements around the problems of housing and urban renewal.[1] It is safe to assume that these kinds of protest are harbingers of a new force in the domestic politics of the advanced societies. In the short run these strategies are not likely to realize great successes, but they do suggest that labor is responding with methods appropriate to the dimensions of the problem and of conceivable import in the long run.

In the core areas of the world system the process of labor transformation we have proposed has its potentially most pernicious effect on three segments of the labor force: (a) displaced and redundant workers from traditional blue-collar industrial jobs; (b) newly "professionalized" groups whose mobility proves to be illusory (e.g. women); and (c) unprotected competitive sector (including migrant) workers. The possible forms of class struggle these groups may undertake separately or collectively, as the common origins of their plight become clear, are difficult to forecast and apt to be confounded with additional considerations of status (e.g. race, sex, nationality, regional location). Rather than enter into loose speculation, we would simply suggest that this is where the theoretical analysis tells us we should look for emergent forms of class conflict that are likely to be critical in the near future.

---

1. Jose Olives Puig, "The Struggle Against Urban Renewal in the 'Cite d'Aliarte' (Paris)," in *Urban Sociology: Critical Essays*, ed. C. G. Pickvance (New York: St. Martin's, 1976), pp. 174–197.

Class struggle in the Third World, of course, is the subject of imposing historical literature and some valuable recent theoretical treatments.[2] Nevertheless, contributions on this topic that develop an explicit link between class conflict and the global economy are less common and devoted primarily to agrarian social organization and peasant movements. This is fitting given the predominantly rural character of most peripheral societies. But rapid worldwide urbanization has only recently been matched with world-systems analyses of class formation and conflict in Third-World cities.[3]

In the well-researched case of agrarian labor protest, analyses begin with what Wolf calls the expansion of "North Atlantic capitalism" or the progressive incorporation of peripheral societies into the global economic system.[4] The metropolitan economy penetrates the agrarian sector in a process that disrupts traditional forms of social organization, converts land from an object of customary rights and obligations into a commodity, and transforms labor from subsistence and petty commodity production into proletarianized wage dependency. As a consequence, the "moral economy"[5] of the peasantry is destroyed and the "middle peasant" radicalized.[6] Peasant revolts are precipitated as attempts to recapture an earlier prosperity and paternalistic order of mutual obligation between landlord and tenant. Recently greater differentiation has been introduced in the forms of protest, ranging from reformist efforts directed at commodity prices and working conditions to nationalist and socialist revolutionary movements depending on particular combinations of the organization of land, capital, and wages.[7] The theory of peasant rebellion has been carefully developed historically[8] and evaluated in comparative empirical studies.[9]

However, what has been relatively neglected as a necessary complement to

2. For example, Richard Sandbrook and Ronald Cohen, *The Development of an African Working Class* (London: Longman, 1975); Andre Gunder Frank, *Lumpenbourgeoisie: Lumpendevelopment: Dependence, Class, and Politics in Latin America* (New York: Monthly Review, 1972).

3. For Example, Paul Lubeck and John Walton, "Urban Class Conflict in Africa and Latin America: Comparative Analysis from a World Systems Perspective," *International Journal of Urban and Regional Research*, 3, No. 1 (March 1979): 3–28.

4. Eric R. Wolf, *Peasant Wars of the Twentieth Century* (New York: Harper and Row, 1969).

5. James Scott, *The Moral Economy of the Peasant: Rebellion and Subsistence in Southeast Asia* (New Haven: Yale University Press, 1976).

6. Hamza Alavi, "Peasants and Revolution," in *Imperialism and Revolution in South Asia*, eds. Kathleen Gough and Hari P. Sharma (New York: Monthly Review, 1973), pp. 291–337; Wolf, *Peasant Wars of the Twentieth Century*.

7. Jeffrey M. Paige, *Agrarian Revolution: Social Movements and Export Agriculture in the Underdeveloped World* (New York: The Free Press, 1975).

8. For example, E. J. Hobsbawm, *Primitive Rebels: Studies in Archaic Forms of Social Movements in the 19th and 20th Centuries* (New York: Norton, 1959); E. J. Hobsbawm, *The Age of Revolution, 1789–1848* (New York: Mentor, 1962); Barrington Moore, Jr., *Social Origins of Dictatorship and Democracy: Lord and Peasant in the Making of the Modern World* (Boston: Beacon Press, 1966).

9. For example, Daniel Chirot and Charles Ragin, "The Market, Tradition, and Peasant Rebellion: The Cast of Romania in 1907," *American Sociological Review*, 40, No. 4, (1975): 428–444; Paige, *Agrarian Revolution*.

this remarkable literature is precisely the full development of a world-systems perspective. The transformative consequences of the global economy visited upon agrarian social organizations are, in principle, equally decisive for urban and national society. The theoretical proposition is amply supported in fact. On the one hand, the same global economic forces affecting agriculture (e.g. commercialization, export production, land concentration) produce urban migration, surplus labor in the urban economy, and transformations in the urban hierarchy.[10]

On the other hand, parallel developments engender qualitative changes in the urban economy such as the destruction of craft and artisan industry, creation of comprador trade, overcrowding of the tertiary sector, urban export industry, and local manufacturing by foreign investors at the expense of indigenous industrial jobs and enterprises. The consequences of incorporation are systemic rather than sectoral.

Theoretically, these collateral and interdependent changes should be equally conducive to labor protest, class struggle, and even revolutionary action. In view of the material presented in previous chapters and related work, the question, therefore, is what can be said generally about urban and societal responses to the process of labor transformation in the periphery.

The hypothesized transformations of semiperipheral and peripheral labor processes have their most telling effects on class three and four workers described previously (Chapter 3). That is, major dislocations occur among: wage workers in capital intensive forms of conventional industrial production that tend, at the same time, to become deskilled and foreign controlled; the overgrown tertiary sector; and the informal economy. In Third World cities these social classes tend to be ecologically interspersed in public and private working class housing developments and irregular settlements of squatters and leaseholders—the Latin American barrios and favelas or the African peri-urban settlements.

Labor protest among these classes and communities is organized around both economic grievances (e.g. industrial actions, protests over consumer prices, merchant strikes) and broader issues of collective consumption (e.g., housing, transport, services, land titles) with the latter predominating. Conventional industrial protests are minimized by the proportionately few but relatively well-paying jobs in capital intensive enterprises, by paternalism (e.g., worker housing), and by mobility opportunities for a significant minority. More common forms of economic protest are actions associated with the cost of food and rent. Although these activities are typically organized by middle and working class consumers, occasionally they originate with shopkeepers protesting official efforts at taxation and price control. With respect to transformations in the semiperipheral labor

---

10. David Slater, "Colonialism and the Spatial Structure of Underdevelopment: Outlines of an Alternative Approach, with Special Reference to Tanzania," *Progress in Planning*, 4, part II (1974): 137–162.

process, protest centers less on industrial problems than marketing and consumption in the tertiary sector.

Yet, the more dramatic forms of protest stem from transformations in the peripheral labor process involving participants in the informal economy around issues of collective consumption. Theoretically, it is here we would locate prototypical urban protest actions such as land invasions, community organization among squatters, and demands for regularized land titles and services. Since, by definition, the informal economy lacks direct wage income, its protest activity is aimed at the indirect or social wage represented by urban services and the security of land tenure.

Protest assumes two general forms based on clientism and autonomous action. The first is governed by instrumentalism and political "realism." Given the lack of political power and great vulnerability to swings in public policy, the urban poor endeavor to use to their advantage government, charitable, and sundry agency efforts at "cooptation" or "mobilization." This allows them to extract a maximum number of concessions, particularly by playing off several patrons against each other, and it may protect them from repression during times of crisis. [11]

Autonomous action is the more radical (and risky) alternative whereby the urban poor organize outside of institutional arrangements to press for more sweeping solutions such as legalized communal ownership of large tracts of land, participation in planning bodies, and bills of "urban social rights."[12] The relative effectiveness of these two general strategies is a complex and unsettled question that depends, in all likelihood, on the constellation of political forces in concrete situations. [13] For present purposes, however, they illustrate cogently the major contours of protest associated with the peripheral labor process.

Less common, though possibly more consequential, Third World revolutionary movements relate closely to the changing conditions of labor. Urban and societal trends toward class inequality that parallel distortions in agrarian social organization also produce revolutionary ferment. When analyzed in terms of broader forces originating in the global political economy, some of the major "peasant" revolutions of the twentieth century prove to have been either urban-based or critically dependent upon rural–urban links. [14]

11. A. Leeds and E. Leeds, "Accounting for Behavioral Differences: Three Political Systems and the Responses of Squatters in Brazil, Peru and Chile," in *The City in Comparative Perspective: Cross-National Research and New Directions in Theory*, eds. J. Walton and L. H. Masotti (Beverly Hills: Sage Publications-Halsted Press, 1976), pp. 193–248.

12. M. Castells, "Movimientos Sociales Urbanos en American Latina: Tendencias Históricos y Problemas Teóricas," mimeo., University of Wisconsin-Madison, 1976.

13. John Walton, "Urban Political Movements and Revolutionary Change in the Third World," *Urban Affairs Quarterly*, 15, No. 1 (September 1979): 3–22.

14. For example, Moore, *Social Origins of Dictatorship and Democracy*; Charles Tilly, "Town and Country in Revolution," in *Peasant Rebellion and Communist Revolution in Asia*, ed. John Wilson Lewis (Stanford: Stanford University Press, 1974), pp. 271–302; Angus W. McDonald, Jr., *The Urban Origins of Rural Revolution: Elites and the Masses in Human Province China, 1911–*

In addition to the previously discussed transformations that predispose rural labor to revolutionary action, related changes contribute momentum and complementary bases. As noted, a key contributor is the growing unemployed and underemployed urban proletariate. The public sector frequently expands beyond productive limits to absorb some of this surplus. As multinational and comprador interests monopolize the internationally linked economy, local merchants and petty entrepreneurs find their livelihood threatened. The urban equivalent of the potentially radical middle peasantry is comprised of: workers in the informal sector, especially those with ties to rural society (e.g., through migratory labor systems); unionized workers, especially those in export-related activities (e.g., transportation workers, stevedores, plantation workers, fabricators of agricultural products); petty traders and merchants; and lesser public functionaries.

The conditions likely to precipitate revolutionary action by these classes also depend importantly, though far from exclusively, on changes in the global economy. Typical are inflationary cycles associated with boom or bust export markets, rising import costs, and rising prices (e.g., of land) associated with speculation based on large comprador profits. Particularly decisive are abrupt reversals in prosperity and declines in real income. Of course, contributing factors are ultimately political and include parallel reversals in the gradual march toward greater political freedoms (e.g., repression of growing unions or popular political associations). These reactions, in turn, tend to come from new developmental coalitions (e.g., of industrialists, merchants, and landowners) organized around externally based modernization policies that are threatened by the organization of popular classes and react defensively.[15]

Naturally, historical, cultural, and social conditions unique to revolutionary societies combine with influences from the global political economy. There is no patent formula that will predict these events even under the most aggravated conditions. We have to appreciate what Moore terms "an adequate realization of the brief and fragile nature of revolutionary upsurges."[16] Our argument is that social revolution is among a series of labor protests and class struggles that must be understood partly through a complex chain of circumstances including transformations in the labor process and, at another level, the internationalization of capital and labor.

1927 (Berkeley: University of California Press, 1978); Ying-Mao Kau, "Urban and Rural Strategies in the Chinese Communist Revolution," in Lewis, ed., *Peasant Rebellion and Communist Revolution in Asia*, pp. 253–270; Christine Pelzer White, "The Vietnamese Revolutionary Alliance: Intellectuals, Workers and Peasants." in Lewis, ed., *Peasant Rebellion and Communist Revolution in Asia*, pp. 77–95.

15. John Walton, *Reluctant Rebels: Comparative Studies of Revolution and Underdevelopment*, 1980, manuscript.

16. Barrington Moore, Jr., *Injustice: The Social Bases of Obedience and Revolt* (White Plains, New York: M. E. Sharpe, 1978), p. 482.

Although we have given equal emphasis to class struggles in the advanced and underdeveloped societies, the most forceful challenges to the present system of global inequality are likely to come from the Third World. In this century most of the imminent "contradictions" of Western capitalism have been resolved in ways that strengthened that order and exploited further the periphery.[17] There are reasons to expect that this alternative will persist as long as it is able. Powerful ideological forces sustain belief in egalitarianism and mobility in the advanced countries. These ideas still reach receptive ears in the Third World (Chapter 4). Present arrangements provide substantial benefits to the powerful classes in the developed societies and their allied dependent elites in the periphery. The working class within and across the advanced countries is divided.

Yet, it is doubtful that these arrangements can persist indefinitely. As we have indicated, resistance is growing along unprecedented lines. Conversely, unyielding constraints are upon us. Today we face a revolution in our fundamental assumptions about development and social progress. We confront limits of growth that are most evidently physical, yet most consequentially human and political. Development and progress are no longer interchangeable. If we are to have progress, or even development, it must depend upon physical and normative limitations on the rate and character of growth. Questions about equity and distribution replace others of productivity and gain. Within the human and environmental limits of development, policy must recognize distributive costs and benefits.

This volume does not begin to develop the kind of normative theory that is needed. It does begin to make the connections between the processes that will figure importantly in future efforts to evaluate the social impacts of interdependent development. It may also contribute some rude realities to what must necessarily be a new conception of social development, the possibilities of such a broadly shared experience, and the values that it would pursue.

17. Douglas Dowd, "Continuity, Change, and Tension in Global Capitalism," in *Social Change in the Capitalist World Economy*, ed. B. H. Kaplan (Beverly Hills: Sage, 1978), pp. 177–195.

References

AFL–CIO
1971   *Needed: A Constructive Foreign Trade Policy. Special Study Commissioned and Published by the Industrial Union Department.* (October): Washington, D.C.
1973   "U.S. multinationals: The dimming of America." Report prepared from the AFL–CIO's Maritime Trade Department's Executive Board Meeting, February 15-16, 1973, and presented to the United States Senate Committee on Finance's Subcommittee Hearings on International Trade. 93rd Congress, 1st Session (February–March).

Alavi, Hamza
1973   "Peasants and revolution." Pp. 291-337 in Kathleen Gough and Hari P. Sharma (eds.), *Imperialism and Revolution in South Asia.* New York: Monthly Review.

Alba, Francisco
1978   "Mexico's international migration as a manifestation of its development pattern." *International Migration Review* 12 (Winter): 485-501.

American Ethnologist
1978   "Political Economy." 5 (August).

Amin, Samir
1974a   "Accumulation and development: A theoretical model." *Review of African Political Economy* 1 (August–November): 9-26.
1974b   *Accumulation on a World Scale: A Critique of the Theory of Underdevelopment.* 2 Vols. New York: Monthly Review Press.
1976   *Unequal Development, An Essay on the Social Formations of Peripheral Capitalism.* New York: Monthly Review Press.

Anderson, Grace M.
1974   *Networks of Contact: The Portuguese and Toronto.* Waterloo, Ontario: Wilfrid Laurier University Press.

Anderson, Perry
1979   *Lineages of the Absolutist State.* London: Verso Editions.

Arizpe, Lourdes
1978   *Migración, Etnicismo y Cambio Económico.* Mexico, D.F.: El Colegio de Mexico.

Arrighi, Giovanni
1973   "Labor supplies in an historical perspective: A study of the proletarianization of the African peasantry in Rhodesia." Pp. 180-234 in G. Arrighi and J. Saul (eds.), *Essays on the Political Economy of Africa.* New York: Montly Review Press.

Babson, Steve
  1973   "The multinational corporation and labor." *The Review of Radical Political Economics.*
          Vol. 5, No. 1 (Spring): 19–36.
Bach, Robert L.
  1978a "Mexican immigration and the American state." *International Migration Review* 12
          (Winter): 536–558.
  1978b "The reproduction of triviality: Critical notes on recent attempts to test the dynamics of
          world capitalism." Department of Sociology, State University of New York. Binghamton,
          New York. (Mimeographed)
Bacha, Edmar
  1976   *Os Mitos de uma Decada.* Rio de Janeiro: Paz e Terra.
Baer, Werner
  1975   "La reciente experiencia brasileña: Una interpretación." *Revista Paraguaya de Sociología*
          34 (September–December): 7–39.
Bairoch, Paul
  1973   *Urban Unemployment in Developing Countries: The Nature of the Problem and Proposals
          for its Solution.* Geneva: International Labor Office.
Balán, Jorge
  1973   "Migrações no Desenvolvimento Capitalista Brasileiro." *Estudos CEBRAP* 5.
  1975   "Regional urbanization under primary-sector expansion in neo-colonial countries." Pp.
          151–179 in Alejandro Portes and Harley L. Browning (eds.), *Current Perspectives in Latin
          American Urban Research.* Austin: Special Publications Series of the Institute of Latin
          American Studies, University of Texas at Austin.
Balan, Jorge, Harley Browning, and Elizabeth Jelin
  1973   *Men in a Developing Society.* Austin: Institute of Latin American Studies and University of
          Texas Press.
Baran, Paul A.
  1957   *The Political Economy of Growth.* New York: Monthly Review Press.
Barnet, Richard, and Ronald Müller
  1974   "Global reach." Part II. *The New Yorker,* December 9.
Barrera, Mario
  1977   "Class segmentation and internal colonialism." Department of Political Science, Univer-
          sity of California at San Diego. (Unpublished manuscript)
Beiguelman, Paula
  1978   "The destruction of modern slavery: A theoretical issue." *Review* II (Summer): 71–80.
Bell, Daniel
  1960   *The End of Ideology: On the Exhaustion of Political Ideas in the Fifties.* Glencoe, Illinois:
          The Free Press.
  1973   *The Coming of Post-Industrial Society: A Venture Towards Social Forecasting.* New York:
          Basic Books.
Bellah, Robert N.
  1958   "Religious aspects of modernization in Turkey and Japan." *American Journal of Sociology*
          64: 1–5.
  1965   *Religion and Progress in Modern Asia.* New York: Free Press.
Bendix, Reinhard
  1962   *Max Weber, An Intellectual Portrait.* Garden City, New York: Doubleday.
  1974   "Inequality and social structure in the theories of Marx and Weber." *American Sociological
          Review* 39 (April): 149–161.
Bienefeld, M.
  1975   "The informal sector and peripheral capitalism: The case of Tanzania." *Bulletin of the
          Institute of Development Studies* 6 (February): 53–73.

Birbeck, Chris
1978   "Self-employed proletarians in an informal factory: The case of Cali's garbage dump."
        World Development 6 (September–October): 1173–1185.
Birnbaum, Norman
1971   *Toward a Critical Sociology.* New York: Oxford University Press.
Blauner, Robert
1972   *Racial Oppression in America.* New York: Harper and Row.
Bluestone, Barry, and Bennett Harrison
1980   *Capital and Communities: The Causes and Consequences of Private Disinvestment.*
        Washington, D.C.: The Progressive Alliance.
Bogardus, Emory S.
1960   *The Development of Social Thought.* New York: Longmans.
Bonacich, Edna
1976   "Advanced capitalism and black/white relations: A split labor market interpretation."
        American Sociological Review 41 (February): 34–41.
Booth, David
1975   "Andre Gunder Frank: An introduction and appreciation." Pp. 50–85 in I. Oxaal, T.
        Barnett, and D. Booth (eds.), *Beyond the Sociology of Development: Economy and Society
        in Latin America and Africa.* London: Routledge and Kegan Paul.
Borah, Woodrow
1963   "Colonial institutions and contemporary Latin America." *Hispanic American Historical
        Review* 43: 371–379.
Bourricaud, François
1967   *Poder y Sociedad en el Perú Contemporáneo.* Buenos Aires: Sur.
Braverman, Harry
1974   *Labor and Monopoly Capitalism: The Degradation of Work in the Twentieth Century.*
        New York: Monthly Review Press.
Brenner, R.
1977   "The origins of capitalist development: A critique of neo-Smithian Marxism." *New Left
        Review* 104: 25–92.
Bromley, Ray
1978   "Organization, regulation, and exploitation in the so-called 'urban informal sector': The
        street traders of Cali, Colombia." *World Development* 6 (September–October): 1161–1171.
Bromley, Ray, and Chris Gerry
1979   "Who are the casual poor." Pp. 3–23 in R. Bromley and C. Gerry (eds.) *Causal Work and
        Poverty in Third World Cities.* New York: John Wiley.
Brownrigg, Leslie Ann
1974   "The role of secondary cities in Andean urbanism" Evanston, Illinois: Center for Urban
        Affairs, Northwestern University. (Mimeographed)
Bukharin, Nikolai
1929   *Imperialism and World Economy.* New York: International Publishers.
1975   *Economics of the Transformation Period.* London: Pluto Press.
1979   "Notes of an economist." (K. Smith, trans.) *Economy and Society* 8 (November): 473–500.
Burawoy, Michael
1976   "The function and reproduction of migrant labor: Comparative material from Southern
        Africa and the United States." *American Journal of Sociology* 81 (March): 1050–1087.
Burgess, Rod
1978   "Petty commodity housing or dweller control? A critique of John Turner's views on housing
        policy." *World Development* 6 (September–October): 1105–1133.
Burns, Leland S., and Wing Ning Pang
1977   "Big business in the big city: Corporate headquarters in the C.B.C." *Urban Affairs Quar-
        terly* 12 (June): 533–544.

Bustamante, Jorge
  1973 "The historical context of undocumented Mexican immigration to the United States." *Aztlán* 3: 257–281.
Calvo, Lino Novas
  1944 *El Negrero, Vida Novelada de Pedro Blanco Fernández Trava.* Buenos Aires: Espasa-Calpe.
Cardenas, Gilbert
  1976 "United States immigration policy toward Mexico: A historical perspective." Department of Sociology, University of Texas at Austin. (Mimeographed)
Cardona, Ramiro
  1968 *Dos Barrios de Invasión.* Boletin No. 21. Bogotá: Asociación Colombiana de Facultades de Medicina.
Cardoso, Fernando H.
  1973 "Associated dependent development: Theoretical and practical implications." Pp. 142–178 in Alfred Stepan (ed.), *Authoritarian Brazil.* New Haven: Yale University Press.
  1974 "Las contradicciones del desarrollo asociado." *Revista Paraguaya de Sociología* 11 (January–April): 227–252.
  1975 *Ideologias de la Burguesia Industrial en Sociedades Dependientes.* Mexico, D.F.: Siglo Veintiuno Editores.
  1977 "The consumption of dependency theory in the United States." *Latin American Research Review* 12: 7–21.
Cardoso, Fernando H., and Enzo Faletto
  1969 *Dependencia y Desarrollo en América Latina.* Mexico, D.F.: Siglo Veintiuno.
Castells, Manuel
  1975 "Immigrant workers and class struggles in advanced capitalism: The Western European experience." *Politics and Society* 5: 33–66.
  1976 "Movimientos Sociales Urbanos en América Latina: tendencias historicas y problemas teoricos." University of Wisconsin, Madison. (Mimeographed)
  1980 *The Economic Crisis and American Society.* Princeton, N.J.: Princeton University Press.
Castles, Stephen, and Godula Kosack
  1973 *Immigrant Workers and Class Struggles in Western Europe.* London: Oxford University Press.
CEBRAP
  1976 *São Paulo, 1975: Crescimento e Pobreza.* São Paulo: Edições Loyola.
CENAPROV
  1979 "Esquema para investigación sobre el problema habitacional en Colombia." Report to the IX National Assembly of Central Pro-Vivienda. Bogotá, October.
Chaney, Elsa
  1979 "The world economy and contemporary migration." *International Migration Review* 13 (Summer): 204–212.
Chernow, Ron
  1978 "The rabbit that ate Pennsylvania: Governor Shapp builds Volkswagen at $70 - million hutch." *Mother Jones* 3 (January): 19–24.
Chicago Sun-Times
  1978 "French firm goes international because 'nobody knew about us'." P. 12, July 2.
Chirot, Daniel and Charles Ragin
  1975 "The market, tradition, and peasant rebellion: The case of Romania in 1907." *American Sociological Review* 40: 428–444.
Chodak, Szymon
  1973 *Societal Development.* New York: Oxford University Press.

Clammer, John
 1975 "Economic anthropology and the sociology of development: 'Liberal' anthropology and its French critics." Pp. 208–228 in Ivar Oxaal, T. Barnett, and D. Booth (eds.), *Beyond the Sociology of Development: Economy and Society in Latin America and Africa.* London: Routledge and Kegan Paul.
Clinard, Marshall B.
 1968 "Urbanization, urbanism, and deviant behavior in Puerto Rico." P. 29 in Social Science Research Center, *Social Change and Public Policy.* San Juan: University of Puerto Rico.
Collier, David
 1976 *Squatters and Oligarchs: Authoritarian Rule and Policy Change in Peru.* Baltimore: The Johns Hopkins University Press.
Cornelius, Wayne A.
 1975a "The impact of cityward migration on urban land and housing markets." Paper presented at the Conference on the Urban Impact of Internal Migration. University of North Carolina at Chapel Hill, September.
 1975b *Politics and the Migrant Poor in Mexico City.* Stanford: Stanford University Press.
 1976 "Mexican migration to the United States: The view from rural sending communities." Department of Political Science, Massachusetts Institute of Technology. (Mimeographed)
Cortén, Andre
 1965 "Como vive la otra mitad de Santo Domingo: Estudio de dualismo estructural." *Caribbean Studies* 4: 3–19.
Dahrendorf, Ralf
 1959 *Class and Class Conflict in Industrial Society.* Stanford: Stanford University Press.
da Silva, Luiz Antonio Machado
 1971 *Mercados Metropolitanos de Trabalho Manual e Marginalidade.* M. A. thesis. Social Anthropology Programme of the National Museum, Rio de Janeiro.
de Andrade, Luis Aureliano Gama
 1976 "Politica Urbana no Brasil: o paradigma, a organização e a política." *Estudos CEBRAP* 18 (October–December): 119–147.
de Andrade, Manuel Correia
 1976 "Os anos trinta no Brasil." *Comunicacoes PIMES* 12 Recife: Universidade Federal de Pernambuco.
Debray, Regis
 1969 "Latin-America: Some problems of revolutionary strategy." Pp. 499–531 in I. L. Horowitz, J. de Castro, and J. Gerassi (eds.), *Latin-American Radicalism.* New York: Vintage.
de Drachemberg, Lyra Pidoux
 1975 "Inmigración y colonización en el Paraguay, 1870–1970." *Revista Paraguaya de Sociología* 34 (September–December): 65–123.
de Janvry, Alain
 1976 "Material determinants of the world food crisis." *Berkeley Journal of Sociology* 21: 2–26.
de Janvry, Alain, and Carlos Garramón
 1977a "Laws of motion of capital in the center–periphery structure." *Review of Radical Political Economics* 9 (Summer): 29–38.
 1977b "The dynamics of rural poverty in Latin America." *Journal of Peasant Studies* 5 (April): 206–216.
Delacroix, Jacques
 1977 "The export of raw materials and economic growth: A cross-national study." *American Sociological Review* 42 (October): 795–808.
de la Torre, Jose, Robert B. Stobaugh and Piero Telesio
 1973 "U.S. Multinational Enterprise and Changes in the Skill Composition of U.S. Employ-

ment." Pp. 127–143. In Duane Kujawa (ed.) *American Labor and the Multinational Corporation*. New York: Praeger.

de Oliveira Marques, A. H.
1972 *History of Portugal*. New York: Columbia University Press.

de Sebastian, Luis
1976 *Investigación evaluativa de los Programas Habitacionales y de Desarrollo de la Comunidad de la Fundación Salvadoreña de Desarrollo y Vivienda Mínima*. San Salvador: Universidad Centroamericana.

de Souza Martins, José
1973 *A Imigração e a Crise no Brasil Agrario*. São Paulo: Livraria Pioneira.

de Vitoria, Francisco
1967 "De Vitoria." P. 30 in *El Pensamiento Politico Hispansamericano*. Buenos Aires: Ediciones de Palma.

Dinerman, Ina
1978 "Patterns of adaptation among households of U.S.-Bound migrants from Michoacán, Mexico." *International Migration Review* 12 (Winter): 485–501.

Donghi, Tulio Halperin
1970 *Historia Contemporánea de América Latina*. Madrid: Alianza Editorial.

Dos Santos, Theotonio
1968 "El nuevo caracter de la dependencia." *Cuadernos del CESO*. No. 10. Santiago, Chile.
1970a "La crisis de la teoria del dessarrollo y las relaciones de dependencia en América Latina." Pp. 147–187 in H. Jaguaribe (ed.), *La Dependencia Politico-Economica de America Latina*. Mexico, D.F.: Siglo Ventiuno.
1970b "The structure of dependence." *American Economic Review* 40 (May): 231–236.

Dowd, Douglas
1978 "Continuity, change and tension in global capitalism." Pp. 177–195. In B. H. Kaplan (ed.), *Social Change in the Capitalist World Economy*. Beverly Hills, Cal.: Sage.

Duarte, Isis
1978 "Marginalidad urbana en Santo Domingo." Paper presented at the First Congress of Dominican Sociology, Santo Domingo, November.

Eckstein, Susan
1977 *The Poverty of Revolution, the State and the Urban Poor in Mexico*. Princeton: Princeton University Press.

ECLA
1969 *Development Problems in Latin America*. Austin: University of Texas Press.

Eisenstadt, S. N.
1961 *Essays on Sociological Aspects of Political and Economic Delolopment*. The Hague: Mouton.

Emmanuel, Arghiri
1972 *Unequal Exchange: A Study of the Imperialism of Trade*. London: New Left Books.
1974 "Myths of Development versus Myths of Underdevelopment." *New Left Review* 85 (May–June): 61–82.

Evans, Peter, and Gari Gereffi
n.d. "Foreign investment and dependent development: Comparing Brazil and Mexico." Harvard University Center for International Affairs, Cambridge, Mass. (Mimeographed).

Fernandez, Raul A.
1973 "The border industrial program of the United States–Mexican Border." *The Review of Radical Political Economics* 5 (Spring): 37–52.

Ferrer, Aldo
1972 *La Economía Argentina, Las Etapas de su Desarrollo y problemas actuales*. Buenos Aires: Fondo de Cultura Económica.

Fortune Double 500 Directory
  1974   New York: Time Inc.
Frank, Andre Gunder
  1967   *Capitalism and Underdevelopment in Latin America.* New York: Monthly Review Press.
  1970   "The development of underdevelopment." Pp. 3–94 in *Latin America: Underdevelopment or Revolution.* New York: Monthly Review Press.
  1972   *Lumpenbourgeoisie: Lumpendevelopment—Dependence, Class, and Politics in Latin America.* New York: Monthly Review Press.
  1979   "Unequal accumulation: Intermediate, semi-peripheral, and sub-imperialist economies." *Review* 2 (Winter): 281–350.
Frank, Robert H., and Richard T. Freeman
  1978   *The Distributional Consequences of Direct Foreign Investment.* New York: Academic Press.
Frankenhoff, C. A.
  1967   "Elements of an economic model for slums in a developing economy." *Economic Development and Cultural Change* 16: 27–35.
Friedman, Jonathan
  1978   "Crisis in theory and transformations of the world economy." *Review* 11 (Fall): 131–146.
Furtado, Celso
  1969   "U.S. hegemony and the future of Latin America." Pp. 61–74 in Irving L. Horowitz, J. de Castro, and John Gerassi (eds.), *Latin American Radicalism.* New York: Vintage Press.
  1971   *Development and Underdevelopment, A Structural View.* Berkeley, Cal.: University of California Press.
  1973   "The Brazilian 'model' of development." Pp. 297–306 in C. Wilber (ed.), *The Political Economy of Development and Underdevelopment.* New York: Random House.
Galbraith, John Kenneth
  1967   *The New Industrial State.* Boston: Houghton Mifflin.
Garcia, Mario
  1975   *Obreros: The Mexican Workers of El Paso, 1900–1920.* Ph.D. dissertation, University of California at San Diego.
Gardner, James A.
  1973   "Urbanization in Brazil." *International Urbanization Survey Report.* New York: The Ford Foundation.
Garrison, Vivian, and Carol I. Weiss
  1979   "Dominican family networks and U.S. immigration policy: A case study." *International Migration Review* 12 (Summer): 264–283.
Geertz, Clifford
  1963   *Peddlers and Princes: Social Development and Economic Change in Two Indonesian Towns.* Chicago: University of Chicago Press.
Geisse, Guillermo
  1974   "La desigualdad de los ingresos: Punto de partido del círculo de la pobreza urbana." Paper presented at the Seminar on New Directions of Urban Research. University of Texas at Austin, May.
Gereffi, Gary
  1978   "Drug firms and dependency in Mexico: The case of the steroid hormone industry." *International Organization* 32 (Winter): 237–286.
  1979   "A critical evaluation of quantitative cross-national studies of dependency." Paper presented at the Panel on Dependency Theory, meetings of the International Studies Association, Toronto, March.
Germani, Gino
  1965   "Hacia una democracia de masas." Pp. 206–227 in Torcuato S. di Tella, Gino Germani, and Jorge Graciarena (eds.), *Argentina, Sociedad de Masas.* Buenos Aires: Eudeba.

1966   "Social and political consequences of mobility." Pp. 364–394 in N. J. Smelser and S. M. Lipset (eds.), *Social Structure and Mobility in Economic Development*. Chicago: Aldine.

Gerry, Chris

1974   *Petty Producers and the Urban Economy: A Case Study in Dakar*. Programme on Urbanization and Employment Research. Geneva: International Labour Office.

1978   "Petty production and capitalist production in Dakar: The crisis of the self-employed." *World Development* 6 (September–October): 1147–1160.

Geschwender, James A.

1978   *Racial Stratification in America*. Dubuque, Iowa: Wm. C. Brown.

Gibson, Charles

1969   "The problem of the impact of Spanish culture on the indigenous American population." Pp. 66–98 in F. B. Pike (ed.), *Latin American History: Select Problems*. New York: Harcourt Brace and World.

Giddens, Anthony

1979   *The Class Structure of the Advanced Societies*. New York: Barnes and Noble.

Gilpin, Robert

1973   *The Multinational Corporation and the National Interest*. Report prepared for the Committee on Labor and Public Welfare, United States Senate, 93rd Congress 1st Session (October). Washington, D.C.: U.S. Government Printing Office.

Gold, David, Clarence Y. R. Lo, and Erik Olin Wright

1975   "Recent developments in Marxist theories of the capitalist state." Parts I and II. *Monthly Review* 27 (October): 29–43 and (November): 36–51.

Goldfrank, Walter R.

1977   "Who rules the world? Class formation at the international level." *Quarterly Journal of Ideology* 1 (Winter): 32–37.

Goldrich, Daniel

1970   "Political organization and the politicization of the poblador." *Comparative Political Studies* 3 (July): 176–202.

Grabois, Giselia Potcngy

1973   *Em Busca de Integração: A Politica de Remoção de Favelas no Rio de Janeiro*. M. A. thesis. Social Anthropology Programme of the National Museum, Rio de Janeiro.

Graciarena, Jorge

1979   "The basic needs strategy as an option: Its possibilities in the Latin American context." *CEPAL Review* (August): 39–53.

Gramsci, Antonio

1971   *Selections from the Prison Notebooks*. Q. Hoare and G. Nowell (trans.) New York: International Publishers.

Guevara, Ernesto

1969   "Message to the tricontinental". Pp. 621–646 in I. L. Horowitz, J. de Castro, and J. Gerassi (eds.), *Latin American Radicalism*. New York: Vintage Press.

Hagen, Everett

1962   *On the Theory of Social Change*. Homewood, Illinois: Dorsey Press.

Hall, Michael M.

1971   *The origins of mass immigration to Brazil*. Ph.D. dissertation, Department of History, Columbia University, New York.

Harberger, A.

1971   "On measuring the social opportunity costs of labour." *International Labour Review* 103 (January–June): 559–579.

Hardoy, Jorge E.

1972   *Las Ciudades en América Latina*. Buenos Aires: Paidos.

1975   "Two thousand years of Latin American urbanization." Pp. 3–56 in J. E. Hardoy (ed.), *Urbanization in Latin America: Approaches and Issues*. Garden City, New York: Anchor Books.

Hardoy, Jorge E., Raul O. Basaldua, and Oscar Moreno
1968   *Política de la Tierra Urbana y Mecanismos para su Regulación en América del Sur*. Buenos Aires: Editorial del Instituto.

Harris, Nigel
1980   "The new untouchables: The international migration of labour." *International Socialism* 2: 37–63.

Hart, Keith
1973   "Informal income opportunities and urban employment in Ghana." *Journal of Modern African Studies* 11: 61–89.

Hawkins, Robert G.
1972   "The Multinational Corporation: A new trade policy issue in the United States." Pp. 161–191 in Robert C. Hawkins and Ingo Walters (eds.), *The United States and International Markets*. Lexington, Mass.: Lexington Books.
1976   "Additional statement." *Foreign Investment and U.S. Jobs*. Hearings before the Subcommittee on International Policy, Committee on International Relations, House of Representatives, 94th Congress, 2nd Session, Part I (January–February), Washington, D.C.: U.S. Government Printing Office.

Hawley, James
1978   "International Banking and the Internationalization of Capital." Pp. 124–137 in Bruce Steinberg *et al.* (eds.), *U.S. Capitalism in Crisis*. New York: The Union for Radical Political Economics.

Hechter, Michael
1976   *Internal Colonialism, The Celtic Fringe in British National Development, 1536–1966*. Berkeley: University of California Press.

Hirschman, Albert D.
1958   *The Strategy of Economic Development*. New Haven: Yale University Press.

Hobsbawm, E. J.
1959   *Primitive Rebels: Studies in Archaic Forms of Social Movements in the 19th and 20th Centuries*. New York: Norton.
1962   *The Age of Revolution, 1789–1848*. New York: Mentor.

Hobson, J. A.
1971   *Imperialism*. Ann Arbor: University of Michigan Press.

Hopkins, Terence K., and Immanuel Wallerstein.
1977   "Patterns of development of the modern world-system." *Review* 1 (Fall): 111–145.

Horowitz, Morris A.
1962   *La Emigración de Técnicos y Profesionales Argentinos*. Buenos Aires: Editorial del Instituto.

Hoselitz, Bert F.
1960   *Sociological Aspects of Economic Growth*. Glencoe, Illinois: The Free Press.

Hughes, H. Stuart
1958   *Consciousness and Society, The Reorientation of European Social Thought, 1890–1930*. New York: Vintage Books.

Hymer, Stephen
1972   "The internationalization of capital." *Journal of Economic Issues* 9: 91–111.

Hymer, Stephen, and Robert Rowthorn
1970   "Multinational corporations and international oligopoly: The non-American challenge." Pp. 57–91 in Charles P. Kindleberger (ed.), *The International Corporation*. Cambridge, Mass.: MIT Press.

207

REFERENCES

Inkeles, Alex
1969 "Making men modern: On the causes and consequences of individual change in six countries." *American Journal of Sociology* 75 (September): 208–225.
International Labour Office
1970 *Employment, Incomes, and Equality: A Strategy for Increasing Production Employment in Kenya.* Geneva.
1974 *Yearbook of Labor Statistics.* Vol. 33. Geneva.
1976 *Urban Development and Employment in São Paulo.* Geneva.
Izquierdo, Gonzalo
1968 *Un Estudio de las Ideologías Chilenas, La Sociedad de Agricultura en el Siglo XIX.* Santiago: Imprenta Técnica.
Jadel, Michael Jay, and John H. Stamm
1973 "The battle over jobs: An appraisal of recent publications on the employment effects of U.S. Multinational corporations." Pp. 144–191 in Duane Kujawa (ed.), *American Labor and the Multinational Corporation.* New York: Praeger.
Jalee, Pierre
1973 *Imperialism in the Seventies.* New York: Third Press.
Kau, Ying-Mao
1974 "Urban and rural strategies in the Chinese communist revolution." Pp. 253–270 in John Wilson Lewis (ed.), *Peasant Rebellion and Communist Revolution in Asia.* Stanford: Stanford University Press.
Kelly, M. P. Fernández
1978 "Mexican border industrialization, female labor force participation and migration." Paper presented at the Meetings of the American Sociological Association, San Francisco, September.
Kidd, Charles V.
1967 *Migration of Health Personnel, Scientists, and Engineers from Latin America.* No. 142. Washington, D.C.: Pan American Health Organization Scientific Publications.
Kiernan, V. B.
1974 *Marxism and Imperialism.* London: Edward Arnold.
Korn, Peggy
1969 "The problem of the roots of revolution: Society and intellectual ferment in Mexico on the eve of independence." Pp. 100–132 in Frederick B. Pike (ed.), *Latin American History: Select Problems.* New York: Harcourt.
Laclau, Ernesto
1971 "Feudalism and capitalism in Latin America." *New Left Review* 67 (May–June): 20 pp.
Leeds, Anthony
1969 "The significant variables determining the character of squatter settlements." *América Latina* 12 (July–September): 44–86.
1974 "Housing-settlement types, arrangements for living, proletarianization, and the social structure of the city." Pp. 67–99 in Wayne A. Cornelius and Felicity M. Trueblood (eds.), *Latin American Urban Research.* Vol. 4. Beverly Hills: Sage.
Leeds, Anthony, and Elizabeth Leeds
1969 "Brazil and the myth of urban rurality: urban experience, work, and values in squatments' of Rio de Janeiro and Lima." Pp. 229–272 in A. J. Field (ed.), *City and Country in the Third World.* Cambridge, Mass.: Schenkman.
1971 "Brazil in the 1960's: Favela and polity." Department of Anthropology, University of Texas at Austin. (Mimeographed).
1976 "Accounting for behavioral differences: Three political systems and the responses of squat-

ters in Brazil, Peru, and Chile." Pp. 193–248 in John Walton and L. H. Masotti (eds.), *The City in Comparative Perspective: Cross National Research and New Directions in Theory*. Beverly Hills: Sage Publications-Halsted Press.

Leeds, Elizabeth
1972 Forms of "Squatment" Political Organization: The Politics of Control in Brazil. M.A. thesis, Department of Political Science, University of Texas at Austin.

Lenin, V. I.
1939 *Imperialism, the Highest Stage of Capitalism*. New York: International Publishers.

Lerner, Daniel
1965 *The Passing of Traditional Society: Modernizing the Middle East*. New York: Free Press.

Levy, Marion J.
1955 "Contrasting factors in the modernization of China and Japan." Pp. 496–536 in S. Kuznets (ed.), *Economic Growth: Brazil, India and Japan*. Durham, N.C.: Duke University Press.

Lewis, W. Arthur
1964 "Unemployment in developing countries." Lectures to the Mid-West Research Conference. (Mimeographed).

Leys, C.
1973 "Interpreting African underdevelopment: Reflection on the ILO report on employment, incomes, and equality in Kenya." *African Affairs* 72: 419–429.

Lipset, Seymour M.
1963 *The First New Nation*. New York: Basic Books.

Lockhart, James
1969 "Encomienda and Hacienda: The evolution of the great estate in the Spanish Indies." *Hispanic American Historical Review* 49 (August): 411–429.
1972 "The social history of colonial Spanish America: Evolution and potential." *Latin American Research Review* 7:6–46.

Lockwood, David
1958 *The Blackcoated Worker: A Study in Class Consciousness*. London: Allen & Unwin.

Lomnitz, Larissa
1975 "Migration and network in Latin America." Pp. 133–150 in Alejandro Portes and Harley L. Browning (Eds.), *Current Perspectives in Latin American Urban Research*. Austin: Special Publication Series of the Institute of Latin American Studies, University of Texas.
1977a "Mechanisms of articulation between shantytown settlers and the urban system." Paper presented at the Symposium on Shantytowns. The Wenner-Gren Foundation, Gloggnitz, Austria, July.
1977b *Networks and Marginality, Life in a Mexican Shantytown*. New York: Academic Press.

Lowenthal, Abraham F.
1974 "Peru's ambiguous revolution." *Foreign Affairs* (July): 799–817.

Lubeck, Paul and John Walton
1979 "Urban class conflict in Africa and Latin America: Comparative analyses from a world systems perspective." *International Journal of Urban and Regional Research* 3 (March): 3–28.

Luxemburg, Rosa
1951 *The Accumulation of Capital*. London: Routledge and Kegan Paul.

McClelland, David
1966 "The impulse of modernization." Pp. 28–39 in Myron Weiner (ed.), *Modernization: The Dynamics of Growth*. New York: Basic Books.

McDonald, Angus W., Jr.
1978 *The Urban Origins of Rural Revolution: Elites and the Masses in Hunan Province China, 1911–1927*. Berkeley: University of California Press.

MacDonald, John S., and Leatrice D. MacDonald
1974 "Chain migration, ethnic neighborhood formation, and social networks." Pp. 226–236 in Charles Tilly (ed.), *An Urban World*. Boston: Little, Brown.

McGee, T. G.
1967 *The Southeast Asian City*. London: G. Bell.
1973 *Hawkers in Hong Kong: A Study of Planning and Policy in a Third World City*. Hong Kong: Centre for Asian Studies, University of Honk Kong.

Magdoff, Harry
1969 *The Age of Imperialism*. New York: Monthly Review Press.

Mandel, Ernest
1975 *Late Capitalism*. London: NLB.
1978 *The Second Slump: A Marxist Analysis of Recession in the Seventies*. London: NLB.

Mangin, William
1967 "Latin American squatter settlements: A problem and a solution." *Latin American Research Review* 2 (Summer): 65–98.

Mannheim, Karl
1936 *Ideology and Utopia*. New York: Harcourt.

Margulies H., and L. S. Bloch
1969 *Foreign Medical Graduates in the United States*. Cambridge, Mass.: Harvard University Press.

Mariategui, Jose Carlos
1971 "The problem of the Indian." Pp. 22–30 in J. C. Mariategui, *Seven Interpretive Essays on Peruvian Reality*. (trans. M. Urquidi) Austin: University of Texas Press.

Marshall, Adriana
1978 *El Mercado de Trabajo en el Capitalismo Periférico: el Caso de Argentina*. Santiago de Chile: PISPAL.

Martinelli, Alberto
1975 "Multinational corporations, national economic policies, and labor unions." Pp. 425–443 in Leon N. Lindberg, Robert Alford, Colin Crough, and Claus Offe (eds.), *Stress and Contradiction in Modern Capitalism*. Lexington, Mass.: D. C. Heath.

Marx, Karl
1957 "Contribution to the critique of Hegel's philosophy of right." Pp. 59–68 in R. Neibuhr (ed.), *Marx and Engels on Religion*. Moscow: Foreign Languages Publishing House.
1962 *Capital*, Vol. II. Moscow: Foreign Language Publishing House.

Marx, Karl, and Friedrich Engels
1939 *The German Ideology*. New York: International Publishers.

Mazumdar, D.
1975 "The urban informal sector." World Bank Staff Working Paper No. 211. Washington, D.C.: World Bank.

Meillassoux, Claude
1972 "From reproduction to production." *Economy and Society* 1 (February): 93–105.

MENSAJE
1962 "Revolución en América Latina." No. 115, December.
1963 "Reformas revolucionarias en América Latina." No. 123, December.

Mercader, Antonio, and Jorge de Vera
1969 *Tupamaros, Estrategia y Accion*. Montevideo: Editorial Alfa.

Mesa-Lago, Carmelo
1978 *Social Security in Latin America, Pressure Groups, Stratification, and Inequality*. Pittsburgh: University of Pittsburgh Press.

Metzger, Walter
1949 "Ideology and the intellectual: A study of Thorstein Veblen." *Philosophy and Science* 16 (April): 125.
Mill, John Stuart
1909 *Principles of Political Economy*. London: Longmans.
Miller, S. M.
1960 "Comparative Social Mobility." *Current Sociology*, IX: 1–61.
Miller, S. M., Roy Bennett, and Cyril Alapatt
1970 "Does the U.S. economy require imperialism?" *Social Policy* 1 (September–October): 13–19.
Mills, C. Wright
1956 *The Power Elite*. New York: Oxford University Press.
1959 *The Sociological Imagination*. New York: Oxford University Press.
Mingione, Enzo
1978 "Capitalist crisis, neo dualism, and marginalization." *International Journal of Urban and Regional Research* 2 (June): 213–221.
Mitchell, Daniel J. B.
1976 *Labor Issues of American International Trade and Investment*. Baltimore: Johns Hopkins University Press.
Mohr, Alberto Fuentes
1971 *Secuestro y Prisión, Dos Caras de la Violencia en Guatemala*. San Jose: Editorial Universitaria Centroamericana.
Moises, Jose Alvaro, and Verena Martinez-Alier
1977 "A revolta dos suburbanos." Pp. 13–63 in CEDEC *Contradições Urbanas e Movimentos Sociais*. São Paulo: Co-edições CEDEC/ Paz e Terra.
Molina, Humberto
n.d. "Una estrategia para el desarrollo urbano." *Revista de Extension Cultural* No. 7. Universidad Nacional de Colombia-Medellin.
Möller, Alois
1979 "Los vendedores ambulantes en Lima." Pp. 415–471 in V. Tokman and E. Klein (eds.), *El Subempleo en América Latina*. Buenos Aires: El Cid Editores.
Moore, Barrington, Jr.
1966 *Social Origins of Dictatorship and Democracy: Lord and Peasant in the Making of the Modern World*. Boston: Beacon Press.
1978 *Injustice: The Social Bases of Obedience and Revolt*. White Plains, New York: M. E. Sharpe.
Morse, Richard M.
1964 "The heritage of Latin America." Pp. 123–177 in Louis Hartz (ed.), *The Founding of New Societies*. New York: Harcourt.
Moser, Caroline
1978 "Informal sector or petty commodity production: Dualism or dependence in urban development?" *World Development* 6 (September–October): 1048.
Moskvichov, L. N.
1974 *The End of Ideology Theory: Illusions and Reality*. Moscow: Progress Publishers.
Mueller, Willard F.
1977 "Recent changes in industrial concentration and the current merger movement." Pp. 7–25 in Maurice Zeitlin (ed.), *American Society, Inc.: Studies in the Social Structure and Political Economy of the United States*. 2nd ed. Chicago: Rand McNally.

Müller, Ronald
  1973   "The multinational corporation and the underdevelopment of the Third World." Pp. 124–151
         in Charles E. Wilber (ed.), *The Political Economy of Development and Underdevelop-
         ment.* New York: Random House.
  1977   "National economic growth and stabilization policy in the age of multinational corpora-
         tions: The challenge of our post market economy." *U.S. Economic Growth from 1976 to
         1986.* Vol. 12, *Economic Growth in the International Economy.* Joint Economic Commit-
         tee, Congress of the United States. Washington, D.C.: U.S. Government Printing Of-
         fice.
Murmis, Miguel
  1969   "Tipos de marginalidad y posición en el proceso productivo." *Revista Latinoamericana de
         Sociología* 2: 43–420.
Musgrave, Pegsy B.
  1975   *Direct Investment Abroad and the Multinationals: Effects on the United States Economy.*
         Report from the U.S. Senate Committee on Foreign Relations' Sub-committee on Multi-
         national Corporations, 94th Congress, 1st Session, August, Washington, D.C.: U.S. Gov-
         ernment Printing Office.
Mutchler, David
  1971   *The Church as a Political Factor in Latin America.* New York: Praeger.
Myint, Hla
  1964   *The Economics of the Developing Countries.* New York: Praeger.
Myrdal, Gunnar
  1957   *Rich Lands and Poor.* New York: Harper and Row.
NACLA
  1975   "Hit and run: U.S. runaway shops on the Mexican border." *Latin America and Empire
         Report* 9 (July–August): 2–30.
  1977   "Electronics: The global industry." *Latin America and Empire Report* 11 (April): 2–25.
Neenan, William B.
  1972   *The Political Economy of Urban Areas.* Chicago: Markham.
Newfarmer, Richard S., and Willard F. Mueller
  1975   *Multinational Corporations in Brazil and Mexico: Structural Sources of Economic and
         Noneconomic Power.* Report from the U.S. Senate Committee on Foreign Relations'
         Subcommittee on Multinational Corporations, 94th Congress, 1st Session, August,
         Washington, D.C.: U.S. Government Printing Office.
North, David S.
  1977   "Illegal immigrants to the United States: A quintet of myths." Paper presented at the
         meetings of the American Political Science Association, Washington, D.C., August.
North, David S., and Marion F. Houston
  1976   *The Characteristics and Role of Aliens in the U.S. Labor Market: An Exploratory Study.*
         Washington, D.C.: Linton.
Nun, José
  1969   "Superpoblación relativa, ejército industrial de reserva y masa marginal." *Revista
         Latinoamericana de Sociología* 5 (July): 178–235.
O'Brien, Philip
  1975   "A critique of Latin American theories of dependency." Pp. 7–27 in Ivar Oxaal, Tony
         Barnett, and David Booth (eds.), *Beyond the Sociology of Development. Economy and
         Society in Latin America and Africa.* London: Routledge and Kegan Paul.
O'Connor, James
  1973   *The Fiscal Crisis of the State.* New York: St. Martin's Press.
  1974   *The Corporation and the State.* New York: Harper and Row.

REFERENCES

O'Donnell, Guillermo
1972 "Modernización y golpes militares: Teoría, comparacion y el caso argentino." *Desarrollo Económico* 47 (October–December): 619–566.
1977 "Estado e aliançãs na Argentina, 1956–1976." Pp. 17–57 in Sergio Paulo Pinheiro (ed.), *O Estado na América Latina.* San Paulo: Co-edições CEDEC/ Paz e terra.
1978 "Reflections on the patterns of change in the bureaucratic-authoritarian state." *Latin American Research Review* 13 (Spring): 3–38.
Omvedt, Gail
1973 "Towards a theory of colonialism." *The Insurgent Sociologist* (Spring): 1–24.
Orejon, Antonio Muro
1945 *Las Leyes Nuevas, 1542–43, Reproducción de los Ejemplares en la Sección del Patronato del Archivo General de Indias.* Sevilla: Escuela de Estudios Hispanoamericanos de la Universidad de Sevilla.
Oteiza, Enrique
1971 "Emigración de professionales, técnicos y obreros calificados argentinos a los Estados Unidos." *Desarrollo Económico* 10 (January–March): 429–494.
Oxaal, Ivan, Tony Barnett, and David Booth
1975 *Beyond the Sociology of Development: Economy and Society in Latin America and Africa.* London: Routledge and Kegan Paul.
Pahl, R. E.
1980 "Employment, work and the domestic division of labor." *International Journal of Urban and Regional Research* 4 (March): 1–19.
Paige, Jeffrey M.
1975 *Agrarian Revolution: Social Movements and Export Agriculture in the Underdeveloped World.* New York: The Free Press.
Pan American Health Organization
1971 *Estudios Sobre Salud y Educación Medica—la Enseñanza de la Medicina.* Serie 4, No. 3. Buenos Aires: Secretaría de Estado de Salud Publica.
Paz, Octavio
1969 "Mexico: la última década." Hackett Memorial Lecture, University of Texas at Austin.
Peattie, Lisa R.
1968 *The View from the Barrio.* Ann Arbor: University of Michigan Press.
1974 "Living poor: A view from the bottom." Proceedings of the Colloquim on Urban Poverty: A Comparison of the Latin American and the U.S. Experience. Los Angeles: UCLA School of Architecture and Urban Planning, May.
Perlman, Janice E.
1976 *The Myth of Marginality, Urban Poverty and Politics in Rio de Janeiro.* Berkeley: University of California Press.
Phelan, John L.
1969 "The problem of conflicting Spanish imperial ideologies in the sixteenth century." Pp. 40–64 in Frederick B. Pike (ed.), *Latin American History: Select Problems.* New York: Harcourt.
Pike, F. B.
1969 *Latin American History: Select Problems.* New York: Harcourt.
Piore, Michael J.
1979 *Birds of Passage, Migrant Labor and Industrial Societies.* New York: Cambridge University Press.
Portes, Alejandro
1969 *Cuatro Poblaciones: Informe Preliminar Sobre Situación y Aspiraciones de Grupos Marginados en el Gran Santiago.* Monograph Report, Land Tenure Center. Santiago de Chile.

1971   "The urban slum in Chile: Types and correlates." *Land Economics* 47 (August): 235–248.
1972   "Rationality in the slum: An essay on interpretive sociology." *Comparative Studies in Society and History* 14 (June): 268–286.
1974   "Modernity and development: A critique." *Studies in Comparative International Development* 9 (Spring): 247–279.
1976a   "Modernization for emigration." *Journal of Inter-American Studies and World Affairs* 18 (November): 395–422.
1976b   "Determinants of the brain drain." *International Migration Review* 10 (Winter): 489–504.
1977   "Labor functions of illegal aliens." *Society* 6 (September): 31–37.
1978   "The informal sector and the world economy: Notes on the structure of subsidized labour." *Bulletin of the Institute of Development Studies* 9 (June): 35–40.
1979   "Housing policy, urban poverty, and the state." *Latin American Research Review* 14 (Summer): 3–24.

Portes, Alejandro and John Walton
1976   *Urban Latin America*. Austin: University of Texas Press.

Poulantzas, Nicos
1975   *Classes in Contemporary Capitalism*. London: New Left Books.

Prebisch, Raul
1950   *The Economic Development of Latin America and its Principal Problems*. New York: United Nations.
1964   *The Economic Development of Latin America in the Post-War Period*. New York: United Nations.

Preobrazhensky, Evgeny
1965   *The New Economics*. Oxford: Clarendon Press.

Puig, Jose Olives
1976   "The struggle against urban renewal in the 'Cite d'Aliarte' (Paris)." Pp. 174–197 in C. G. Pickvance (ed.), *Urban Sociology: Critical Essays*. New York: St. Martin's Press.

Quijano, Anibal
1971   *Nationalism and Capitalism in Peru. A Study in Neo-Imperialism*. New York: Monthly Review.
1974   "The marginal pole of the economy and the marginalized labor force." *Economy and Society* 3: 393–428.

Ray, Talton F.
1969   *The Politics of the Barrios of Venezuela*. Berkeley: University of California Press.

Reynolds, L.
1965   "Wages and employment in a labour surplus economy." *American Economic Review* 55: 19–39.

Rivas, Edelberto Torres
1974   "Poder nacional y sociedad dependiente: Notas sobre las clases y el estado en Centroamérica." *Revista Paraguaya de Sociología* 29 (January–April): 179–210.

Roberts, Bryan R.
1973   *Organizing Strangers*. Austin: University of Texas Press.
1976   "The provincial urban system and the process of dependency." Pp. 99–132 in A. Portes and H. Browning (eds.), *Current Perspectives in Latin American Urban Research*. Austin: Institute of Latin American Studies and The University of Texas Press.
1978   *Cities of Peasants. The Political Economy of Urbanization in the Third World*. London: Edward Arnold.

Romero, Mauricio
1980   "Nuevas Perspectivas Ocupacionales y Cambios en la Estrategia de Reproducción de la

Fuerza de Trabajo" ILO Technical Mission to the Ministry of Labor and Social Security. Bogota. (Mimeographed).

Romo, Ricardo
1975 *Mexican Workers in the City: Los Angeles, 1915–1930.* Ph.D. dissertation, University of California at Los Angeles.

Rosenblum, Gerald
1973 *Immigrant Workers: Their Impact on American Labor Radicalism.* New York: Basic Books.

Rostow, Walt
1978 *The World Economy: History and Prospects.* Austin: University of Texas Press.

Rowthorn, Bob
1971 "Imperialism in the seventies—Unity or rivalry." *New Left Review* 69 (September–October): 31–59.

Samora, Julian
1971 *Los Mojados: The Wetback Story.* Notre Dame, Indiana: University of Notre Dame Press.

Sanchez, Manuel Moreno
1971 *Crisis Política de Mexico.* Mexico, D.F.: Editorial Extemporáneos.

Sandbrook, Richard, and Ronald Cohen
1975 *The Development of an African Working Class.* London: Longmans.

Santa Cruz, Anibal Pinto
1962 *Chile: Un Caso de Desarrollo Frustrado.* Santiago: Editorial Universitaria.

Schapera, Issac
1974 *Migrant Labour and Tribal Life.* London: Oxford University Press.

Schmitt, Karl, and David Burks
1963 *Evolution or Chaos: Dynamics of Latin American Government and Politics.* New York: Praeger.

Schmukler, Beatriz
1979 "Diversidad de formas de las relaciones capitalistas en la industria argentina." Pp. 309–351 in V. Tokman and E. Klein (eds.), *El Subempleo en America Latina.* Buenos Aires: El Cid Editores.

Scott, James
1976 *The Moral Economy of the Peasant: Rebellion and Subsistence in Southeast Asia.* New Haven: Yale University Press.

Shils, Edward
1955 "The end of ideology." *Encounter* 5 (November): 53.

Silvert, Kalman H.
1969 "Peronism in Argentina: A rightist reaction to the social problem of Latin America." Pp. 340–390 in F. B. Pike (ed.), *Latin American History: Selected Problems:* New York: Harcourt.

Singer, Paul
1976 *Economia Politica da Urbanização.* (Third edition). São Paulo: Editora Brasiliense.

Sito, Nilda, and Luis Stuhlman
1968 *La Emigracion de Cientificos de la Argentina.* Bariloche, Argentina: Fundacion Bariloche.

Skidmore, Thomas E.
1969 "The death of Brazilian slavery." Pp. 134–171 in F. B. Pike (ed.), *Latin American History: Selected Problems.* New York: Harcourt.
1973 "Politics and economic policy making in authoritarian Brazil, 1937–1971." Pp. 3–46 in Alfred Stepan (ed.), *Authoritarian Brazil, Origins, Policies, and Future.* New Haven: Yale University Press.
1976 *Preto no Branco, Raça e Nacionalidade no Pensamiento Brasileiro.* Rio de Janeiro: Paz e Terra.

REFERENCES

1977   "A case study in comparative public policy: The economic dimensions of populism in Argentina and Brazil." Washington, D.C.: Latin American Program of the Wilson Center, Working Paper #3.

Slater, David
1974   "Colonialism and the spatial structure of underdevelopment: Outlines of an alternative, with special reference to Tanzania." *Progress in Planning*. Vol. 4, part II.

Soares, Glaucio Dillon
1977   "The web of exploitation: State and peasants in Latin America." *Studies in Comparative International Development* 12 (Fall): 3–24.
1978   "After the Miracle." *Luso-Brazilian Review* 15 (Winter): 278–301.

Solberg, Carl
1970   *Immigration and Nationalism, Argentina and Chile, 1890–1914*. Austin: University of Texas Press.

Sorel, Georges
1950   *Reflections on Violence*. T. E. Hulmes (trans.), New York: The Free Press.

Spencer, Herbert
1914   *Principles of Sociology*. New York: Appleton.

Stein, Stanley, and Barbara Stein
1970   *The Colonial Heritage of Latin America*. New York: Oxford University Press.

Stern, James L.
1972   "Consequences of plant closure." *Journal of Human Resources* 7 (Winter): 3–25.

Stevens, Rosemany A., Louis W. Goodman, and Stephen S. Mick
1974   "What happens to foreign-trained doctors who come to the United States?" *Inquiry* 11 (June): 112–124.

Stobaugh, Robert
1972   "How investment abroad creates jobs at home." *Harvard Business Review* (September–October): 118–126.

Stoddard, Ellwyn R.
1976   "A conceptual analysis of the 'alien invasion': Institutionalized support of illegal Mexican aliens in the U.S." *International Migration Review* 19 (Summer): 157–189.

Stork, Joe
1975   *Middle East Oil and the Energy Crisis*. New York: Monthly Review Press.

Sunkel, Osvaldo
1972   *Capitalismo transnacional y desintegracíon nacional en América Latina*. Buenos Aires: Nueva Visión.

Szulc, Tad
1965   *Winds of Revolution: Latin America Today and Tomorrow*. New York: Praeger.

Szymanski, Al
1977   "Capital accumulation on a world scale and the necessity of imperialism." *The Insurgent Sociologist* 7 (Spring): 35–53.

Tabb, William K.
1978   "The New York City fiscal crisis." Pp. 241–266 in William K. Tabb and Larry Sawera (eds.), *Marxism and the Metropolis: New Perspectives in Urban Political Economy*. New York: Oxford University Press.

Thomas, Brinley
1973   *Migration and Economic Growth*. (Second edition). London: Cambridge University Press.

Tilly, Charles
1974   "Town and country in revolution." Pp. 271–302 in John Wilson Lewis (ed.), *Peasant Rebellion and Communist Revolution in Asia*. Stanford: Stanford University Press.
1978   "Migration in modern European history." Pp. 48–72 in William M. McNeill and Ruth

216

REFERENCES

Adams (eds.), *Human Migration, Patterns and Policies*. Bloomington: Indiana University Press.

Tokman, Victor E.

1978 "An exploration into the nature of informal–formal sector relationships." *World Development* 6 (September–October): 1065–1075.

1978a "Competition between the informal and formal sector in retailing: The case of Santiago." *World Development* 6 (September–October): 1187–1198.

1978b "Informal–formal sector interrelationships." *CEPAL Review* (January–June): 99–134.

Tolosa, Hamilton C.

1975 "Macro-economics of Brazilian urbanization." *Brazilian Economic Studies* 1: 227–274.

Turner, John F. C.

1968 "Uncontrolled urban settlements: Problems and policies." *International Social Development Review* 1: 107–130.

1976 *Housing by People*. London: Marion Boyars.

Turner, John F. C., and R. Fichter

1972 *Freedom to Build*. New York: Collier.

U.S. Immigration and Naturalization Service

1976 *Annual Report 1975*. Washington, D.C.: U.S. Government Printing Office.

United States Senate

1975 *Implications of Multinational Firms for World Trade and Investment and for U.S. Trade and Labor*. 93rd Congress, 1st Session (February), Washington, D.C.: U.S. Government Printing Office.

Urquidi, Victor, and Sofia Mendez Villarreal

1975 "Importancia economica de la zona fronteriza del norte de Mexico." Paper presented at the Conference on Contemporary Dilemmas of the Mexican-United States Border, The Weatherhead Foundation, San Antonio.

Valenzuela, Arturo

1978 *The Breakdown of Democratic Regimes, Chile*. Baltimore: Johns Hopkins University Press.

Vaitsos, Constantine

1974 *Intercountry Income Distribution and Transnational Enterprises*. London: Oxford University Press.

Vekemans, Roger, and Ismael Silva Fuenzalida.

1969 "El concepto de Marginalidad." Pp. 15–63 in DESAL. *Marginalidad en America Latina: Un ensayo de diagnostico*. Barcelona: Herder.

Vekemans, Roger, and Ramon Venegas

1977 "Marginalidad y promocion popular." *Mensaje* 149 (June): 218.

Villena, Guillermo Lohman

1957 *El Corregidor de Indios en el Peru bajo los Austrias*. Madrid: Ediciones de Cultura Hispanica.

Wallerstein, Immanuel

1974a *The Modern World-System I: Capitalist Agriculture and the Origins of the European World-Economy in the Sixteenth Century*. New York: Academic Press.

1974b "The rise and future demise of the world capitalist system: Concepts for comparative analysis." *Comparative Studies in Society and History* 16 (September): 387–415.

1976a "A world-system perspective on the social sciences." *British Journal of Sociology* 27: 343–352.

1976b "Semi-peripheral countries and the contemporary world crisis." *Theory and Society* 3: 461–483.

1977 "Rural economy in world-society." *Studies in Comparative International Development* 12 (Spring): 29–40.

1979 "Development: Theories, research designs, and empirical measures." Paper Presented at the "Thematic Panel on Development," meetings of the American Sociological Association, Boston, August.
1979 "Kondratieff up or Kondratieff down?" *Review* 4 (Spring): 663–673.
Wallerstein, Immanuel, William G. Martin, and Torry Dickinson
1979 "Household structures and production processes: Theoretical concerns plus data from southern Africa and nineteenth century United States. Binghamton, N.Y.: Fernand Braudel Center. (Mimeographed).
Walton, John
1976 "Urban hierarchies and patterns of dependence in Latin America: Theoretical bases for a new research agenda." Pp. 43–69 in A. Portes and H. L. Browning (eds.), *Current Perspectives in Latin American Urban Research*. Austin: Special Publications Series of the Institute of Latin American Studies, The University of Texas at Austin.
1979 "Urban political movements and revolutionary change in the Third World." *Urban Affairs Quarterly* 15 (September): 3–22.
1980 *Reluctant Rebels: Comparative Studies of Revolution and Underdevelopment* (Manuscript).
Ward, Barbara
1964 "The uses of prosperity." *Saturday Review* (August 29): 191–192.
Watkins, Alfred, and David Perry
1978 *Sun-Belt Cities*. Beverly Hills, Cal.: Sage Publications.
Weber, Max
1958 "The social psychology of the world religions." Pp. 257–301 in Hans H. Gerth and C. Wright Mills (eds.), *From Max Weber: Essays in Sociology*. New York: Oxford University Press.
1962 *The Sociology of Religion*. Ephraim Fischoff (trans.) Boston: Beacon Press.
Webster, David
1979 "The political economy of survival." *Work in Progress*. University of Witwatersrand (November 10): 57–64.
Weeks, John
1975 "Policies for expanding employment in the informal urban sector of developing countries." *International Labour Review* 91 (January): 1–13.
White, Christine Pelzer
1974 "The Vietnamese revolutionary alliance: Intellectuals, workers and peasants." Pp. 77–95 in John Wilson Lewis (ed.), *Peasant Rebellion and Communist Revolution in Asia*. Stanford: Stanford University Press.
Wilson, Francis
1972 "International migration in Southern Africa." *International Migration Review* 10 (Winter): 451–488.
Wolf, Eric R.
1969 *Peasant Wars of the Twentieth Century*. New York: Harper and Row.
Wolfe, Alan
1974 "New directions in the Marxist theory of politics." *Politics and Society* 9: 131–159.
Wolpe, Harold
1975 "The theory of internal colonialism: The South African case." Pp. 229–252 in Ivar Oxaal, Tony Barnett, and David Booth (eds.), *Beyond the Sociology of Deveopment. Economy and Society in Latin America and Africa*. London: Routledge and Kegan Paul.
Wright, Erik Olin
1976 "Class boundaries in advanced capitalist societies." *New Left Review* 98 (July–August): 3–41.

REFERENCES

Wright, Erik Olin, and Luca Perrone
1977 "Marxist class categories and income inequality." *American Sociological Review* 42 (February): 32–33.
Yalour, Margot Romano, Maria M. Chirico, and Edith Soubie
1969 *Clase Obrera y Migraciones*. Buenos Aires: Editorial del Instituto.
Zea, Leopoldo
1953 *El Positivismo en Mexico*. Mexico, D.F.: Ediciones Studium.

Index

Juan G. Espinosa and Andrew S. Zimbalist. Economic Democracy: Workers' Participation in Chilean Industry 1970-1973

Richard Maxwell Brown and Don E. Fehrenbacher (Eds.). Tradition, Conflict, and Modernization: Perspectives on the American Revolution

Harry W. Pearson. The Livelihood of Man by Karl Polanyi

Frederic L. Pryor. The Origins of the Economy: A Comparative Study of Distribution in Primitive and Peasant Economies

Charles P. Cell. Revolution at Work: Mobilization Campaigns in China

Dirk Hoerder. Crowd Action in Revolutionary Massachusetts, 1765-1780

David Levine. Family Formations in an Age of Nascent Capitalism

Ronald Demos Lee (Ed.). Population Patterns in the Past

Michael Schwartz. Radical Protest and Social Structure: The Southern Farmers' Alliance and Cotton Tenancy, 1880-1890

Jane Schneider and Peter Schneider. Culture and Political Economy in Western Sicily

Daniel Chirot. Social Change in a Peripheral Society: The Creation of a Balkan Colony

Stanley H. Brandes. Migration, Kinship, and Community: Tradition and Transition in a Spanish Village

James Lang. Conquest and Commerce: Spain and England in the Americas

Kristian Hvidt. Flight to America: The Social Background of 300,000 Danish Emigrants

D. E. H. Russell. Rebellion, Revolution, and Armed Force: A Comparative Study of Fifteen Countries with Special Emphasis on Cuba and South Africa

John R. Gillis. Youth and History: Tradition and Change in European Age Relations 1770-Present

Immanuel Wallerstein. The Modern World-System I: Capitalist Agriculture and the Origins of the European World-Economy in the Sixteenth Century; II: Mercantilism and the Consolidation of the European World-Economy, 1600-1750

John W. Cole and Eric R. Wolf. The Hidden Frontier: Ecology and Ethnicity in an Alpine Valley

Joel Samaha. Law and Order in Historical Perspective: The Case of Elizabethan Essex

William A. Christian, Jr. Person and God in a Spanish Valley